The Fabrication of Social Order

D1553596

The Fabrication of Social Order

A Critical Theory of Police Power

Mark Neocleous

Pluto Press

LONDON • STERLING, VIRGINIA

First published 2000 by Pluto Press
345 Archway Road, London N6 5AA
and 22883 Quicksilver Drive, Sterling, VA 20166–2012, USA
www.plutobooks.com

British Library Cataloguing in Publication Data
A catalogue record for this book is available from the British Library

ISBN 0 7453 1489 9 hbk
ISBN 0 7453 1484 8 pbk

Library of Congress Cataloging-in-Publication Data

Neocleous, Mark, 1964–
    The fabrication of social order : a critical theory of police power / Mark
Neocleous.
        p.   cm.
    Includes bibliographical references.
    ISBN 0–7453–1489–9
    1. Communist state. 2. State, The. 3. Police power. 4. Liberalism. 5. Social
control. 6. Social security. I. Title.
    JC474.N47 2000
    363.2'3–dc21
                                                                    00–022301

09 08   07   06   05   04   03   02   01   00
10 9   8   7   6   5   4   3   2   1

Designed and produced for Pluto Press by
Chase Production Services, Chadlington, OX7 3LN
Typeset from disk by Marina Typesetting, Minsk, Belarus
Printed in the EU by T. J. International, Padstow

Contents

Acknowledgements   vii
Preface   ix

1 'Police Begets Good Order'   1

- Mastering the masterless; imposing order   1
- Excursus on the 'peculiarities of the English', or, Aristotle in Britain   9
- Mastering the market; imposing work   11

2 Liberalism and the Police of Property   22

- From police to political economy?   22
- From rule of police to rule of law?   29
- The state of liberal order: interest, independence, property   34
- Towards security   41

3 Ordering Insecurity I: Social Police and the Mechanisms of Prevention   45

- 'The well ordering and comfort of civil society'   47
- Political economy and social police   56
- Towards social security   59

4 Ordering Insecurity II: On Social Security   63

- The fabrication of wage labour   66
- Border patrols: classes, criminals and claimants   79
- The metaphysics of the proper: medical police, pigs and social dirt   84
- Towards the legal reconstruction of police work   89

5 Law, Order, Political Administration   92

- Arrest and police 'illegality'   95
- Administration and the rationality of police: discretion   99
- 'Wonderful and marvellous things': the mythology of modern law and order   106
- Formless power and ghostly presence: the state of the police   115

Notes   119

Index   157

Acknowledgements

Parts of the argument in what follows have been tried out in the following articles: 'Policing and Pin-making: Adam Smith, Police and the State of Prosperity', *Policing and Society*, Vol. 8, 1998; 'Policing the System of Needs: Hegel, Political Economy, and the Police of the Market', *History of European Ideas*, Vol. 24, 1998; 'Social Police and the Mechanisms of Prevention: Patrick Colquhoun and the Police of the Poor', *British Journal of Criminology*, Vol. 40, 2000; and 'Against Security', *Radical Philosophy*, 100, 2000.

I am grateful to Clive Emsley and Barry Godfrey for making available unpublished material, despite the fact that they had little real sense as to how I might use it.

I thank Stuart Elden for his careful reading of the manuscript, David Stevens for making me sharpen up my critique of liberalism, Debbie Broadhurst for making me spend more time on the 'unpoliced', and KK for making the difference.

Preface

Anyone who considers questions of power cannot help but be struck by the ubiquitous nature, emotional force and political pull of the idea of order. This book contains an argument about the role of police in the fabrication of social order. As such, it consists of a set of mutually reinforcing claims about the historical role of police, the relevance of the police concept to social and political thought, and the ideological nature of the concepts of law, order and security.

The concept of police has had a peculiar history. Where it once occupied a central place in the work of major thinkers on the grounds that policing was so obviously a central part of state power and thus integral to civilized life, for many years the concept has been relegated to the backwater of 'police studies'. Police science, once a central means of understanding and sustaining the exercise of state power, has been reduced to the study of crime and law enforcement and thus absorbed into the discipline of criminology. In one sense then, the police concept has been handed over to criminology. But as Paul Rock has noted, the empirical and policy-oriented focus of criminology, having made criminologists conciliatory and catholic, and having reduced their research to a civil trade in one another's ideas, has shifted the discipline away from the theoretical and argumentative mode which once characterized it.[1] Stuck in the discipline of criminology, most research on the police has eschewed any attempt to make sense of the concept itself. As we shall see, having encouraged the view that policing, like the criminal law of which it is supposedly part, is no more and no less than a set of instruments to manage something called crime, criminology has become little more than ideology.[2]

In contrast to this conciliatory and catholic approach, the police concept would appear to have found its natural home in the work of those operating within a Foucauldian theoretical framework. A range of writers have latched on to Foucault's interest in the idea of police and tried to use it as a tool for making sense of what they consider to have been the major historical transformations in government.[3] The problem with much of this work is the opposite to that found in criminology. With their tendency to latch on to over-inflated categories, Foucauldians use the police concept so abstractly that it comes to look as though it is yet one more synonym for 'power', 'discipline' and 'governmentality'. This has an added negative effect, which is that for all their discussions of policing as a form of governmentality, Foucauldians barely mention the police institution itself, to the extent that one begins to think that policing and the police have nothing connecting them at all.[4] One searches high and low in Foucauldian texts for police officers themselves to appear and play a part in the exercise of power or the disciplinary project. For them, the police idea is emptied of the humiliations administered both on the street and in the police station, the thud of the truncheon and the gratuitous use of 'discretionary' force. In other words, the Foucauldian texts are stripped of any sense that police has anything to do with violence and thus state power.

In this sense the Foucauldians, for all their bravado about undermining the central assumptions about power in the social sciences, replicate one of the main features of mainstream sociological work. Much recent work on the sociology and politics of sexuality, to take one example, utilizes the police concept to make sense of the way in which sexual behaviour is structured through relations of power (that is, is 'policed').[5] The problem with this literature is that the term is so taken for granted that no real explication of the concept ever takes place. As such, one is left unsure of the extent of the variety of forms policing can take and, as with the Foucauldians, the connection between these forms, the police institution and the state is left unclear.

The argument in this book operates at a critical distance from these positions. I partly seek to recover the concept of police from the backwater of 'police studies'[6] and to resituate it into the mainstream of social and political theory. To do this I shall initially seek to recover part of the original meaning of police as it emerged with the collapse of feudalism. The tendency in police studies is to treat the police as something that emerged in the early nineteenth century – even an astute writer on police such as Egon Bittner comments that 'the police, as we know it today, is a creature of English society in the second quarter of the nineteenth century'.[7] Such an approach leads to the forms of policing that existed prior to, say, the formation of the Metropolitan Police in London in 1829, as being rewarded with merely cursory glances by way of prefatory antiquarianism.[8] The older and broader conception of police is mentioned, but otherwise the assumption implicit in police studies is that the 'real' police only emerges with the coming of the uniformed forces for the prevention of crime and enforcement of law. Yet even a cursory glance at the content of the early police idea reveals that central to the original police mandate was 'good order', in the broadest possible sense, and that policing took the form of a range of institutions concerned with far more than crime. Part of the argument in this book is that although during the late eighteenth and nineteenth centuries the institutional form of police was transformed under pressure from a new hegemonic liberalism, the *raison d'être* of the police function remained. Only by grasping this *raison d'être* can we make sense of the police project. One of the central themes in this book is therefore that police and policing should not be identified with *the* police, and that one must stifle the impulse to equate police with men in uniform.[9] Policing is undertaken partly by the uniformed public police, but their actions are coordinated with agencies of policing situated throughout the state. In other words, part of the purpose of this book is to encourage the use of an *expanded* concept of police, to reflect the expansive set of institutions through which policing takes place. Since, as I shall argue, the core of the police project remains the question of poverty and thus the condition of the class of poverty, and since state institutions for the administration of poverty are generally understood by the term 'social policy' and administered through the institutions of the welfare state, the expanded concept of police shall be thought of as *social police* and presented as the project of *social security*.

The term is also expanded in that it accommodates the orginal French use of the word as a subject noun (*la police de Paris*), as an object (*faire la police*) and as a transitive verb (*policer*). As noun, verb and adjective 'police' was historically used to describe the way order was achieved, and part of the argument here is to suggest that it is through policing that the state shapes and orders civil society. 'Police' should therefore be as important a concept to social and political theory as 'sovereignty', 'legitimacy', 'consent', 'social contract', 'violence', and all of the other concepts regularly used by theorists grappling with the nature of state power. As the first chapter will show, the history of police is the history of state power, and the overlapping consensus that this power is rooted in the control of the exercise of force – a consensus stretching from Hobbes to Weber – should suggest that the police, as one of the institutions which has been granted the right to exercise this force, needs to be understood in the wider context of the state. As a consequence, any theory of police must involve a theory of state power; conversely, any theory of state power must necessarily consist of a theory of police. To try to discuss police without discussing state power is like trying to discuss the economy without mentioning capital.[10] It is for this reason that social and political theory need the police concept.

Most recent attempts at developing a theory of the state seem to have accepted that the idea of police belongs with criminology, and have therefore ignored the police concept. Yet criminology has for the most part ambled along without any real concept of the state, let alone a theory of it. Even were it the case that crime is the main concern of policing, that in itself should have meant focusing on the state: since the state declares what is or is not a crime, it would seem to follow that the concept of the state would be at the heart of criminology. Yet this is far from being the case. In conventional criminology, the exercise of state power through the operation of the law is acknowledged only formally, and its mode of operation is treated as unproblematic. Such a separation of police from state power generally helps in making the methodological claim that is supposed to ground 'police studies' as an autonomous enterprise. But even 'radical criminology' has often failed to distinguish between types or forms of state, to locate the state historically, and has thus equally failed to develop a theory of the state. What is striking about key texts within 'radical criminology' such as Taylor, Walton and Young's *The New Criminology*, published in the heyday of Left critiques of traditional criminology in the 1970s, is the absence of discussion of the state.[11] Likewise, while Foucauldians have latched on to the police concept, they have retained their distaste for any use of the state concept.

As well as arguing that social and political theory in general need the concept of police, this book has a more political aim: to reassert the importance of the police concept to materialist theory in particular. I aim to give some theoretical weight to the concept of police in order to state its case to be part of the conceptual and theoretical arsenal of Marxism. The book argues that 'police', along with its equally fetishized sister concepts of 'order', 'security' and 'law', is a central category in the self-understanding of bourgeois society. In one sense then, this book is an inquiry into a category of bourgeois society.[12] But in a more explicit Marxist sense the book holds that police is one of the *supreme* concepts of bourgeois society, and that we can better understand the exercise of power in bourgeois society by utilizing this concept for a critical theory of society. Attempts within Marxism to grapple with the idea of police have often succumbed to a rather crude functionalism, tending to settle for the argument that the police institution acts as a repressive agency, crushing working-class struggles and guarding private property.[13] Even one of the most sophisticated Marxist theorists of law, Pashukanis, treats the police in this way.[14] The argument here distances itself from other Marxist arguments concerning police by showing that policing has been central not just to the repression of the working class and the reproduction of order, but to the *fabrication of order*.[15] To show, in other words, the centrality of the historically massive police operation on the part of the state to the consolidation of the social power of capital and the wage form: as order became increasingly based on the bourgeois mode of production, so the police mandate was to fabricate an order of wage labour and administer the class of poverty.

This does not mean that I am seeking to develop a 'Marxist criminology'. While such a thing has been attempted before, most notably in the heyday of radical criminology in the 1970s, I am unconvinced about what a 'Marxist criminology' would actually look like. As Paul Hirst has argued, to try to 'apply' Marxism to a pre-given field of sociology such as criminology modifies and distorts Marxist concepts to suit a non-Marxist purpose.[16] 'Criminology', in that sense, is incompatible with the object of study and the conceptual structure of Marxism.[17] Rather, given the centrality of police to the exercise of state power over a class society, to develop a materialist conception of police means nothing more than developing the Marxist theory of the state.

The present work is therefore a development of my earlier attempt at developing just such a theory. In *Administering Civil Society* I tried to rethink the state–civil society distinction through the category of political administration via an immanent critique of Hegel's account of the law and administration of civil society, Marx's understanding of state power and class struggle, and Foucault's work on administration.[18] I argued that we need to address the constitutive power of the state over civil society and the way this power is expressed via a law-and-administration continuum. We need the state–civil society distinction, I argued, but we also need to recognize the importance of the range of mechanisms by which the state orders civil society, which since 1834 have taken the form of what I call political administration. Part of the argument was that materialist theory has too easily succumbed to a crude use of the base–superstructure metaphor, and that what is actually needed for a Marxist theory of the state is a recognition of the ways in which the state fashions civil society, in particular by helping to make the working class. In developing the argument I suggested, largely in passing, that the constitutive power of the state can be understood as the *policing* of civil society by the state. Using the concept in passing, however, left it theoretically undeveloped. Although I do not think the overall thrust of the argument in the book was affected by this, the present work tries to develop the argument by focusing on the role of police in the fabrication of a central component of bourgeois order, namely wage labour (Chapter 4) and by arguing that the police institution should be considered as the exercise of *administration* as much as *law* (Chapter 5).[19]

The argument is therefore in part a critique of liberalism and the liberal assumptions which permeate much of the thinking on police. The emergence and consolidation of industrial capitalism and liberal ideology also generated new ways of thinking about the politics of order, and thus to a radical revision in the way the police is understood. This revision mystified xiv The Fabrication of Social Order

the nature of police power, not least because the genius of liberalism was to make the police appear as an independent, non-partisan agency simply enforcing the law and protecting all citizens equally from crime. Concomitantly, liberalism glossed over the power of property and subordination of labour to capital through which order is sustained in contemporary society. Liberalism's misunderstanding of the nature of police power, bound up with the liberal sanctification of law and security, is part and parcel of liberalism's unwillngness to specify the precise nature of the dynamics of state power. These issues are addressed in Chapter 2, where the liberal recoding of the politics of order is discussed, and developed further in Chapter 5 in the context of contemporary debates surrounding the police. The point is not to hammer home liberalism's theoretical blindspots – which are plain for all to see – but to use this as a critical springboard to sustain the argument about the role of police in the fabrication of social order.

Athough this book is situated politically within materialist theory – indeed, *because* the book is situated within materialist theory – it is not situated intellectually within any particular discipline. It aims to avoid the 'specialization-induced intellectual poverty'[20] brought about by the academic attempt to remain 'disciplined' (in both senses of the term). Because any act of writing cannot account for its reception, it ought not to try to ensure its comprehensibility to readers it thinks it knows. Writing relying too much on a sense of one's audience tends to reiterate the arguments in texts already familiar to the audience.[21] Situating oneself too rigidly within a particular discipline often tends to burden one's argument so much so that, as Ben Agger puts it, one ends up arguing nothing in particular, repeating the tired and true, rearranging the footnotes and references of others.[22] Indeed, one might push the argument further and suggest that the social intervention of a text is measured not by its popularity among a particular audience, nor by being comfortably situated firmly within a particular discipline and its rubrics, nor by the fidelity of the socioeconomic reflections it contains, but rather by the violence (Barthes) or intellectual trespass (Butler) that enables it, in Barthes's terms, to *exceed* the laws that a society, an ideology, a philosophy or a discipline establish for themselves in order to agree among themselves a historical intelligibility. It is this excess that writing should aim to be.[23]

It is in this spirit of excess that the book contains no proposals for reform. The reader searching for how to make the police and social policy more democratic (more representative, more accountable, less racist, less oppressive, and so on) is best advised to read another book. Like *Administering Civil Society* and critical theory in general, this book is an attempt to write about administration and against administration in an overly administered world, a world in which administration has the power to sub-sume even the attempts to write against it. Given how frequently argu-ments concerning the police and policy start out looking like critique and end up in apology (evidence of the extent to which law, administration, police and state power present themselves as natural – the 'way things are' – and thus beyond critique), the only hope for a text such as this is that it inspires others to continue the critique of power and administration, on the basis of which something other than 'reform' might take place.

1
'Police Begets Good Order'

Mastering the masterless; imposing order

From the late fifteenth century political discourse in Europe centred very much around the concept of police. Originating in French-Burgundian *policie* in the fifteenth century, the word 'police' spread across Continental Europe and generated a range of words adopted from the French-Burgundian: *'Policei'*, *'Pollicei'*, *'Policey'*, *'Pollicey'*, *'Pollizey'*, *'Pollizei'*, *'Politzey'*, *'Pollucey'*, and *'Pullucey'*. Though the spelling of the word varied, the meaning remained constant, denoting the legislative and administrative regulation of the internal life of a community to promote general welfare and the condition of good order (as encapsulated in phrases such as 'police and good order' or 'good police and order'), and the regimenting of social life (as in 'regiment and police'). The instructions and activities considered necessary for the maintenance of good order were known as *Policey Ordnung*, or *Polizeiordnungen* – police ordinances – and referred to the management and direction of the population by the state. In giving rise to the *Polizeistaat* they referred, in effect, to the 'well-ordered police state'.[1]

There are a number of reasons why 'police' or *'Polizei'* emerged at this time, all of which are traceable to the collapse of feudalism. The determining characteristic of feudalism as a mode of production was the unity of economic and political domination. Serfdom as a mechanism of surplus extraction was simultaneously a form of economic exploitation and politico-legal coercion. With the growth of trade and industry, the division of labour, the mobility of labour, and the increasing importance of a money economy, the estates-based social order was gradually weakened and with it the unity of political and economic oppression which the lord exercised over the serf. The result was the displacement of politico-legal coercion towards a centralized (and militarized) summit. Diluted at local level, political and legal power came to be increasingly concentrated at a 'national' level. The slow emancipation of the serfs from their traditional system of domination led to their simultaneous impoverishment and beginnings of their proletarianization. The massive depopulation following the Black Death of 1349 led to a doubling of wages and an increase in the mobility of labour, along with the transformation of a large number of labour services into cash rents. With the increased mobility of labour, villeins could slip away from their manors and labourers demand more wages. At the same time, such individuals and the groups from which they emerged were increasingly radicalized. The early half of the sixteenth century, for example, saw revolts across Europe: the *Communeros* in Spain in 1520–21, followed by the *Germanias* in 1525–26; the German Peasants' Revolt of 1524–26; the revolts of English textile workers in 1525–28 followed by more widespread revolts in 1536–37; the *Grande Rebeyne* in Lyon in 1529; the revolt of the *Straccioni* at Lucca in 1531–32; plus numerous urban revolts in towns across Europe.[2] The aristocracy also found itself facing an increasingly powerful (in economic terms at least) mercantile bourgeoisie, especially in the developing towns.

Concomitantly, the growth of towns also helped undermine the traditional forms of authority and social distinctions between estates, creating conditions for new 'lifestyles' which, combined with the increase in new forms of economic activity, led to a growth in consumption. New opportunities emerged for gambling, drinking, adultery, blasphemy and, more generally, the opportunity to 'wander' (though this term was often a euphemism for begging and vagrancy) much further than was traditionally possible. The increase in town living also meant an increased concern over hygiene in the towns, which were subject to a different set of health and cleanliness problems. Moreover, as towns developed so many of the matters which had previously come under the jurisdiction of the Church now came within the jurisdiction of urban authorities, and thus required new forms of managing them. This also helped undermine the authority of the Church, which was to come under increasing pressure with the Reformation – it is not for nothing that, despite the word originating in French Burgundian, police regulations first took a firm hold in the Protestant states of Germany and then only later in Catholic states such as France, Spain and Italy.

Police therefore emerged as part of an overall concern with the increasing 'social disorders' that were said to be plaguing the state. As the established and customary relations of the feudal world began to collapse, the old systems of authority were increasingly undermined. New means and practices for the constitution of political order were necessary and thus new concepts with which to understand them. In its origins 'police' thus presupposed a breakdown of the estate-based order which had previously given form to the social body. Where previously the estates had formed the foundation of order, so as they began to break down new means were necessary to re-form that order. The absolutist state stepped in to impose this order amidst a society of increasingly independent 'individuals', free (or at least relatively so) from their historic submission to the direct authority of the lord. In conceptual terms, these independent individuals appeared as a 'dissolute condition of masterlesse men, without subjection to Lawes, and a coercive Power to tye their hands'.[3] As 'masterless men', free from the traditional authorities that existed under feudalism, their social, economic and political condition appeared to undermine social order: as masterless men they were considered disorderly. It is in this context that the police project has its roots.

In its concern with good order amidst the breakdown of the old system of authority, police held an incredibly broad compass, overseeing and administering a necessarily large and heterogeneous range of affairs. In some sense police was without parameters, since it was to see to everything that might be necessary to maintain order within a community. The police mandate extended to the minutiae of social life, including the means of comfort, public health, food and wine adulteration, expenses at christenings, weddings and funerals, the wearing of extravagant clothing, the behaviour of citizens at church or during festivities, the maintenance of roads, bridges and town buildings, public security, the regulation of the provision of goods and services, the performance of trades and occupations, religion, morals and manners, and the behaviour of servants towards their masters. The stated aim of the Strasbourg police ordinance for 1628, for example, was the correction of 'disorder and contempt of good laws...all kinds of wrong-doing, sin and vice'. It dealt with moral questions such as Sunday observance, blasphemy, cursing and perjury, provided rules for the bringing up of children, keeping domestics, spending at weddings and christenings, and dealings between innkeepers and guests. It also dealt with sumptuary regulations, the status of Jews, rules governing funeral celebrations, the prevention of usury and monopolies, the condition for good trading, and contained rules concerning gaming, and breaches of the peace. In other areas police ordinances also concerned themselves with weights and measures, brewing and baking, and the serving of drinks.[4] Even 'frivolity' and associated 'extravagances' such as gluttony came under the eye of police power, as did the sale and consumption of alcohol, scarce commodities – such as coffee in Prussia – or commodities felt to be too important to leave 'unpoliced', such as grain in France.[5] Carnivals and other festivities were increasingly banned or restricted, and the police also engaged in censorship and pursued those with unacceptable religious, social or political views.[6] Surveillance was also an important aspect of policing. One French lieutenant of police, Sartines, boasted to Louis XV that where three men were talking on the street, at least one of them worked for him, while in late-eighteenth-century Russia it was widely assumed that everybody's words and actions were watched to such an extent that there may have been no social circle without a spy.[7] Police also included overseeing the educational institutions on behalf of the Crown – in order to ensure that teaching encouraged loyalty to king, church, order and labour – and paid attention to families and their domestic problems, ranging from unruly children to love triangles, exemplifying the police commitment to the family as part of the foundation of social order. Thus as Duschesne noted in his *Code of Police* of 1757, 'the objects which it [police] embraces are in some sense indefinite'.[8]

Many of these activities have been dealt with at length by others, and it is not my concern to repeat their findings. Rather, the aim here is to draw out some initial points concerning the early notion of police, which will then be developed more fully in later chapters. It can be seen that from the outset police was for the most part concerned not with criminal activity but with activities potentially damaging to communal good order. In other words, preventing crime was not integral to the definition of police; crime prevention has never been the *raison d'être* of police. Police referred to everything needed for the maintenance of civil life and existed wherever human life was organized communally and freemen or subjects conducted themselves in an orderly, modest, courteous and respectable fashion.The French police commissaire and police theorist Nicolas Delamare, whose *Traite de la Police* (begun in the 1670s and published between 1705 and 1738) was the most influential French text on police, being owned and read by foreign princes, local officials and jurists as well as the highest judicial and administrative officials in France, treats the object of police as 'the general and common good of society'. This is because police from its origins has been a form of *governing* rather than the exercise of law: 'the *science* of governing men', as the Paris police commissioner Jean-Charles Lemaire, educated in the works of Delamare but echoing a common belief among police theorists, put it in 1770, or 'the science of maintaining the welfare of a state, the science of governing', according to the Austrian police theorist Sonnenfels.[9] As such police was as much concerned with *administrative regulation* as with law-enforcement. 'That which is called Police, having as its only object service to the King and to public order, is incompatible with the obstacles and subtleties of litigated affairs and derives its functions far more from the Government than from the Bar', notes Delamare.[10] Moreover, the best way to understand police is as an *activity* rather than an institution, a *function* rather than an entity. Given that the key to this science of governing men was felt to be the institution and maintenance of order in the community, we can agree with Knemeyer that the ultimate concern of police was the abolition of disorder.[11] As Peter the Great wrote to the chief magistrate of St Petersburg: '*The Police begets good order.*'[12]

The activity of abolishing disorder, however, shifted as policing developed in conjunction with the shifts in the nature of both state power and the transformation from feudalism to capitalism. One can divide the history of police into three stages. The first two are separated by the Thirty Years War (1618–48), while the third stage emerges in the late eighteenth century and is consolidated in the nineteenth century.[13] Part of the general argument in this book is that there is a consistency in the police function throughout these stages, a consistency that resides in the centrality of police to not just the *maintenance* or *reproduction* of order, but to its *fabrication*, and that at the heart of this fabrication is work and the nature of poverty. This presents police as a far more productive force than many assume, in the sense that the police project is intimately connected to the fabrication of an increasingly *bourgeois* order, achieved through the *exercise of state power*. The 'stages' therefore parallel stages of state formation (early modern, absolutist, representative) and the rise and consolidation of a system of bourgeois rule (widely understood as 'modernity'). It is in the second and third stages that the productive capacities of police come into their own. The purpose of this chapter is to excavate the early police idea and pin down some of its key characteristics. It is therefore the first two stages that will initially concern us here; the third stage will be the focus of the chapters to follow.

In its first stage policing was characterized by *ad hoc* reactive measures. The police project was to maintain the structure of manners threatened by the decay of the existing Estates and the crisis provoked by the Reformation. Because the major activity of policing in this phase was formed through a reaction to emerging social problems and crises it can be thought of as a form of 'emergency legislation', passed without breaking with legal tradition. Nor did it usurp the power of the Estates; indeed, it often co-operated with the Estates, even into the seventeenth century. In its second stage policing changed from being an improvised set of legislative and administrative emergency responses to a more active and conscious interventionist form of social regulation grounded on the principle of good order and in search of what in German was understood as the *gemeine*

Nutz (general welfare) or *gemeine Beste* (common good) of the population. As Marc Raeff notes, in the sixteenth and early seventeenth centuries police legislation was almost entirely negative. Note was taken of unsatisfactory conditions and violations of existing laws, and regulations were issued to correct these defects and stop the decline – to bring back the *'gute Policey'* – thereby restoring the normal and proper order. In the course of the seventeenth century, in contrast, police legislation and ordinances acquired a positive cast: 'its aims no longer were to restore and correct abuses and defects but rather to create new conditions, to bring about changes and introduce innovations'. The dynamic and positive nature of this process is captured in the German notion of *Beste* which has connotations of a hypothetical state to be pursued and a goal to be actively worked for.[14]

To make sense of some of these changes we have to recognize that behind the early police concept lies an essentially conservative political project. Jeffrey Minson and Mitchell Dean have argued that in its original terms police was conservative in the sense that it was aimed at the reform – in the sense of returning to an original shape – of whatever appeared disorderly. Police was thus originally an attempt at the *re*-formation of the social body via an attempt to regulate everything which went unregulated. 'While it is true that [early police] measures were designed to prevent disorder, violence, and crime, their primary function would seem to be the reformation, by juridical means, of relations of authority and service which had been previously ensured by the customary bonds of the serf to his manor and the labourer to his master.' As such, the measures can be seen 'as instances of the conservative aspect of police in so far as they are concerned with a re-formation of feudal social relations and codes of obligation and service by means of the regulation of the plebeian masses'.[15] But in its second stage police was less concerned with *re*-forming a social body of increasingly obsolete social Estates, and more with actively shaping the social body according to certain ends – the ends of the state and the production of wealth. Police ordinances from then on created *new* law enacted by a sovereign power as deliberate acts of will and reason.

This shift is closely connected with a major shift in the concept of order that occurs during the same period. Order in the feudal and early modern world meant fixity, constancy and immutablility. The order in question was natural and divine, and thus included the planets and all of nature. 'Divine providence imposes an order on all things', Aquinas wrote in the thirteenth century, citing the Apostle's claim (in Romans 13, 1) that 'all things that are, are set in order by God'.[16] The idea of a 'great chain of being' fed into the Tudor and Elizabethan idea of order. Historians have often used Ulysses' 'degree' speech in Shakespeare's *Troilus and Cressida* as an example of this:

> The heavens themselves the planets and this centre,
> Observe degree, priority and place,
> Insisture, course, proportion, season, form,
> Office, and custom, in all line of order.[17]

Social order was thus merely part of a wider universal order, natural and divinely ordained; social disorder was thus seen as unnatural and against divine law, but was prevented by the existence of a superior unifying order. Towards the end of the sixteenth and into the seventeenth century, however, the idea of order was gradually transformed, increasingly understood not as divine but as man-made. Concomitantly, social order was also increasingly seen as being structured politically.[18] A number of writers during this period begin to signal this shift in focus. For example, although in his *Laws of Ecclesiastical Polity* Richard Hooker still accepts that sovereignty is divinely ratified, he also notes that all human laws are 'made for the ordering of politic societies'. Some men 'gave their consent *all to be ordered* by some whom they should agree upon'. Thus while Hooker retains some aspects of the older conception of order as natural and divine, he also believes that it is something to be achieved through political society: 'this order of things and persons in public societies is the work of polity'.[19] Likewise for James I, laws represent the king's definitive ordering of society. Although this power is given a pre-modern ideological gloss by being placed in the context of divine ordination, it is clear that for James I order is continually actualized through the creative powers of sovereignty.[20]

By the mid-seventeenth century the idea of social order had been largely emancipated from cosmology and replaced by the essentially Hobbesian belief that order is constituted by the sovereign. At the same time as the state began to acquire the power of being able to fabricate order out of the increasingly disorderly social world, the concept of order no longer reflected something transcendental, natural and divine, but instead was discursively structured around the concept of sovereign power – 'the mortal God', as Hobbes dubbed the Leviathan. Thus whereas police in its first stage was legitimated through being part of the traditional law and justice of an Estates-based and theologically ordained social order, in the second stage the political development of absolutism and the economic power of increasingly capitalist socioeconomic relations undermined the traditional authority of the Estates, with the result that police came to express the power of the sovereign body and not merely the political consequences of social change. Having taken centre stage in international politics through the Peace of Westphalia (1648) the state now came to play a more active role in internal politics too, being seen by rulers, philosophers and natural law theorists as going beyond the preservation of order and justice in the face of perceived crises and having the task of actively promoting the general welfare and common good by fostering its productive energies, through which the welfare and prosperity of the state would itself be improved. The general acceptance that man had a creative responsibility for order was the wider backdrop for the recognition that social order could be created – indeed, *had* to be created – by the state. Thus one central theme in political theory in this period is that man creates an order (civil society and the state) and simultaneously transfers his creative power to part of his creation (the state), which then uses it to order civil society.[21] And as the sovereign state came to be seen to have the power to fabricate order, so the key institutional mechanism through which this fabrication was achieved – police, policy – became legitimated.

Given the need to fabricate order by actively re-forming the social body, European states instituted increasingly active, interventionist and wide-ranging police through its second stage: the establishment of the *lieutenant de police* for Paris (later known as the *lieutenant-général de police*) was imitated by Tsar Peter with his imperial police administration (*politsiia*) in St Petersburg (1718) and across the country from 1733, Friedrich II's police director in 1742 and Maria Theresa's police commissioner in 1751. In all of these regimes the almost universal powers and interests of police in the earlier centuries acted as the foundation for the active and dynamic principle within the systems of 'enlightened absolutism'. In the wider context of both political history and the development of political thought in which the idea of *raison d'état* had come to occupy centre stage, the problem of police was conceptualized as the problem of the state: the condition of the order which was to be maintained by police was the order of the state. For some writers 'policing' thus refers to all those areas where, as we might now put it, state power enters into social life. For this reason police was fundamental to *raison d'état* and writings on police were simultaneously investigations into the nature of state power – the first German rendering of the concept of 'reason of state', for example, appeared in the title of a translation of Botero's work *Della ragion di stato* (1589), which was translated as *Johannis Boteri Grundlicher Bericht Anordnung guter Polizeien und Regiments* (1596).[22] It is for this reason that Foucault rightly refers to the statism implicit in the police concept.[23] In this sense we can say that early discourse on policing was simultaneously a discourse on *Polizeistaat* or 'police state', implying a state which engages in wide-ranging internal administration, welfare and surveillance. Given both the negative connotations of the phrase 'police state' in the twentieth-century – the term came into general English usage in the 1930s as a means of conceptualizing the emerging totalitarian regimes – and the problematic liberal assumptions which underlie it – to which I return in Chapter 5 – a far better means of understanding *Polizeistaat* is as an early *welfare* state. For example, Brian Chapman has argued that the first 'police states' were dedicated to three purposes: the protection of the population, the welfare of the state and its citizens, and the improvement of society in all its aspects. Likewise Reinhold August Dorwart, in his account of *The Prussian Welfare State before 1740*, suggests that the only reason we do not equate *Polizeistaat* with *Wohlfahrsstaat* is because we are captives of twentieth-century definitions of police state and welfare state. He notes that the definition of the early welfare state as a *Polizeistaat* may best be observed in the identification of the borrowed French term with the German phrases, *gemeine Nutz* and *gemeine Beste*. 'From the French *polir* ("to establish good order") the word *Polizei* was adopted into the German legal language in the early sixteenth century. As there was no German equivalent, it could not be translated precisely; it connoted order, welfare, security'. By the eighteenth-century *Polizei* had become synonymous with *Wohlfahrt* or *gemeine Nutz*.[24] Given that the twentieth-century 'welfare state' is also characterised by and understood in terms of its wide-ranging *policy*, it makes as much sense to think of the policing of the common good or general welfare as a form of policy, and to think of *Polizeistaat* as 'policy state'.[25] Doing so would then enable us to place the adminstrative techniques of the police search for the common good in the wider intellectual context of the philosophical concern for the general welfare and happiness.[26] This is an important point to which I shall return throughout the book, but there is a broad point about the history of ideas and national context that is pertinent to mention at this juncture.

Excursus on the 'peculiarities of the English', or, Aristotle in Britain

Translating 'police state' as 'policy state' is especially useful in the English context, for at first glance it would appear that the tradition of discourse on police being discussed here is absent from British political thought. Though 'constables', 'watchmen', 'yeomanry' and other offices were known, the first official use of 'police' only occurred in December 1714 in Queen Anne's appointment of Commissioners of Police for Scotland, a body of men charged with the task of the general administration of the country. Thereafter the word gradually seeps into the English language, but only very slowly. As late as 1789 Bentham noted that although the term had been imported into Britain, it 'still retains its foreign garb'.[27] It is easy to conclude from this that in terms of its origins 'police' is an essentially 'Continental' concept. In the eighteenth century there was a widespread myth that the English system, having resisted absolutism in favour of the 'liberty of the subject', had no need for such a broad police concept, and this assumption became part of the rhetoric of a certain Whigish trend and liberal mythologizing in British police studies, a subject to which I shall return at several points below.

Although the idea of 'police' may appear to have been alien to British political discourse, the range of policies, projects and practices were remarkably similar in Britain to those on the Continent. While many of these practices may not have been understood as 'police', the meaning of this term was in fact captured in an English equivalent, 'policy', which also derives from the old French *policie*. As we have seen, 'police' and 'policy' were used in rather undifferentiated but broadly parallel ways across Europe into the sixteenth century and after. Hence the meaning given to the earliest mentions of 'policy' in the *Oxford English Dictionary* range from 'an organized state' (1390) or 'an organized and established system or form of government or administration' (1387), with particular reference to the decisions of rulers, urban conditions, and good conduct. Francis Bacon, for example, uses 'policy' as interchangeable with 'government' in *The Advancement of Learning* (1605), and on one occasion refers to government as 'the policing of cities and commonalties'. Likewise James I comments on 'how soone Kingdomes began to be setled in civilitie and policie', while Sir Walter Raleigh notes that 'Policy is an Art of Government'.[28] Like police, policy relies on the notion of what is to be policed (as opposed to 'policied'). It is for this reason that historians of police often slip between 'police' and 'policy' – as in John LeDonne's comment on policing in Russian towns that 'to administer the collectivity was to police it, to formulate a single *policy* of interdependent parts', or G.R. Elton's use of 'police' and 'policy' more or less interchangeably in his work on the Reformation[29] – and why historians of ideas often translate *Polizeistaat* as 'policy state'. In practical terms what this means is that England in the seventeenth and eighteenth centuries was not 'an almost unpoliced society', but that the agents of policing were understood as carrying out *policy* rather than being *police*.[30]

The reasons for the adoption of the different terms in different countries is partly due to the nature of translations of Aristotle's *Politics* from the thirteenth century onwards. In France and Germany the key terms of Aristotle's text – *polis* and *politeia* – were often translated as 'police', whereas in England they were translated as 'Commonwealth' or 'policy'. Despite the different translation, the meaning of the term 'policy' was understandably more or less the same as that of the French 'police'. The first English translation of Aristotle's *Politics* in 1598 translated *politeia* as 'policy' and defined it as 'the order and description, as of other offices in a city, so of that which hath the greatest and most soveraine authority: for the rule and administration of a Commonweale, hath evermore power and authority joined with it: which administration is called policie in Greek, and in English a Commonweale'. This was because the first English translations of Aristotle's text were from an earlier French translation of the Latin version. It was only later, with the first direct translation into English from Greek in 1776, that *politeia* was defined independently of either the concepts police or policy, as the 'form of government...the ordering and regulating of the city'.[31]

Mastering the market; imposing work

A notable feature of the police concern over the welfare and common good of society was that it took the interests of the state as its starting point. This touches on two key aspects of the first two stages of police. First, the contribution of police to state power occurred partly through the identification of the interests of the state and the social body and, second, that welfare and the general good were to be achieved via the police of the state of prosperity.

In the discourse of police during the first two stages, 'state' and 'civil society' are interchangeable terms; the state is synonymous with the social body.[32] It is for this reason that texts on policing are replete with such phrases as 'the great society is the state' and 'the welfare of the ruler and the happiness of the subjects can never be separated'.[33] This identification is understandable, given the range of functions that fell under the label of 'police'. Given the general order mandate under which it operated, the police appear to have possessed a pre-emptive right to inquire into the operation of 'private' enterprises and homes. But the use of the term 'private' here, as in Gerhard Oestreich's account of social disciplining or Dorwart's account of the Prussian welfare state, is a misleading anachronism.[34] There is no evidence for a conception of 'private life' or 'civil society' independent from the state in the period in question. Only with the development of liberalism would the idea of a 'private' sphere be separated from the 'public', or 'civil society' be separated from 'the state', with the former in both cases being defended as a sphere free from state intervention. The same point can be made regarding the relationship between 'state' and 'economy'. It is only in the late eighteenth century that 'oeconomy' becomes separated from its prior integration with questions of state power or sovereignty and isolated as an independent realm known as 'the economy'. These points will be developed in Chapter 2. For the moment, the point is that for the police project in the absolutist period 'the economy' and 'civil society' were not conceived of as autonomous realms and thus potentially subject to government intervention; rather, they were always already political.

To grasp the importance of this point we need to recognize that the shift from the first to the second stage of police was made in conjunction with the development of what became known in German-speaking areas as cameralism (*Cameralwissenschaft*) and the rise of a science of police (*Polizeiwissenschaft*). Although publications on police were extensive in German-speaking areas – a 1937 bibliography listed no fewer than 3,215 titles published between 1600 and 1800 under the heading 'science of police in the strict sense', and it has more recently been claimed that there are some 14,000 cameralist tracts[35] – these had their equivalents in non-German-speaking areas too. The term *Kammer* was derived from Latin and Greek and originally referred to the apartment where those concerned with the management of the revenues of a principality assembled, but came to denote systematized governmental procedure. Cameralism drew together a whole range of practices, and the theories concerning those practices, that on political and intellectual grounds liberal thought would later draw apart. In his *Einleitung in die Oeconomischen-, Policey- und Cameral-Wissenschaften* (*Introduction to the Economic, Police and Cameral Sciences*, 1727), for example, Justus Christoph Dithmar outlines how 'cameralia' teaches the administration of the prince's personal domain, 'oeconomica' the general administration of production, and '*Polizeisachen*' the preservation of the state (which Dithmar analyses through Prussian police ordinances). But he considers all three as subdivisions of the general *Polizei*. Similarly, Johann Heinrich Gottlob von Justi tries to distinguish between cameral science, oeconomy and police, but concedes that cameralism and police are inseparable – 'the police expert must sow if the cameralist is to reap' – and includes under *Oekonomie* all the general rules of management, including those which apply to the municipal and agricultural spheres. This refers equally to the routines of the emergent bureaucratic state. Thus although the main focus of *Polizeiwissenschaft* was the content of the routines being followed and the nature of the order being instituted via statutes, constituting as such a set of theories concerned with the detailed conditions for the institution and maintenance of order, this concern was intimately bound up with oeconomy. For Justi, police science is 'the first part of the *Oekonomie* of the state', and it is the duty of the police theorist to specify the nature of the political management of the economy, from taxation to mining practices. In one sense this notion of 'oeconomie' is not dissimilar to what would later become bourgeois political economy: for von Justi *oekonomie* is the science 'concerned with the goods and gainful occupation of private persons'. Yet this is understood as 'the great management of the state', an exercise to maintain and increase the resources of the state.[36] In other words, 'political economy' and 'police' were not separate fields of enquiry for cameralism. A Chair in *'Oeconomie, Policey und Kammer-Sachen'* and another in *'Kameral-Ökonomie and Polizeiwissenschaft'*, established by Friedrich Wilhelm I of Prussia in 1727,[37] are indicative of how close these fields of enquiry were conceived, as are the titles of key cameralist texts such as that mentioned by Dithmar, or Joseph von Sonnenfels's *Grundsätze der Policey, Handlung und Finanz* (1765). As Tribe points out, the objects found under the heading of *Cameralwissenschaft* are also found under *Oeconomy*.[38] The same is true of *Polizeiwissenschaft*. Police theorists therefore recognized the diversity of social life and the importance of productive and active economic performance, but sought to draw them both into a unity. It is for this reason that the same objects are found under 'cameralism', 'Oeconomie' and 'Police'.

The identification of state and civil society on the one hand and the concerns of police with the concerns of political oeconomy on the other meant that as much as cameralism and police science were essentially discourses on state power and the order of sovereignty, so state power and the general state of prosperity were interchangeable terms. Given the commitment to happiness and the perceived necessity of prosperity for happiness, this meant that the main interest of police was the development of commerce and the production of wealth. This was especially true of the second stage of police, when the positively conceived and dynamically executed activity of the state came to treat wealth and its cultivation as fundamental to the common good and general welfare. In the aftermath of the Thirty Years War and the formation of standing armies in the wake of the Peace of Westphalia, the state was left with no alternative but to manage society towards greater prosperity, in order to provide a healthy fiscal foundation for the financing of modern warfare and international relations. In order to sustain its status in the international order, the state had to maintain a condition of prosperity via administrative and legislative manipulation of the population. This was done with the use of a set of doctrines and policies that have become known, though not unproblematically, as mercantilism.

Mercantilism has been defined in different ways – as 'carrying the point of view of capitalistic industry into politics' in order to encourage 'the development of the state as a political power' (Weber), or as a 'system of State-regulated exploitation...the economic policy of an age of primitive accumulation' (Dobb) – but all definitions of it recognize the state as the heart of mercantilist doctrine. As a state-directed economic policy concerned with the wealth of nations, mercantilism identifies the state of prosperity with the prosperity of the state: for mercantilism, the state is both the subject and the object of policy, as Eli Hecksher puts it.[39] Thus the characteristic creations of mercantile policies were the royal manufactures and state-regulated guilds in France and the chartered companies in England. Unsurprisingly, many have therefore treated mercantilism and cameralism as more or less interchangeable terms.[40] Both presuppose an identification of the interests of state with those of society, and thus operate with the assumption of state 'intervention' (as it would later become) into the economy. The traditional instruments of both – laws, decrees and regulations issued by the sovereign power – are the same, as are the final goals – the strengthening of state power via the bolstering of the might of the sovereign and the prosperity of the state, to be achieved through the encouragement of a general state of prosperity.

Whatever the exact nature of the relationship between mercantilism and cameralism, the language of both is much the same, with the net effect that both identify the state of prosperity with the prosperity of the state. Moreover, for the state of prosperity to be achieved, and for the state to be a state, the population had to be policed. Policing mechanisms designed to facilitate the growth of the money supply, population, foreign trade and mining thus became integral to the development of the state itself as well as the condition of prosperity. In this sense we can say that one of the fundamental concerns of policing is with the state of prosperity: the wealth of nations. To this end police theorists argued that the state should secure a flourishing trade and devote its power to the preservation and increase of the resources of private persons in particular and the state of prosperity in general, by overseeing the foundations of commerce. For Justi, 'All the methods whereby the riches of the state may be increased, in so far as the authority of the government is concerned, belong consequently under the charge of the police.'[41] In arguing this way I am not, *pace* Hull, trying to *reduce* the cameralist and police view of civil society to economic activity; rather, I am trying to draw out and specify the grounds for the police view of order. As much as one might point to the police concern with sexuality, for example, it makes little sense to describe this as part of the search for order 'for order's sake' as Hull does. As Hull goes on to say, 'the cameralists' fixation on the *Kammer* (treasury) often led them to emphasize the economic aspects of civil society, seemingly to the exclusion of all others'.[42]

The commitment to a state of prosperity was not, however, thought of as a commitment to a system of *laissez faire*; nor was it a demand for 'state ownership'. Rather, it was an argument for the simultaneous control and support of commerce in order that the wealth of the state be increased. Prosperity, on this basis, involved mastering the market. In France, for example, Delamare had argued for a politicized understanding of the economy as part of the theory and practice of police. This was especially true as regards trade in key commodities such as grain, giving rise to what Charles Tilly has described as the 'food-centered conception' of police power. As Steven Kaplan puts it, 'the grain trade was too important to be left to the grain traders', to the extent that the hallmark of the well-ordered police state was the high standard of its 'grain police'. Authorities 'tracked grain from the time it was seeded until bakers made it into bread, watching its movement from hand to hand and trying to keep it optimally visible and reassuringly ubiquitous by enforcing certain rules of conduct and exchange. This surveillance was called the police of provisioning.' Any trader who wished to trade in grain, for example, had to first register with the police, giving their names, addresses, details of where they made their purchases, the names of their correspondents, the location of their storehouses or magazines, the anticipated scale of their trade, and the usual place of destination. Certain groups of person, such as *laboureurs* and *fermiers*, were prohibited from dealing in grain while others, such as bakers, were allowed to buy grain for the exercise of their profession but forbidden from reselling it. The grain itself had to be registered and have a certificate of purchase as a kind of 'passport', and the buying merchant had to inform the police of the amount, price and quality of the merchandise he had purchased. The police would also enter bakeries, open sacks and barrels looking for illegal supplies and workers, and, not least, would set the price of bread and change it each time grain prices rose or fell. Not only was the merchant meant to be unable to hide anything about his trade, he was also expected to be traceable at any moment and willing to modify his trade in a way declared publicly useful by the police.[43] Similar policing mechanisms existed across Europe, from the 'police granaries' of Russia to the 'market police' of Austria.[44] The purpose of this police of the grain trade, along with the police of a whole range of other trades, was clear: the police believed that they could prevent artificial shortages and violent price oscillations and thus satisfy one of the basic subsistence needs of the population in a regular and predictable fashion. This would promote public tranquillity: guaranteeing the food supply was crucial to guaranteeing order. Commodities such as grain were too important to be left to the vagaries of the market and corrupted by the search for profit; they had to be subject to the authority of police.

Prosperity, however, cannot be separated from the concomitant concern with subsistence in general, the state of work and, most crucially, the condition of poverty. Behind the police of the state of prosperity as the basis of order was a more specific concern over the place of the poor and the potential threat posed by the new 'class' of poverty to the emerging structures of private property. 'Order' is hardly threatened unless there is a force which appears to possess the potential of undermining it, and as bourgeois social relations began to stamp themselves across the face of society the major threat appeared to be the labouring poor. Thus the need to shape the workforce played an increasingly significant part in policing. From an early stage, then, one finds pamphlets specifically on the police of alms or the police of the poor – *La Police de l'almonse de Lyon* (1530) and *La Police des pauvres de Paris* (1544), for example. More generally, one finds that the poor had a presence in texts on police, either as beggars and vagrants (or at least, potential beggars and vagrants) or as a general category subject to police, as Pasquale Pasquino's outline of the relationship between police and the state of prosperity makes clear.[45] This is because the administration of poverty was and is the heart of the police project. By virtue of its concern with the production of wealth, policing meant (and, I shall argue, continues to mean) policing the class of poverty.

In one sense this implies a set of *immobilizing* practices. Part of the intention in ensuring adequate provisions was the straightforward strategic one of forestalling the disorder arising in times of general need. According to police commissioner Lemaire, a good display of food 'sustains the poor, encourages them; it removes and banishes from their minds the fears and uncertainties most capable of causing them to contemplate the ruin and misery which pursue them and which, in excess, drive them to despair'. Or as Leray de Chaumont, a French entrepreneur deeply involved in financing and organizing the royal grain reserve for Paris, put it in more explicitly political terms in 1766: 'if 800,000 people [in Paris] were to lack bread for six hours, *everything* would blow up'.[46] In other words, the science of police can be traced to the fear that the forerunners of the proletariat would invade property.[47] But it also the case that the science of police can be traced to the understanding that the forerunners of the proletariat were *essential* to property. Of the 'free and rightless proletariat' created by the breaking-up of feudalism and the forcible expropriation of the people from the soil, Marx comments:

On the one hand, these men, suddenly dragged from their accustomed mode of life, could not immediately adapt themselves to the discipline of their new condition. They were turned in massive quantities into beggars, robbers and vagabonds...hence at the end of the fifteenth and during the whole of the sixteenth centuries, a bloody legislation against vagabondage was enforced throughout Western Europe. The fathers of the present working class were chastised for their enforced transformation into vagabonds and paupers.

The argument in this book is partly an attempt to develop Marx's comment that the 'bloody legislation' and 'bloody discipline' which created a class of wage labour was a product of the 'police methods to accelerate the accumulation of capital by increasing the degree of exploitation of labour'.[48] The more interesting aspect of police in this period is therefore its *mobilizing* work. Whereas in its immobilizing activities police sought to render disorderly elements harmless, in its mobilizing activities it sought to fashion these elements into a mobile and active workforce. This project would culminate in the fabrication of wage labour in the third stage of police, as we shall see in Chapters 3 and 4.

The police of poverty was regarded as a necessity because of the perceived connection between all forms of 'disorderly' behaviour, such as begging, crime, gambling and drinking. Instead of working, a French royal declaration of 1686 put it, the poor 'give themselves up to beggary, and in becoming addicted to idleness, commit robberies and fall unfortunately into many other crimes', a point reiterated some 80 years later in the committee established to devise measures for the suppression of begging and vagrancy.[49] These were understood as a threat to public propriety and the common good. The police distinguished between groups according to the degree of danger they appeared to pose to the common good – domestic labourers, prostitutes, the young, religious and political groups – but the most significant part of this enemy was the growing class of poverty (and its social cousin, the 'class' of vagrants), which was most in need of being mobilized for work. The idea expressed in the royal declaration just cited is repeated in the work of police theorists. Sonnenfels, for example, argued that 'there are only two roads open to make one's livelihood if one does not have an inherited fortune: work or crime'.[50] Ostensibly, the concern over vagrancy and begging was a concern that those persons engaged in such activities were more likely to engage in criminal activity, but in some sense the greatest 'crime' was thought to be the idleness itself, since this deprived the state of the vagabond's contribution to prosperity and was at the heart of all other disorderly behaviour. It is almost as if all disorderly activities were subsumed under the category of 'idleness'.[51] At the heart of this approach to poverty was a combination of the understanding that the prosperity and strength of the state depended on the productive power of the labour force, with the fear that the producers of wealth were the same group who could potentially become a burden on the relief system. In France, Colbert sought to promote the taxable wealth of the nation by encouraging the growth of the *manufacture* (the manufactory), centralizing production in a factory. This would strengthen the state by employing the poor in operations either founded by royal patent or at least sufficiently policed such that the industry would not be subject to periodic crises. The more of the poor who could be forced into manufactories, the more people there would be to pay taxes, with the added benefit that the manufactory enabled a firmer disciplining of the labour force: workers were to be subject to detailed control over when they worked, the conditions in which they worked, the length of holidays they were entitled to, the kind of behaviour allowed at work, and so on. This was based on the central mercantilist doctrine, expressed by Colbert in his advice to the Aldermen of Auxerre in 1667, that 'since abundance always results from labour and poverty from idleness, [the] most important task is to find means to restrain the poor and to set them to work'.[52] A century later in Austria Sonnenfels argued that the government should prevent idleness, and presented ways of doing this: preventing begging, careful inspection to ensure that everyone in the state is earning a living, checking all useless occupations akin to vagrancy, reduction of the number of students, good discipline of the servant class and, finally, workhouses and penal institutions as a means of ensuring that these methods work.

Though the police theorists lacked a political economy finely tuned enough to pinpoint the precise nature of the relationship between poverty and wealth, they nonetheless knew what the broad connection was: when they looked at beggars and vagrants, they saw able-bodied (but lazy, ignorant and potentially rebellious) workers witholding their labour and thus not producing wealth. The solution was clear: 'the philosopher's stone, so long sought after, has been found – it is work'.[53] Sonnenfels's comment that 'society should demand that every citizen ought to work' expressed the founding principle of police.[54] As Foucault notes,

> Police is the totality of measures which make work possible and necessary for all those who could not live without it; the question Voltaire would soon formulate, Colbert's contemporaries had already asked: 'Since you have established yourselves as a people, have you not yet discovered the secret of forcing all the rich to make all the poor work? Are you still ignorant of the first principles of the police?'.[55]

The outcome was a series of measures to impose work. Whereas the measures against vagrancy and begging in the first stage of police were largely merely punitive – early police ordinances laid down that, for example, all unemployed people should be expelled from the city or that they be whipped or put in the galleys – in the second stage they became more actively interventionist and 'positive', seeking to mobilize the resource that the vagabond possessed. Although expulsion and other measures still existed,[56] the general thrust of the policing of the poor was increasingly towards institutions of confinement across Europe – workhouses, *hopitaux generaux*, *Zuchthausern*, *Tuchthuizen*, *Armen- und Wohlfahrtsanstalten* – in which they could be set to work. In France this took the form of the *enfermement des pauvres*, the enclosing of the poor in 'hospitals' under the overall authority of the police. Under Louis XIV institutions such as the General Hospital of Paris were designed to serve as a refuge for the 'true' or 'deserving' poor and as a penal workhouse for vagabonds and beggars. This process of *enfermement* accelerated greatly with the royal edict of 1724 and, in the light of the failure of this edict to fully eradicate vagabondage, the creation in 1768 of new workhouses, the *depots de mendicite* under the direct authority of the central state, to ensure that beggars and vagabonds were removed from society. The 1724 edict held that the deserving poor would receive shelter, food and assistance in the nearest hospital, while the 'undeserving' would be given two weeks to find work. Those who could not find work on their own would be housed in the hospital and put to work on public projects or in the workhouse. A similar scheme operated with the *depots* instituted from 1768, which were estimated to have detained 230,000 persons from 1768 to 1790.[57]

Now, it is widely accepted that absolutism revealed a new and modern conception of the state, from which the bourgeois state proper would slowly develop. Gerhard Oestreich has also argued that the 'the establishment of social discipline was the effective achievement of absolutism' and Perry Anderson has shown that capitalism was *nurtured* by the absolutist state, despite the absolutist tendency to defend the domination of the landed aristocracy.[58] To these points we can add that this nurturing of capitalism occurred via the *intensified policing of the poor* in the second stage of police. The primary aim of this policing was not to confine persons under some great scheme of incarceration or 'great confinement', as Foucault calls it, however productive this might be, but to help fashion a labour force outside the institution by making the able-bodied beggar and vagrant offer their labour power for sale on the market. This was the process by which the feudal workforce was 'forcibly expropriated from the soil, driven from their homes, turned into vagabonds, and then whipped, branded and tortured by grotesquely terroristic laws into accepting the discipline necessary for the system of wage-labour'.[59] Short of that, they should be made to work in hospitals or on public work projects. The eighteenth-century workhouse, like its nineteenth-century successor, peformed a joint task: it instilled labour discipline into the poverty-stricken yet idle or unemployed poor, and it encouraged industrious workers to believe that the only option to the discipline of 'free' labour was the discipline of the workhouse. The hospitals, workhouses and other places of confinement should be thought of not as a grand project of confinement of the marginal individuals and social lepers of modern society – the elderly, mentally ill, invalids and orphaned children – but as part of the project of constructing a modern workforce trading its labour power for a wage. As such, policing should be thought of as at the centre of the construction of a new form of order. In the eighteenth century this was increasingly a *bourgeois* order, though not yet fully so. The vagrant's key characteristic in this sense was as a symbol of *disorder*, an act of defiance against order in all senses of the term (without work, without place, without family).[60] This is the basis of the interest in education in the writings of the police theorists – to teach discipline and orderly behaviour[61] – and their desire to ban festivals, on the grounds that these disrupted the production process by undermining the temporal rhythms of the newly emerging social order, wasted energies best expended at work and encouraged disorderly behaviour.[62]

Having emerged as a response to the fear of 'masterless men', police helped transform these masterless men into rational calculating individuals in pursuit of clearly defined economic goals. Its concern for the prosperity of the state meant that it had to encourage wealth production, and thus the productivity of labour, as the foundational activity of modern society. It therefore prioritized productive activity in the material and economic sphere. That is, its mobilizing work was the mobilization *of* work. In other words, the policing of prosperity began the process of the making of the working class, a process which would only be completed once a new form of master had properly emerged on the historical stage.

In his work on the well-ordered police state, Marc Raeff claims that in succeeding in creating conditions and mental attitudes favourable to productive enterprise, police legislation abolished its own *raison d'être*.[63] Creating rational calculating individuals brought to the surface a major underlying tension in the police idea. This tension is best captured in the Latin phrase used by Foucault when grappling with the idea of police: *omnes et singulatim* – everyone together and each individually. The project of imposing work meant rationalizing individual material activity, but this undermined the demand that all work together under some common good.

This underlying tension was compounded by the emergence of an alternative doctrine in the eighteenth century which focused on the same rational individual and self-interested economic agent. This emergent doctrine was to pose the greatest challenge to police theory by undermining its central claims and by presenting an ideological defence of another sort of order. That doctrine was liberalism, and the new form of order was to be the rule of capital.

2
Liberalism and the Police of Property

1776 was a good year for liberalism. Mentioned in the previous chapter in the context of translations of Aristotle's *Politics*, 1776 was important for liberals as the year which saw publication of Adam Smith's *Wealth of Nations*, the American revolution, and texts defending the revolution such as Thomas Paine's *Common Sense*. In one sense this chapter is *about* 1776, for in it we shall explore the implications of the rise of liberalism on the police concept. Although the full implications will only become clear in later chapters, it is worth spending some time on discussion of the issues surrounding the rise of liberalism in the late eighteenth century, for it will be recalled that I suggested that the third stage of police could be taken as beginning in this period.

There are two broad issues to be addressed. First, the challenge to police science posed by liberalism formed a key part of the dynamic clash that took place in the late eighteenth century between rival versions of the state of prosperity. Second, liberalism also came to argue for the rule of law over the rule of police. The first two sections of this chapter focus on these two issues respectively. The discussion then brings these points together to tease out some of the main theoretical contours of an increasingly hegemonic liberal ideology, to link these to the rise of a society increasingly dominated by the power of capital, and to spell out the implications of these for the police concept and the idea of social order.

From police to political economy?

Adam Smith's *Inquiry into the Nature and Causes of the Wealth of Nations* has long been known as a text written against both the mercantilist assumption that a surplus on the balance of trade is the main source of wealth and the agriculturalist belief that agriculture is the only productive sector. Vivienne Brown has noted that in its attack on both these versions of political economy the *Wealth of Nations* reconceptualizes them in such a way that they both come to occupy the same theoretical space, a space from which the *Wealth of Nations* could then detach itself. One concept crucial to effect this transformation is that of 'police'.[1] In this sense the concept of police is of paramount importance in Smith's work. Yet between the *Lectures on Jurisprudence* (1762–64) and the *Wealth of Nations* (1776) the concept undergoes a dramatic change.

In the *Lectures on Jurisprudence* Smith uses the concept of police in a way familiar to us from Chapter 1. Noting the historical origins of the term – although it is borrowed from the French it can in fact be traced back to the Greek idea of 'policy' or 'politicks', both of which refer to 'the regulation of a government in generall' – Smith regards the main task of government as 'promoting the opulence of the state'. This task is defined as 'police' – a broad heading under which a discussion of a wide variety of issues takes place, including the propensity to truck, barter and exchange, and the division of labour. 'Whatever regulations are made with respect to the trade, commerce, agriculture, manufactures of the country are considered as belonging to the police'. For Smith police has three aspects: (1) cleanliness, (2a) security against accidents such as fires, (2b) security attained through patrols and guards, and (3) the cost of provisions and the maintenance of the market. Where (1) and (2a) are 'too trifling' to be considered a branch of jurisprudence, (2b) and (3) are both considered part of the police. Yet it soon becomes clear that the supply of readily available cheap commodities supersedes the patrols and guards needed for security. Consequently, it is the smooth operation of the market – the cheapness and supply of commodities – that is the most important branch of police.[2]

Smith believes that crime is a product of the socioeconomic conditions prevalent in society, and of the condition of the poor in particular. For Smith, the condition of dependence experienced by many servants has a detrimental effect: if too many are employed by one household and economic conditions force that household to dispense with some of its servants, then they are thrown into a situation in which they are liable to commit crimes. Smith notes that although Paris has far more police regulations and statutes than London, it nonetheless has more crime, a fact he attributes to the nature of the development of commerce in the two nations: in Paris 'the spirit of the feudall government is not so intirely abolished as it is here'. The higher crime rate of Paris is due to the much higher number of servants in France. The 'idle and luxurious' life they lead 'renders them altogether depraved both in mind and body' such that when their masters render them redundant they are unable to support themselves by work; the consequence is that they turn to crime. In England, in contrast, where the convention is now to have no more than one servant each, there is less likelihood that the servant will be dispensed with, and thus less people set adrift. 'We see too that in this town [Glasgow], where each one seldom has above one man servant, there are few or no capitall crimes committed, and those that are, most commonly by strangers; whereas at Edinburgh, where the resort of the nobility and gentry draws together a vast number of servants who are frequently set adrift by their masters, there are severall every year.' Smith's specific point – that 'it is the custom of having many retainers and dependents which is the great source of all the disorders' – in fact rests on a far more general historical point: that the extent of crime is linked to the degree to which a country or city has retained feudal relics. Those that have not, that is, those that have commerce and manufacturing as the predominant means to a state of prosperity, experience less crime. In other words, 'the establishment of commerce and manufactures' gives workers an independence and is thus 'the best police for preventing crimes'.[3]

Given that Smith regards the *Lectures on Jurisprudence* as a contribution to the debate about the promotion of opulence and the state of prosperity, the centrality of police to these conditions means that the *Lectures* are in some sense a positive contribution to eighteenth-century discourse on police, resonating with the themes found in police science. As Howard Caygill has noted, the same four major functions of government – justice, revenue, arms and police (policy) – are identified by both Smith and Frederick the Great. In his *Political Testament* (1752) Frederick the Great notes that 'government rests on four great pillars: on the administration of justice, prudent taxation, the maintenance of discipline in the army, and finally, the art of co-ordinating the measures for the preservation of the interest of the state, which is called policy'. In opening the *Lectures* Smith declares that 'there are four things which will be the design of every government': justice or internal peace, the opulence of the state (police), taxation as a form of revenue and protection from foreign injuries.[4] Smith's reference to the origins of the term in ancient Greek and not just the French is presumably intended to circumvent the negative connotations of spies and despotism associated with police on the Continent at the time.

By the *Wealth of Nations*, however, Smith's use of the concept of police has altered dramatically. This is exemplified in the now famous example of the pin-factory, which is commonly understood through Smith's discussion of it in the *Wealth of Nations*. In the latter text it appears in Chapter

I of Book I and is used to illustrate the principle of the division of labour. But in the *Lectures* the pin-factory makes its appearance under the heading of 'police', and its role in reducing crimes by helping to sustain a state of prosperity is highlighted. Moreover, in the *Wealth of Nations* police gets few very specific mentions, virtually all of which have negative connotations, denoting economic systems in which the state favours the industry of either town or country. In this context 'police' is part of the wrong type of government. Thus police may keep the market price of a commodity above the natural price and is associated with 'foolish' rules. In the context of European government police is considered as an obstruction to the free circulation of labour and in the context of the government of China, Egypt, Indostan, ancient Greece and ancient Rome police is described as the severe and sometimes violent policy of favouring agriculture or limiting the movement of labour.[5] We can thus agree with Brown that the word 'police' in the *Wealth of Nations* is not used as a self-description as it had been in the *Lectures on Jurisprudence*. As Brown notes, whereas in the *Lectures* 'police' denotes the general heading under which its own discussion of economic topics could be organized, in the *Wealth of Nations* this is no longer the case. In the latter text the word 'police' is used negatively to denote systems of state regulation to which the *Wealth of Nations* is opposed.[6]

Although in the *Lectures* Smith relates a society's crime rate to the degree to which it has become properly commercial having abandoned feudal practices, he lacks the means of conceptualizing a state of prosperity outside of the concept of police and thus, implicitly at least, the prosperity of the state. As in the science of police, Smith identifies plenty and the state of prosperity as the key issue, treats questions of what would later become the separate discipline of 'political economy' as a branch of jurisprudence and subsumes its central concerns under the category of police. Although he immediately narrows down the focus by dismissing the extra-economic concerns of police as 'too mean and trifling a subject to be treated of in a system of jurisprudence', this nevertheless leaves political economy as the main branch of police. The *Lectures* are thus to be seen as a contribution to our understanding of 'the opulence of the state'.[7] In the *Wealth of Nations*, however, poverty and labour are dealt with through a new conceptual tool – the self-generating and self-regulating commercial society. The state of prosperity is therefore rethought as a condition of the social rather than of the state itself. As such, the sovereign body is discharged from 'the duty of superintending the industry of private people, and of directing it towards the employments most suitable to the interest of the society'. The statesman who seeks to direct the desire for private gain into socially useful ends 'would not only load himself with a most unnecessary attention, but assume an authority which could safely be trusted, not only to no single person, but to no council or senate whatever'. Since every person 'becomes in some measure a merchant', the 'natural effort of every individual to better his own condition' is sufficiently 'capable of carrying on the society of wealth and prosperity'. Social good comes from the pursuit of private interest, guided as this interest is by the 'hidden hand'.[8] Duncan Forbes has suggested that the most original contribution made by the Scottish Enlightenment was to destroy the 'Legislator Myth'.[9] Part of Smith's contribution to this was to free political thought from the vision of police as the prime mechanism of the power of the 'legislator'. The tasks of the sovereign body are narrowed down to internal and external security and of providing the sort of public works and institutions which it is not in the interest of any individual to supply.

Precisely why this transformation takes place in Smith's work is a matter of speculation, but we can make some fairly safe claims. Smith's distance from the concept of police by the time of the *Wealth of Nations* may well have been a result of a greater acquaintance with these doctrines gained from his time spent on the Continent between delivering his lectures on jurisprudence and writing the *Wealth of Nations*. Smith left Glasgow in January 1764, spent some 18 months in Toulouse and a few months in Geneva and then Paris, before returning to Scotland via London.[10] During this period a debate was taking place in France over the liberalization of the grain trade, with some favouring a 'system of natural liberty' and others a 'system of police'. In a Declaration of May 1763 and a further Edict of July 1764 the government of Louis XV broke with the provisioning tradition in France. The king renounced the old police and thus the very premises upon which the provisioning of grain had been based, proclaiming instead an era of liberty in which grain would be freed from the policing mechanisms to which it had hitherto been accustomed. This opened the trade to anyone who wanted to participate, abolished laws requiring merchants to register their transactions, permitted off-market transactions and repealed the tolls levied on grain in transit. In making his declarations the king made a major contribution to the process of liberalization – 'absolutism in the service of liberalism', as Kaplan describes it – which had been demanded by influential writers. In his *Essai sur la police général des grains* (1753), for example, Claude-Jacques Herbert struck at the heart of police by claiming that in intervening in the supply of grain the police had merely driven prices higher or helped dry up the sources of supply. As such it was failing to secure the happiness of the people: 'The more we wanted to perfect this Police [of grain] the more we strayed from the right path.'[11] Other writers in the 1750s also helped shape more liberal ideas on police by attempting to rethink the conditions of prosperity. The most prominent of these were Quesnay and Turgot. Although the physiocrats would later become one of Smith's main targets, they nonetheless helped develop the liberal critique of police by identifying the right of property with total liberty – this was the period in which the term *laissez faire* became increasingly common.[12] Grain was a commodity like any other, the argument went, and as such should be left to free trade as part of the wider system of liberty.

When Smith travelled in France, then, he would have encountered an ongoing debate which, to oversimplify somewhat, boiled down to a battle between the 'police' or the 'liberty' of the grain trade. Underlying the arguments for both was the assumption that one would better lead to order; Turgot, for example, was concerned with bringing both *liberté* and order to French markets. Smith was certainly aware of some of these debates. The outline of the jurisprudential terrain at the beginning of the *Lectures* would appear to have been adopted from the sections on police in Bielfield's *Institutions politiques* (1760), and on more than one occasion he cites Herbert's *Essai*.[13] It has also been argued that Smith's personal contact with Turgot and Quesnay was 'the most exciting passage in Smith's intellectual development, second in importance only to his early contact with Hume'.[14] Moreover, despite the Royal edicts encouraging the debate on the liberalization of the grain trade, and the 'seasonally lenient police' practised in France, the fact that when Smith was travelling there the grain trade was beginning one of its periodic crises which lasted the best part of a decade (from 1765 through to 1775) meant an intensification of the policing mechanisms at this time.[15] Thus in the context of a debate concerning the nature of liberty and police, Smith also encountered police intervention of the most powerful kind. It is not too far-fetched to suggest that this brought home to Smith the dangers of policing prosperity beyond merely protecting internal security and preventing crime. It is also perhaps pertinent that other writers within the Scottish Enlightenment during these years had also shifted attention away from police in a way that had affected Smith. Adam Ferguson, for example, had argued that 'the great object...is to secure to the family its means of subsistence and settlement; to protect the industrious in the pursuit of his occupation; to reconcile the restrictions of police, and the social affections of mankind, with their separate and interested pursuits'.[16]

The effects of Smith's change of orientation regarding police were far-reaching, and we have yet to explore its full implications. First, however, we need to spell out the political and intellectual background to it. Given

Smith's reputation as a political economist, it may well appear as though police science was displaced by political economy – that his work is part of an overall shift 'from police to political economy', as Steven Kaplan describes this period.[17] But as Donald Winch has pointed out, Smith was sparing in his use of the term 'political economy', partly because rival writers had used the term, such as Sir James Steuart in his *Inquiry into the Principles of Political Economy*, but also because Smith saw political economy as but one part of the much larger inquiries on which he was engaged. Smith defines political economy in the introduction to Book 4 of the *Wealth of Nations*:

> Political oeconomy, considered as a branch of the science of a statesman or legislator, proposes two distinct objects; first, to provide a plentiful revenue or subsistence for the people, or more properly to enable them to provide such a revenue or subsistence for themselves; and secondly, to supply the state or commonwealth with a revenue sufficient for the publick services. It proposes to enrich both the people and the sovereign.[18]

As Winch points out, the fact that Smith defines political economy as a branch of the science of a statesman or legislator reminds us that the *Wealth of Nations* began life as those parts of Smith's *Lectures* dealing with the subordinate questions of 'police, revenue and arms'; Peter Miller has also usefully pointed to the origins of political economy in the effort to further the power and wealth of the state.[19] Thus despite the differences between the *Wealth of Nations* and Smith's earlier texts, the *Wealth of Nations* can be seen as the logical end of seventeenth- and eighteenth-century arguments that only the statesman or sovereign can recognize and defend the common good of the nation, a common good defined in terms of wealth. In this sense rather than obliterating the police notion entirely, in the way that 'from police to political economy' suggests, Smith's work can in some sense be seen as his own version of 'the great system of public police', his contribution to 'the perfection of police'.[20] As much as Smith may have opposed the absolutist tendencies of police science, he did not oppose a new understanding of police. And the basis of this new understanding is less political economy and more a new set of *liberal* ideals. While J.G.A. Pocock's strictures against the loose use of 'liberalism' in accounting for intellectual changes in the late eighteenth century are understandable,[21] it is nonetheless clear that Smith saw his project as an argument for *liberal government* rather than 'political economy'. He distinguishes the system of natural liberty from Colbert's mercantilism, for example, by arguing that 'instead of allowing every man to pursue his own interest his own way, upon the liberal plan of equality, liberty and justice, he bestowed upon certain branches of industry extraordinary privileges, while he laid others under as extraordinary restraints'. And on subjects as diverse as colonies, banking, the corn trade, the professions, exports, the rewards paid to labour, and individual social vices, Smith makes it quite clear that it is liberal arrangements that should be favoured.[22]

It is such liberal arguments which eventually give rise to a new vision of the perfection of police. But to fully grasp the significance of Smith's contribution here we need to identify the wider ideological context in which other writers helped develop the liberal vision of order and police, not least through the idea of the rule of law.

From rule of police to rule of law?

Reflecting on politics in the 1860s, the German liberal Eduard Lasker made the following observation:

> Rule of law and rule of police are two different ways to which history points, two methods of development between which peoples must choose and have chosen...The true man is the independent citizen. Every citizen should and must be independent, for each has to see to his own welfare. He has no other claim on the state than protection from injurious force.[23]

Lasker was reflecting on the transformation of Prussian society, defending the rule of law from the rule of police. This defence goes back to the development of liberal thought in the late eighteenth century, and played some part in the transformation of the idea of police being traced here, for liberal writers initially came to *oppose* the rule of law to the rule of police, separating legislative and judicial acts from the far more limited function of preventing crime and protecting internal security (order).

In Germany the most important thinkers challenged the principles of police and *Polizeistaat* in the name of an independent civil society with specified rights for its members. In Kant's classical defence of Enlightenment as man's emergence from his self-incurred immaturity and the courage to be wise, for example, the emphasis on the use of one's own understanding and the ability to work one's own way out of immaturity not only requires the public to be left in a state of individual freedom, but also that the courage to use one's own understanding be defended by a system of laws. This would be a 'civil state' under the rule of law, in which people

live as subjects with equality before the law and are free to pursue their
freedom as the basis for self-development. Kant's defence is conducted partly
in terms of the question of happiness, the universal obsession of the eighteenth century. Whereas the cameralists and philosophers such as Leibniz
saw the main political project as the communal happiness – for Justi, for
example, 'the ultimate aim of each and every republic is therefore unques-
tionably the common happiness', or 'the common blissful happiness
[gemeinschaftliche Gluckseligkeit] of ruler and subjects', while for Leibniz
the most perfect society seeks 'the general and supreme happiness'[24] – Kant
proposed an alternative eudemonism more consistent with the rule of law
than a system of police. 'Men have different views on the empirical end of
happiness and what it consists of, so that as far as happiness is concerned,
their will cannot be brought under any common principle.' 'The sovereign [who] wants to make the people happy as he thinks best...becomes a
despot.' The sovereign power should content itself merely with guaranteeing the equal freedom of all before the law and protecting their security,
so that 'each remains free to seek his happiness in whatever way he thinks
best'. This necessarily limits the role of police. It is not that 'the police are
of no positive benefit', but that 'their main business is merely to prevent
the violence of which citizens stand in mutual fear, in order that each may
pursue his vocation in peace and security'.[25]

Kant is supported here by a number of other writers. Wilhelm von
Humboldt, for example, distinguishes between police as the state providing security and police as the state offering 'positive welfare'. 'A State, then,
has one of two ends in view; it designs either to promote happiness, or
simply to prevent evil...If it restricts its concerns to the second of these
objects, it aims merely at security; and I would oppose this term security to
every other possible end of State agency, and comprise these last under the
general heading of Positive Welfare.' By 'positive welfare' Humboldt understands the Polizeistaat, for it oversees subsistence by managing the poor
laws and encouraging culture, industry and commerce, regulates the financial markets and controls imports and exports, and tries to remedy or
prevent natural disasters. 'All such institutions', for Humboldt, 'have harm-
ful consequences, and are irreconcilable with a true system of polity.' In
considering police, then, we 'must overlook the fact that those regulations
which do not relate to security, but are directed to the positive welfare of
the citizen, are most commonly classed under this heading [police laws]
since it does not fall in with the system of classification I have adopted'.
On this view police laws are to be conceived of in the most limited fashion: 'they either restrict actions whose immediate consequences are likely
to endanger the rights of others; or they impose limitations on those which

usually lead ultimately to transgressions of the law; or, lastly, they may specify what is necessary for the preservation or exercise of the power of the State itself'.[26]

Highlighting the rule of law over the rule of police was also a common theme in America as it appropriated certain ideas from Europe and then handed them back again as the central principles of a good polity. Some of the founding fathers there toyed with using 'police' as part of the theoretical arsenal of America's vision of a good society. Shortly after he became governor of Virginia in 1779, for example, Jefferson proposed to the College of William and Mary a Chair in Law and Police as a means of achieving his vision of good training for republican citizens. As Christopher Tomlins points out, the chair is symbolic of the relationship between law and police in Jefferson's thinking, implying a state built not just to realize a liberal capitalist society but also the general well-being and happiness of the population. It is also indicative of the fact that from roughly the time of the revolution Americans had a range of alternative options regarding the best polity open to them; it is at this moment that the language of police entered American political discourse.[27] Unsurprisingly, it did so with its old European notions intact: 'police' was taken to refer to general regulations coextensive with 'government', and the management of communal good order and collective happiness. But instead another vision won out, that of Madison and Hamilton, for whom the main concern was a more limited vision of security; as such they proposed a vision of the state which privileged law over politics and thus strictly limited the role of police within the framework of the rule of law. The insistence in *The Federalist Papers* on a *reverence* for the law appeared to turn law into the sovereign power. 'In America *the law is king*', Thomas Paine famously noted.[28] This idea of law became a central component of the self-understanding of the US constitution: that government should be 'a government of laws, and not of men'. As Tomlins notes,

> Between the Revolution and the beginning of the nineteenth century, law became *the* paradigmatic discourse explaining life in America... [L]aw moved from an essentially peripheral position as little more than one among a number of authoritative discourses through which the social relations of a locality were reproduced...to a position of supreme imaginative authority from which, by the end of the century, its sphere of institutional and normative influence appeared unbounded.

This had an important effect on the police concept:

In the newly created republic, therefore, as the discourse of police emerged...it encountered the competing discourse of law claiming to provide the language of rule in the new polity and also invoking, hastily transmuted into a language of consent, its own independent heritage as a superordinate source or mode of rule *in itself*. The subsequent nineteenth-century fate of police, indeed, is an apt illustration of the power of this ideology.[29]

This is not to say that liberal constitutionalism surrounding the rule of law won out immediately. Both Tomlins and William Novak[30] make clear the extent to which the theory and practice of police powers in the older sense of the term continued well into the nineteenth century, operating alongside the newer liberal assumptions and practices. The reasons for this are explored in Chapters 4 and 5 below. The point here is that the *myth* of liberal constitutionalism certainly won out.

This myth involved pitting the *Rechtstaat* against the *Polizeistaat*, the rule of law against the rule of police. Part of liberalism's solution to the problem of social order was to hand it over to law: order became law's empire. In this new liberal constitutionalism, the well-ordered police state was to be superseded by a secure state founded on a system of rights, in which the rule of law would defend the citizen from excessive state interference and police power. Because liberalism came to view order through the lens of law, police had to be viewed through this lens. No longer an almost universal force with unlimited powers to pursue the common happiness, police was reconceptualized as a more limited force with clearly specified powers and focused on the prevention of crime and internal security. Concomitantly, economic activity came to be seen as an essentially 'private' concern and segregated from public management. In other words, the liberal vision sought to separate the broader tasks of welfare and administration from 'police', reducing the latter to the far narrower task of the protection of law and order through the prevention and detection of crime. By the late eighteenth century this had transformed cameralism and police science which, despite remaining as an intellectual doctrine in the nineteenth century,[31] gradually found itself overwhelmed by liberal political economy and jurisprudence. Chairs in cameralism were increasingly being taken by writers of a more 'liberal' persuasion – the starting point was the Chair in Cameral Science in Milan being given to Beccaria, 'the Italian Adam Smith',[32] in 1768 – and writers who still identified with the older police science felt obliged to rethink it in accordance with liberal doctrine concerning law. Thus Robert von Mohl, whom Mack Walker suggests was in many ways the last of the cameralists, felt obliged to publish on 'Police

Science According to the Principles of the Legal State [*Rechtstaat*]' (in 1837).[33] This ascendant liberal doctrine also had an effect on police arrangements. In France, for example, the gradual liberalization intensified after the revolution which, having declared that there was no authority superior to the law, came to associate 'police' with the old regime, while in Prussia the 1795 legal code was to produce a *Rechtstaat* rather than a *Polizeistaat*. In Austria the major police reforms in 1782 distinguished between the 'welfare' and 'security' functions of police. Count Johann Anton Pergen, president of the government of Lower Austria and then later head of the Imperial ministry for police, argued that to bring about any kind of improvement in the police the narrower law-and-order aspects of the police would have to be separated from the broader concept of *Polizeiwissenschaft* – police work had to be 'specialized' and freed from its historical concern with the general good.[34]

We have then what appears to be a joint conceptual transition – from police to political economy, from the rule of police to the rule of law – which some have suggested displaced the police paradigm. On the one hand political economy and the rule of law, rooted in the language of rights and limited government and centred on an independent civil society understood according to the natural laws of political economy. On the other hand the police paradigm, centred on the political domination of civil society via the management of the population through police mechanisms and the ideological identification of civil society with the state. I shall argue that rather than being displaced (by political economy, the rule of law, or anything else) the police concept was in fact transformed. As we have already begun to see, the heart of the transformation was an attempt to rethink the project of police in liberal terms, but to flesh out the argument we need to recognize the wider context of the liberal re-reading of the nature of order and, concomitantly, state power.

Whereas for the police theorists the basis of sovereignty was the 'vertical' relation between ruler and ruled, sovereign and subjects, rich and poor, and was shot through with the politics implicit in the identification of state with civil society, for liberalism the basis of sovereignty is more 'horizontal' than vertical, resting on a civil society in which every individual expresses their natural propensity to truck, barter and exchange. Here the political relation is oriented towards what Michael Shapiro has called a 'robust version of the social'.[35] No longer concerned with the fabrication of social order from above by the state, late-eighteenth-century liberalism repudiated *raison d'état* and focused instead on the cultivation of an autonomous civil society. This created a theoretical myopia concerning the state from which liberalism never properly recovered, a myopia captured most clearly in Smith's recourse to the 'hidden hand', which is symptomatic of not just a 'failure of reason', as Wendy Motooka describes it, but of political delusion too – the delusion that civil society and the commercial order can exist without being fabricated by the state.[36] This *closing off of the question of the state* and its constitutive power over civil society imposed a *liberal theoretical closure* on the idea of police. In helping shift political analysis away from an 'interventionist' political rationality to a 'non-intervention-ist' one, the question of order was transposed from the terrain of police to the terrain of commerce. Far from being the *antithesis* of police, then, late-eighteenth-century liberalism involved a *rethinking* of the police concept in new, liberal terms.

In doing so liberalism faced a major difficulty, connected to the fact that the notion of police had positive as well as negative connotations. 'Positive' in the sense that it connoted general well-being, health and welfare and thus the *presence of order*; negative in the sense that it connoted spying, censorship, the excessive management of trade and thus the *absence of liberty*. The positive and negative seemed to go hand in hand. That is, the order entailed a lack of liberty. To transform the police idea, liberalism therefore required an alternative notion of social order. Perry Anderson has commented that the prevalent property system is the nodal intersection between law and economy, and it is around and through the points of this intersection that liberalism engaged in what Colin Gordon has described as a radical recoding of the politics of order.[37] To consider this recoding we need to further enter the terrain of liberal ideology. In doing so we need to consider four key concepts in the 'house of bourgeois ideas':[38] interest, independence, property and security.

The state of liberal order: interest, independence, property

The idea of interest first came to play a crucial role in political thought in the seventeenth century in relation to the Prince and the state. But at the end of the seventeenth and beginning of the eighteenth centuries the meaning of interest was gradually transformed from the political (reason of state, will of the prince) to the economic. As J.A.W. Gunn points out, 'interest' made the journey from the council chamber to the market-place very quickly. As interest became increasingly thought of in economic terms, so interest of state was considered to be 'plenty', facilitating mercantilist and cameralist doctrines identifying prosperity and the state. This also meant that the concerns of 'private individuals' and those of the 'public' or 'community' might be described in the same terms, thus facilitating the process of identifying the two.[39] However, as interest came to be one of the key operative principles of eighteenth-century thought and was gradually given an economic meaning, it was soon found applicable to the activities of these individual economic actors. Thus there was what Albert Hirschman describes as a 'semantic drift' of the term 'interest' toward economic advantage and money-making on the part of individuals.[40] Nowhere is this clearer than in Smith's work, where interest is presented as the core motivating dynamic of social action:

> It is not from the benevolence of the butcher, the brewer, or the baker, that we expect our dinner, but from their regard to their own interest. We address ourselves, not to their humanity but to their self-love, and never talk to them of our own necessities, but of their advantages. No one but a beggar chuses to depend chiefly upon the benevolence of his fellow-citizens.[41]

Smith's reconfiguration of 'passion' and 'vice' into 'advantage' and 'interest' has been well researched, most notably by Hirschman. My concern here is with the role of this reconfiguration in transforming the police idea. Smith was echoing anti-police arguments centred on interest found on the Continent. In his essay on the police of grain, for example, Herbert identified self-interest as the foundation of all human activity. 'It is the destiny of humanity', he wrote, 'to be highly motivated only by personal interest.'[42] The material welfare of the whole society is therefore advanced when everyone follows their own interest rather than adheres to a common plan imposed from above. Instead of being 'policed' as a means of integrating it with the common good, interest can be given free reign as the core feature of social order and the good polity.

For Smith and other liberal writers of the late eighteenth century, this idea of 'interest' was integrally linked to the notion of independence. As we have seen Smith note, it is the condition of *dependence* within obsolete social structures – 'the custom of having many retainers and dependents' – that leads to crime and disorder: 'independency is the best police for preventing crimes'. In commercial society individuals are free to truck, barter and exchange – to change trades as they please – because they are not tied into relationships of dependence. The key to commercial society is thus the independence associated with the individual economic actor. It is only the establishment of commerce and industry which brings independence, in contrast to the 'violent' practice of police in Indostan and ancient Egypt in which sons are made to follow their fathers' occupations.[43] Likewise for Kant, the defence of equal freedom under the rule of law is based on the assumption that each citizen is his own master. The civil and lawful state

requires not only the freedom of each as a human being and the equality
of each as a subject, but also 'the *independence* of each member of the commonwealth as a citizen'. Although this is defined in a rather circular
fashion, as 'all who are free and equal under existing public laws', and
although Kant is clearly unsure about who qualifies as his own master, as
citizen and thus as independent, it is nonetheless clear that for Kant 'independence' is a central category for understanding the status of the members
of the civil state, and that this independence is rooted in economic activity – a man 'must be his own master and have some property to support
himself'.[44]

The use of independence here served to transform the language of political discourse in a way conducive to the ruling class project and which
was to also have an important effect on the police idea. In feudal and
preindustrial society 'dependency' meant subordination. Like 'interest',
'independence' was initially a term that appplied to bodies only, such as
churches, and then came to be applied to individuals. The earliest definition of 'dependence' given in the *Oxford English Dictionary* is 'to be connected
with in a relation of subordination; to belong to as something subordinate'.
A dependent person was one who relied on another for 'maintenance,
support, supply, or what is needed'. The context of this was a social order
in which subordination was the norm: virtually everyone was subordinate to someone else. As such, no stigma was attached to being dependent.
However, with the increasing domination of the bourgeois social form and
its concomitant monetization and commodification of human relations,
'dependence' assumed the mantle of stigma, coming to refer to a negative
and deviant state. The citizen was an independent person who knew his
own interest; dependence, the negative state of subordination, was deemed
antithetical to citizenship. Thus the icons of dependency were the slave,
the housewife and the pauper.[45]

In effect, as part of its wider ideological project, liberalism gave birth to
the idea that *any* system of police should be founded on the liberty of the
independent economically active and self-interested individual. This undermined the police view that the population needed to be protected from
the ravages of commercial activity and that 'order' required the extensive
policing of the means of subsistence. As I argued towards the end of the
previous chapter, while the cameralists and police theorists sought to
encourage independent activity as the basis of work, they could never quite
give up the idea that such self-interested independence would be damaging to the social fabric and undermine the common good. They saw as the
opposite of police not liberty, but chaos. The police idea therefore became
fraught with tensions. On the one hand, and in the spirit of the market

sytem which it helped bring about, it implied the pursuit of self-interested independence. On the other hand, and more in line with its search for order, it could not but fail to see that the pursuit of individual interest was anti-social and therefore in need of mastering. Thus police theorists could never quite give up the idea that independent and self-interested individuals had to be policed in such a way as to make their interests coincide with the general good.

The reason for this is because for the police theorists of the eighteenth century, order was still considered a unified concept encompassing the organization of labour both inside and outside production. It was only when political economy established itself as an independent science that wider questions of political and legal order were separated out and dealt with separately under the heading of jurisprudence, while the production of wealth and thus order in the factory could be dealt with under the heading of 'economics'. It is an illusion partly arising from the artificial development of political economy as a discipline that the science of police only came into being to deal with problems of order outside production, and beyond the limits of factory discipline, when in point of fact the science of police understood the centrality of labour both inside and outside the factory, and did so because it worked with a conception of a unified order.[46] It is this understanding that I shall explore in the context of the fabrication of a bourgeois order through police power in Chapters 3 and 4 below.

Part of the increasingly hegemonic liberal ideals was a theoretical distinction between state and civil society, identifying self-interested market-based activity as the operating principle behind civil society. This essentially *depoliticized* the state of prosperity. Liberalism's move away from the identification of police as a positive condition of the good polity occurred as liberal writers increasingly identified the constitutive feature of social life as self-seeking individuals operating through a civil society guided only by the hidden hand. On this model the fundamental mechanism of society – the market – not only generates wealth but is also the prime mover behind societal development and has important consequences in terms of personal liberty – only with the freedom to truck, barter and exchange does one get the political liberty of the citizen. A properly commercial society requires the rule of (liberal/bourgeois) law; a society in which the (liberal/bourgeois) law functions rests on the commercial freedom and independence of its citizens. Commerce makes liberty possible; liberty makes commerce possible. A commercial society thus creates a new world order after its own image. Note for example Montesquieu's comment that 'the spirit of commerce brings with it the spirit of...order'.[47] Police action, as the archetypal expression of state power, is thus removed from the centre stage of historical development. Hence the shift in Smith's discussion of the pin-factory, from being one moment in the articulation of police power contributing to the wealth-producing capacities of a *politically constituted* social order, to being a site of autonomous social relations and thus the foundation of the wealth of nations.

It is imperative to note, however, that in developing this new notion of order liberalism was engaged in a massive reconfiguration of the notions of both order and property, which meant abolishing all connotations of power and hierarchy within these terms. Property originally consisted in whatever resources enabled one to do one's part in keeping good order; and the normal understanding of order was hierarchy. This was entirely consistent with the meaning of order. To order means to not only put things in their place, but to rank, grade or class them accordingly. By definition then, order connotes a disciplined hierarchy, as its derivations 'subordinate' and 'insubordinate' testify. The feudal and early modern conception of order as part of the great chain of being accepted the inherently hierarchical meaning of order, even when social order came to be understood as politically constituted. Richard Hooker, for example, comments that 'if things or persons are to be ordered, this doth imply that they are distinguished by degrees'.[48] The family, immediate community, society, commonwealth, body politic and the natural world all exemplified the hierarchical nature of order. Thus to say that the 'police beget good order', or that the police fabricate order, was to say that the police ensured that things took their place within a hierarchy. Police regulations were often based on the understanding that the order to be made and maintained was of a hierarchical nature, down to the sumptuary regulations concerning dress. In contrast, in its presentation of order as a system of independent property-owning individuals equally pursuing their self-interest, liberalism glossed over the fact of hierarchy connoted in one of its central concepts.

In reconstituting social order around a different strategy of coordination centred on property, liberalism had to perpetuate the myth propounded by Locke that 'every man has a property in his own person'. 'The property which every man has in his own labour, as it is the original foundation of all other property, so it is the most sacred and inviolable', Smith states.[49] Having identified the abolition of dependence as the key to social order, the new liberal semantics had to treat *wage labour* as the form of independence for the bulk of the population. (The more recent attempts to eradicate the 'culture of dependency' in liberal democratic states merely replicate this bourgeois ideological presupposition.) Indeed, real dependency for the poor appeared to consist of the *absence* of wage labour; hence the status of the pauper or vagabond. But as Marx points out, 'individuals *seem* independent...but they appear thus only from someone who abstracts from the *conditions*, the *conditions of existence* within which these individuals enter into contract'. 'In the ordinary run of things, the worker can be left to the "natural laws of production", i.e. it is possible to rely on his dependence on capital, which springs from the conditions of production themselves, and is guaranteed in perpetuity by them.' A 'very Eden of the innate rights of man', capital–labour relations were (and still are) presented as free from all forms of dependency (despite Smith's own calculation that 'in every part of Europe twenty workmen serve under a master for one that is independent'). The assumption that every man becomes in some measure an independent merchant is indicative of the ideological gloss liberalism placed on relations of subordination and social domination, the subordination of labour to the 'silent compulsion of economic relations'.[50]

As eighteenth-century liberalism came to highlight and fetishize the individual actor, the umbilical cord between property and sovereignty was seemingly broken. In the seventeenth century and into the eighteenth the connection between 'property' and 'propriety' was still clear. Although the terms are now usually treated separately (aside from hangovers such as 'proprietor' to describe the owner of a business), in the eighteenth century property-as-propriety was taken for granted: witness the way that between the first (1690) and third edition (1698) of his *Two Treatises*, Locke replaced many of the references to 'propriety' with 'property'. Locke's comment that every man has a property in his own person should be read alongside his suggestion that man is 'Proprietor of his own Person'.[51] The reason property and propriety were so closely connected was that ownership of property meant sovereign power over it. But liberalism came to encourage the view that property and sovereignty are of a fundamentally different nature. Where the latter was taken to be rule over people, the former was treated as simply rule over things. Here liberalism played on the Roman distinction between *dominium*, the rule over things by the individual, and *imperium*, a vertical relationship of domination between a political authority (usually, though not necessarily, the prince) and its subordinates.[52] This obscured the fact that *dominium* over things is also a form of *imperium* in a different form: the rule over people via property ownership.[53] To state the point in more obvious terms: it obscured the fact that property is a form of power. *Dominium* is still a form of subjugation – not only does it allow rule over people through the power of property, but it facilitates the treatment of human beings as if they were property.

Moreover, it is pertinent to note that while as a slogan the rule of law was a rallying cry for the liberal bourgeoisie against the arbitrary power of the *ancien régime*, its flip side was that it was used to oppose not only arbitrary power from above, but also 'mob rule' from below. 'Mob' was an abbreviation of the Latin *mobile vulgus*, a term developed by the ruling class in the eighteenth century as a coda for the poor and thus the emergent working class as the lower *order*.[54] Thus the rise of the rule of a supposedly formally equal system founded on private property in fact generated new concepts founded on the underlying hierarchical relations of power within the system.

One of the major ideological achievements of the rise of liberalism was therefore its ability to gloss over the fact that property really was an exercise of power and a form of hierarchy, in the context of a society ever more focused on capital. Writing of the eighteenth century, E.P. Thompson has argued that 'property and the privileged status of the propertied were assuming, every year, a greater weight in the scales of justice, until justice itself was seen as no more than the outworks and defences of property and of its attendant status'.[55] Until it was abundantly clear, that is, that the masterless men brought into being by the breakdown of feudalism were now faced with a new form of master: capital. Capital had by this point been simultaneously enthroned and consecrated; the Divine Right of Kings had become the Divine Right of Property. Capital had become King.[56] Not for nothing is the central category of modern property ownership the same as one of the central categories of law and state power. As Peter Linebaugh has noted, in criminology as in economics no word is more powerful than 'capital', denoting on the one hand the power of the state over deliberate death, and on the other the power of private property as the condition (the 'stock') of life.[57] Where historically the vagrancy laws involved refusenik members of the forerunners of the proletariat being put to death at the hands of the state, in the eighteenth century an increasing number of crimes against property were treated in the same fashion: resistance to capital was met by capital punishment. Capital offences against property aside, the subordination of labour in the order of property was abundantly clear from the multitude of statutes dealing with employment. Acts such as the Statute of Labourers (1349), the Statute of Artificers (1563) and the later aptly named Master and Servant Acts made it clear that the relationship between capital and labour was fundamentally unequal: despite being 'contractual' and thus treating master and servant as formally equal, the law regarded the servant as of lower 'status'. As Holdsworth notes in his *History of English Law*, 'the relation between master and servant under the statutes, though contractual in its origin and in some of its incidents, gave rise, like the marriage contract, to a status of a particular kind'.[58] The law thereby compelled the labourer to accept the order imposed by his or her employer regardless of the reasonableness of the order in question; refusal to accept orders frequently meant arrest and imprisonment. In other words, refusal to be disciplined by the power of capital by refusing to obey the order of the master was a *criminal offence*. Against this, Smith's idea that every man is a merchant is revealed as the archetypal liberal myth.

In effect, liberalism ignored the fact that the mastery and discipline formerly exercised by police was increasingly coming to be exercised by capital. Concomitantly, it ignored the fact that the rule of law remains the rule of men. Rather than opposing oppressive regimes, liberalism was in fact a way of refocusing and even intensifying the power over individuals inaugurated in absolutist programmes of police found in cameralism and police science.[59] In other words, it was possible for liberalism to transform the police concept in the late eighteenth century because the exercise of power and domination was slowly being transferred from police to capital; the disciplinary logic of police was being superseded by the disciplinary logic of the market.[60] Formally, of course, capital possessed no 'police power' as such (although in some countries employers entitled their rules 'police regulations'). But the ability to hire and fire, set wages, formulate rules of work, charge fines, stop wages and myriad other forms of power were to all intents and purposes unlimited, so long as labour failed to act in unison. It is for this reason that one historian describes the power of capital as 'police-style discipline'.[61] For all its condemnation of the tyranny of police, late-eighteenth-century liberalism happily condoned the tyranny of capital.

Towards security

It is within liberalism's ideological recoding of the politics of order, the nature of property and the question of the state that its rethinking of the police concept must be placed. Historically, the trick was to make policing consistent with the rule of law and a liberal polity. Having painted an ideological gloss on the tyranny of capital and having ignored the gradual assumption of increasing powers of domination of capital over labour, liberalism transformed the police idea by restricting it to 'law and order' in the narrowest sense – the prevention of crime and disorder via the enforcement of law by a professional body of public officials forming a single institution with a clearly defined and limited role and subject to the rule of law. This vision of police became the dominant one in political discourse and in the self-understanding of police, and formed the basis of the theoretical foundation of the third stage of police, for this was the period when the earlier notion of police as the good ordering of society by the state was being overtaken by a new understanding of police as a body of officials charged with preventing and detecting crime – a body charged with *enforcing* the law while simultaneously limited by it.

A comment by the economist Paul Samuelson concerning the twentieth-century 'libertarian' is suggestive as to the reason why liberalism did not just abandon the police concept.

> I will tell you a secret. Economists are supposed to be dry as dust, dismal fellows. This is quite wrong, the reverse of the truth. Scratch a hard-boiled economist of the libertarian persuasion and you find a Don Quixote underneath. No lovesick maiden ever pined for the days of medieval chivalry with such sentimental impracticability as some economists long for the return to a Victorian marketplace that is completely free. Completely free? Well, almost so. There must, of course, be the constable to ensure that voluntary contracts are enforced and to protect the property rights of each molecule which is an island unto itself.[62]

Since laws and government are ultimately 'instituted for the defence of the rich against the poor, or of those who have property against those who have none at all',[63] there must be some force designed to implement such laws. There must be some force to provide *security*, in other words.

The English word 'security' comes from Latin *securitas/securus*, in turn derived from *sine cura*. *Sine* – meaning without – and *cura* – meaning troubling; solicitude; carefulness, or to have a care or be anxious about; attention; pains; anxiety; grief and sorrow; diligent; guardianship; concern for persons and things – together give us *sine cura*: to be without care, free from cares and untroubled. *Securitas* is consequently defined as freedom from concern and danger or, looked at from a slightly different angle, safety and security.[64] Yet early notions of security also referred to something quite different, even contradictory. The *Oxford English Dictionary* gives several examples of the way security was thought of as a *negative* state: 'our vayne glory, our viciousness, avarice, ydleness, security' (1564); 'they...were drowned in sinneful securitie' (1575); and Shakespeare has Hecate declare in *Macbeth* that 'security is mortal's chiefest enemie'.[65] Security here is a careless, dangerous and in some cases sinful confidence. This meaning has now been lost as, far from being a careless, dangerous or sinful state, security has come to form the highest moment of order. It will therefore become an important concept for the argument in this book.

As a political concept *securitas* took on political prominence with the motto *Securitas Publica* – the safety or defence of empire – and eventually transformed into the idea of security of state. Hence the Act of Security (1704), passed by the Scottish Parliament excluding Queen Anne's successor from the throne unless conditions of government were enacted securing the independence of the kingdom. But just as the notion of interest shifted from politics to the market-place in the eighteenth century, so too did the notion of security. In doing so security became the cornerstone of the liberal bourgeois mind, which came to identify security with the freedom and liberty to pursue one's individual self-interest.[66] In contrast to the Hobbesian view of security as the foundation of the absolute powers of the sovereign, liberalism came to treat security and liberty as more or less synonymous. One can see this in Smith's references to the liberty and security of individuals in the same breath, Montesquieu's claim that 'political liberty consists in security', and Bentham's suggestion, in his work of the 1780s at least, that 'a clear idea of liberty will lead us to regard it as a branch of security'.[67] Almost identical claims are made by a range of other writers in the liberal tradition: 'if population be connected with national wealth, liberty and personal security is the great foundation of both' (Ferguson); 'the design and end of government, viz. freedom and security' (Paine); 'the people, having no political liberty, would have no *security* for the continuance of the same laws' (Priestly); 'the loss of security' is 'the loss of liberty' (Paley); 'I would call security, if the expression does not seem too abrupt to be clear, the assurance of legal freedom'(Humboldt).[68] It was even found to be part of English constitutional law during this period.[69]

This identification of liberty with security should be understood as part of the articulation of a certain vision of security; the word 'freedom' designated a range of activities which occurred outside the political realm. As Arendt points out, as security became the decisive criterion of freedom, it came to imply the security of an undisturbed development of the life process of society as a whole. In other words, 'security' for liberalism came to refer to the 'the liberty of secure possession', as Joyce Appleby puts it; that is, the liberty of private property.[70] Government exists 'for the security of property', Smith tells us, presenting us with a triad of concepts which are run so closely together that they are almost conflated: 'liberty, security, property'.[71] The concept of security thus became the ideological guarantee of the egoism of the independent and self-interested pursuit of property within bourgeois society. In doing so, security became *the supreme concept of bourgeois society*.[72]

Liberalism's radical recoding of the politics of order turned police into a range of 'security measures' consistent with liberal principles; that is into a *technique of liberal security*.[73] Part of the argument in the chapters to follow will be to rework the connection between police and security in such a way as to move the theory of police beyond the parameters defined by liberalism. I shall do this by arguing that the liberal identification of security with liberty and property in fact masks an underlying *insecurity* at the heart of the bourgeois order – the insecurity of property – which is deeply connected to the question of class. As Gordon notes, 'the question of class, as the problem of making an industrial market economy *socially* possible, becomes, from the bourgeois point of view, an essential part of the politics of security'.[74] As the working class were gradually incorporated into the body politic so the question of security became a class issue. I shall develop this argument by pushing to its limits Marx's suggestion that security is the supreme concept of class society. The recognition of the insecurity of the class system of private property meant that security came to be thought of as something to be *achieved* rather than merely conflated with liberty and property and left at that. Writers who recognized this, such as G.W.F. Hegel and Patrick Colquhoun, did so because they understood that security is imposed on civil society by the state through the exercise of police power. In some fundamental sense then, security *is* the concept of police, as Marx puts it.[75] Security is part of the rationale for the fabrication of order. In terms of the demand for order in civil society, it is under the banner of 'security' that police most often marches.

3
Ordering Insecurity I: Social Police and the Mechanisms of Prevention

It has been said that Hegelian property theory is a sublation of liberalism.[1] *'To sublate'* has a twofold meaning, Hegel tells us. 'On the one hand it means to preserve, to maintain, and equally it also means to cause to cease, to put an end to.' Thus 'what is sublated is at the same time preserved; it has only lost its immediacy but is not on that account annihilated.[2] Sublation is thus a process through which the internal contradictions of concepts are resolved. One of the themes of this chapter will be the way that the work of both Hegel and Colquhoun can be thought of as a sublation of some of the key concepts of late-eighteenth-century liberalism. The insight made by Hegel, but developed more fully by Colquhoun, is that 'police' must be understood in the context of wider questions concerning property and commerce on the one hand and poverty and indigence on the other. Put simply: a massive and intensive police operation on the part of the state is a necessary feature of civil (i.e. class) society for the simple reason that the class of poverty and the indigent rabble generated by civil society in turn pose a threat to private property and commerce, rendering civil society insecure. Civil society therefore needs to be policed – to be *made secure* – by the state. Both Hegel and Colquhoun try to develop a general theory of police as part of their wider understanding of the order of capitalist modernity, and thus help in developing an expanded concept of police beyond the parameters of liberalism.

Given that the theory being developed here is to be shaped through a reading of Hegel and Colquhoun, it is worth pointing initially to some peculiarities regarding their work. Concerning Hegel, the first thing to note is that although the concept of police is central to Hegel's political philosophy it has been barely examined in the secondary literature on Hegel. The tendency in commentaries on Hegel's political thought is to point to the very general nature of the meaning of the term for him, namely that he uses the term to refer to more than a predominantly uniformed institution for the prevention and detection of crimes, and to then pass this off as simply referring to 'public authority'. This is an approach facilitated by the nature of some translations of Hegel's work. Knox, for example, in the first English translation of the *Philosophy of Right*, tells us that '*Polizei*...has a wider sense than that conveyed by "police" in English' and thus 'in what follows it is generally translated "public authority"'.[3] Likewise the translators of Hegel's lectures of 1817–18 claim that he 'uses the word *Polizei* to denote what we would call "the public authority" or government regulation of industry and commerce'. Consequently, they add, 'this is how we have translated it except for where the reference is clearly to the police as agency of law enforcement'.[4] This kind of translation has encouraged the general tendency of shying away from attempting a fuller exploration of the concept.[5] In contrast to the wealth of literature on Hegel's concept of the corporation there is a marked absence of discussion about his concept of police, an absence that is especially striking given that Hegel treats police and corporations alongside each other in the *Philosophy of Right*. The second peculiarity is that despite the importance of police in his work, Hegel does not develop the concept at any length. The third peculiarity is that Hegel is hardly ever mentioned in general work on police within 'police studies'. This is perhaps odd, given the obvious importance of the concept to Hegel and the importance of Hegel to political thought in the last two centuries.

In many ways Colquhoun suffers from the opposite problem. Largely ignored by political theorists, Colquhoun has long been a key figure in British police studies. Radzinowicz, for example, gives Colquhoun a central role in the volume on police in his *History of English Criminal Law*: 'Colquhoun was the first major writer on public order and the machinery of justice to use "police" in a strict sense closely akin to modern usage.' For T.A. Critchley, Colquhoun's ideas 'represent an important link between the old and the new', and for Charles Reith, Colquhoun is the second of three of the 'outstanding creators of the British police'.[6] He has even been dubbed 'the patron saint of the police institution'.[7] But here lies the problem. Radzinowicz's and Critchley's references to the 'modern' and 'new' are partly attempts to highlight the idea of prevention in Colquhoun's work. Although more recent interest in his work has been among those developing new ways of understanding power and poverty[8] or those investigating the nature of 'private' policing,[9] the main reason for the attention given to

Colquhoun by writers in mainstream British police studies has long centred on the idea of prevention.[10] The problem is that since the new police is commonly said to have involved the emergence of preventive policing, commentators searching for the origins of the new police have focused on the preventive principle in Colquhoun's work. They have tended to assume that since the new police emerged as an agency for the prevention of crime, so those working on preventive policing before 1829 must have had in mind the kind of force that emerged in 1829. But in reading Colquhoun through the lens of 1829 they have distorted his significance, imposing on him a reading of police that depends too heavily on twentieth-century criminological assumptions. The result is a failure to recognize the importance of Colquhoun's work as a *theory* of police, his understanding of the insecurity of property, and his recognition of the need to fabricate a class society. It is these aspects of Colquhoun's work that I shall appropriate and rethink in this and the following chapter.

'The well ordering and comfort of civil society'

The starting point for both Hegel and Colquhoun is the insecurity of private property within civil society. Hegel treats police as part of ethical life. Of the three moments of ethical life – family, civil society and the state – Hegel introduces the police as one of the integrating mechanisms of civil society. In one sense the aim of police is straightforward: 'the police should prevent crimes'. But the much wider scope of the police indicates that for Hegel the prevention of crimes is brought about in an indirect fashion. For the broader aim of the police is 'to mediate between the individual and the universal', to 'care for the particular interest as a *common* interest'. As such the police should provide not only security for individuals and property, but also welfare, street-lighting, bridge-building, the pricing of daily necessities, public health, and the founding of colonies.[11]

There are significant reasons why Hegel introduces the police into civil society and thinks of it in this way. The subtitle of the *Philosophy of Right – Natural Law and Political Science in Outline* – reveals the book's origins in Hegel's lectures on natural law and politics. The standard approach to such topics was to begin with either family or individuals (possessive or otherwise), then to move on to the state, in the process justifying the existence of private property. In what has been called the 'Hegelian transformation of political philosophy'[12] Hegel breaks with this by inserting civil society between the spheres of family and state, a civil society which contains the market as one of its most active forces. The significance of this is threefold. First, although Hegel discusses police in the section on civil society, he is in fact referring to those activities through which the state organizes and administers civil society: 'the *executive power*...also includes the powers of the *judiciary* and the *police*'.[13] Second, this draws attention to the fact that although Hegel is adopting a key liberal concept – civil society – he treats civil society as dependent upon far more extensive state power than most liberals. And, third, the core issue in this administration of civil society by the state is the nature of the market and the problem of poverty.

Despite being heavily influenced by Smith's political economy – from the Jena period onwards he uses the example of the pin-factory and reproduces Smith's figures when discussing the division of labour[14] – Hegel remained far from convinced that the market is a spontaneous and self-regulating mechanism in the way Smith implied. The influence of Smith on Hegel lies more in Smith's explanation of how wealth is produced. Beyond that, Hegel's notion of the market is more akin to that of Sir James Steuart, a writer whom one could describe as a British cameralist.[15] Like Steuart, Hegel understands the market as a system which is constantly on the verge of going wrong and which therefore needs policing. 'The differing interests of producers and consumers may come into collision with each other, and even if, *on the whole*, their correct relationship re-establishes itself automatically, its adjustment also needs to be consciously regulated by an agency which stands above both sides.'[16] The background to this is Hegel's understanding of the insecurity brought about by the existence of a class of poverty, which is a necessary condition of civil society. 'The emergence of poverty is in general a consequence of civil society, and on the whole it arises necessarily out of it.' As such, there is no solution to it: 'The important question of how poverty can be remedied is one which agitates and torments modern societies especially.'[17] The problem, however, is not poverty per se, but the fact that from the class of poverty a further, more dangerous 'class' can emerge.

> When a large mass of people sinks below the level of a certain standard of living...that feeling of right, integrity, and honour which comes from supporting oneself by one's own activity and work is lost. This leads to the creation of a *rabble*... Poverty in itself does not reduce people to a rabble; a rabble is created only by the disposition associated with poverty, by inward rebellion against the rich, against society, the government, etc.[18]

While charity may offer some help, it is no solution. The state's police power is the main mechanism for overseeing poverty. But the crucial point here is this: the police is equally no solution. Since it cannot abolish poverty, because to do so would abolish civil society, all the police can do is to prevent the poverty-stricken class from becoming a criminalized and pauperized rabble. It is at this point that the work of Patrick Colquhoun becomes pertinent.

Like Hegel, Colquhoun's starting point is the insecurity of property, which he takes to be a result of imperfections in the criminal law and the lack of an 'active principle' regarding the police of the metropolis.[19] Estimating that in 1795 there were some 150 offences on the statute books with execution as their punishment, Colquhoun notes that the rationale for this is prevention, yet this is precisely what severe punishment *fails* to achieve. Despite a 'bloody code' which saw the execution of large numbers of people for increasingly petty crimes, the crime rate in London was still high; according to Colquhoun there were some 115,000 people in London supporting themselves by criminal or immoral means, resulting in a net loss to the metropolis of over two million pounds a year. The criminal law merely punished the inexperienced criminal severely while leaving the experienced criminal free to commit more crimes.[20]

Colquhoun suggests a number of solutions. One is Beccaria's argument that instead of severity, the criminal law should be based on certainty. Another is a shift in the style of punishment, focused on the use of the penitentiary.[21] But the main way to reduce crimes, Colquhoun argues, is less through the style of punishment and more through the prevention of crimes in the first place. While in England property is ravaged and threatened, Colquhoun argues that in many European countries this is not the case, claiming that in many European cities people rarely bolt their doors or windows at night. Thus 'security [of property] does not proceed from *severe punishments*, for in very few countries are they more sanguinary than in England. It is to be attributed to a more correct and energetic system of Police, joined to an early and general attention to the education and morals of the lower orders of the people; aided by a system of industry and sobriety.'[22] At its core is the belief that society needs not just sensible laws but also 'a watchful police, aided by a correct system of restraints' to *prevent* crimes occurring and thus obviate the need for punishment. Wise legislatures know that it is better to prevent rather than punish crimes: 'the prevention of crimes and misdemeanours is the true essence of Police'.[23]

The idea of prevention was hardly original to Colquhoun. Beccaria had already influentially argued that 'it is better to prevent crimes than to punish them', and in Britain the Fielding brothers had also expressed the need for some form of 'General Preventive Plan' or 'preventive machine'.[24] What is original is Colquhoun's attempt to do what neither Beccaria nor the Fieldings manage, namely, to integrate the general idea of prevention into a theory of police. It is worth noting that despite their importance in establishing a force of permanent, paid officers for the systematic gathering, analysis and distribution of information regarding crimes (the Bow Street Runners), and despite the widespread agreement on their central importance to police history in Britain,[25] Henry Fielding never used the word 'police', and John Fielding's main concern was to defend the term from its sinister foreign connotations.[26]

Colquhoun's preventive plan was to involve breaking with the five separate jurisdictions in London in which a few watchmen and constables were expected to prevent crime and keep the peace, and establishing a uniform and centralized system. This 'Criminal Police' – a significant title to which we shall return – would carry out many of the functions of the magistrates. It would license and regulate those activities which encouraged frauds, such as hawkers and pedlars, pawnbrokers, hackney coaches, fortune tellers and alehouses, and would regulate those areas the proper supervision of which would prevent crime, such as customs and excise, stamps, game laws, friendly societies, the highways and vagrancy. Aside from this, the police would compile 'a general and complete register of every known offender' and lists of stolen property, enabling a complete knowledge of the state of the criminal population and their activities; he approvingly cites the fact that 'at the commencement of the troubles in France' the Lieutenant General of the National Police there had no less than twenty thousand suspect or depraved characters of the criminal variety on his register.[27] These activities would be carried out by a group of men 'who would give *their whole attention to* the criminal department of the Police' on a centralized and national basis, with a Board of Commissioners of police maintaining the registers and managing the force overall in terms of salaries and uniforms. The scheme should be applied nationally and operate under a 'Minister of the National Police' (the Home Secretary).[28]

Clearly then Colquhoun's work must be understood as an argument for the protection of liberty and security of property via the prevention of crime, as we have seen many commentators note. But the focus on *crime* prevention disguises the breadth and originality of Colquhoun's thought, the key to which lies in the definition of police Colquhoun introduced in later editions of his *Treatise*. The famous opening of the later editions runs as follows:

Police in this country may be considered as a *new Science*; the properties of which consist not in the Judicial Powers which lead to *Punishment*, and which belong to Magistrates alone; but in the PREVENTION AND

DETECTION OF CRIMES, and in those other Functions which relate to INTERNAL REGULATIONS for the well ordering and comfort of Civil Society.[29]

Colquhoun's emphases are significant here. Like Hegel, Colquhoun sees civil society as something to be ordered, and this is the project of police. 'The Criminal Police' is one aspect or branch of this project. It is essentially this aspect or branch (or something like it) which became institutionalized as *the* police from 1829. The other integral part is the Municipal Police. Noting that various Acts of Parliament have established a system 'which may be denominated *municipal regulations*, such as *paving, watching, lighting, cleaning, and removing nuisances; furnishing water; the mode of building houses;* the system *established* for *extinguishing fires*, and for regulating *coaches, carts*, and *other carriages*; with a variety of other useful improvements, tending to the comfort and convenience of the inhabitants', a list to which he later adds the sewage system, signs and signposts, and gutters and balconies, Colquhoun makes the point that these regulations for the well ordering and comfort of civil society are part of the system of police: he describes Acts of Parliament outlining the management of the city as containing 'a complete and masterly system of *that branch of the Police* which is connected with municipal regulations'; the regulations explain 'by what means *the system of Police*, in most of its great features, is conducted in the metropolis'.[30]

The crux of this lies in the connection Colquhoun makes between crime, indigence and poverty. It is significant that Colquhoun presents *The State of Indigence* (1799) and the later *Treatise on Indigence* (1806) as part of the overall argument found in his *Treatise on the Police*: his continual cross-referencing between the texts is indicative of his basic working assumption that the problem of poverty is part of the wider problem of police.[31] Colquhoun's initial thoughts on this, in *The State of Indigence*, are that the poor be placed within Houses of Industry, or Work-rooms, where they 'should receive whole of their earnings and a meal besides'. This would cut the expense to the parish and end begging. The modest and deserving poor would receive relief while the idle and profligate would be compelled to labour for their subsistence. The Chief Commissioners overseeing these places would then be in a position to keep a register of those applying for relief and in receipt of it, exercise legal powers through constables to compel the idle and destitute to come before the Commissioners for examination, and keep a check on the morality of those in receipt of relief.[32] In other words, in his earlier attempts to grapple with the police of the poor Colquhoun was a fully-fledged supporter of early arguments for a workhouse system operating a test of eligibility for work. Given the five classes of the poor identified by Colquhoun – useful poor, vagrant poor, indigent poor, aged and infirm, and poor infants[33] – the 'great art' is to establish a system whereby those verging on indigence may be kept in the class of useful labour and those who are able but not willing to work (vagrants) be compelled to do so. At this stage in his work then, Colquhoun's criticism that in the present system 'the Police...has provided no place of industry in which those who were disposed to reform might find subsistence in return for labour' should be seen in the light of his proposals in *The State of Indigence* for work-rooms and tests of ability to labour as 'a most important branch of Police'.[34] Indeed, it is the very core of the police system, since if this part of the system is effective then crimes will reduce and the Criminal Police be as little active as possible.

In the later *Treatise on Indigence*, however, the concern with the work-house has diminished somewhat. He criticizes the workhouse for debasing the mind of the labouring people, being 'gaols without guilt, punishment without crime', for rewarding in a roundabout way vice and idleness, and therefore in dire need of improvement.[35] His failure to suggest what kind of reforms would constitute improvement is because by the time of the *Treatise on Indigence* he has developed a key theoretical presupposition which comes to determine his approach to poverty and thus his overall approach to police in later editions of the *Treatise on Police*: namely, the distinction between poverty and indigence.

In Colquhoun's writings from the 1790s the distinction between poverty and indigence lacks any real theoretical importance. Sometimes he works without the distinction at all, distinguishing instead between 'the *noxious* and the *blameless* and useful part of the community'. At other times he refers to the differences between the poor and the indigent but without spelling out the theoretical or practical importance of the distinction: 'The principal object of this [meat and soup] Charity is not only to afford a temporary relief to the indigent, sober and industrious.'[36] Once he starts dealing with the issue of indigence more directly, however, in the 1799 text on *The State of Indigence* he begins to recognize the importance of labour to the production of wealth, and thus the importance of poverty, and starts to separate poverty from indigence. 'Labour is absolutely requisite to the existence of all Governments; and it is from the Poor only that labour can be expected...It is not *Poverty* therefore, that is itself an evil.' Instead 'the evil is to be found only in *Indigence*, where the strength fails, where disease, age, or infancy, deprive the individual of the means of subsistence, or where he knows not how to find employment when willing and able to work'.[37] By the 1806 *Treatise on Indigence* this has become a categorical distinction between poverty and indigence of fundamental theoretical importance.

> *Poverty* is that state and condition in society where the individual has no surplus labour in store, and, consequently, no property but what is derived from the constant exercise of industry in the various occupations of life; or, in other words, it is the state of every one who must labour for subsistence.
>
> *Poverty* is therefore a most necessary and indispensable ingredient of society, without which nations and communities could not exist in a state of civilization. It is the lot of man – it is the source of *wealth*, since without *labour* there would be *no riches*, no *refinement*, no *comfort*, and no *benefit* to those who may be possessed of wealth.
>
> *Indigence* therefore, and not *poverty*, is the evil...It is the state of any one who is destitute of the means of subsistence, and is unable to labour to procure it to the extent nature requires. The natural source of subsistence is the labour of the individual; while that remains with him he is denominated *poor*; when it fails in whole or in part he becomes *indigent*.[38]

Although some have rightly pointed to Bentham's prior use of this distinction, to present Colquhoun as doing little more than following Bentham here is misleading.[39] Colquhoun has been badly served by being presented as a 'Benthamite', a label which often obscures more than it reveals. In this context Colquhoun is in fact more Malthusian than Benthamite – it is significant that the *Treatise on Indigence* and the later editions of the *Treatise on Police* appear after the publication of Malthus's hugely influential *Essay on Population* (1798). Following Malthus rather than Bentham, Colquhoun was a crucial figure in effecting a conceptual break in the notion of the 'labouring poor' that was to become a crucial conceptual device in ruling class strategies thereafter. And, far more than Bentham, Colquhoun integrated this conception into the vision of preventive police.[40] In the eighteenth century the labouring poor was one undistinguished mass. Although some attempts were made to distinguish between poverty and pauperism, or the deserving and undeserving poor, in general 'labourers' and 'poor' were spoken of interchangeably, and often amalgamated in the term 'labouring poor'. No distinction existed between the 'poor' and those in receipt of poor relief (say, 'the indigent' or 'paupers') because relief was so extensive that it would have meant stigmatizing most of the population with the term 'pauper'.[41] Only when a new sense of the social problem had emerged in the nineteenth century was the continuum of the labouring poor broken and a categorical distinction established between the labouring poor and the indigent pauper.[42] This fact will become central to the argument in Chapter 4 below, but the point here is that this distinction between poverty and indigence not only forms the theoretical foundation of Colquhoun's understanding of poverty, *it also shapes his conception of police*. What Malthus contributed to political economy, Colquhoun reasserted as the basis of police science. It is thus the key to understanding his idea of the Municipal Police and, as such, his notion of prevention.

This is due to Colquhoun's fundamental belief that 'from indigence is to be traced the great Origin and the Progress of Crimes'.[43] The key to Colquhoun's science of police is that the Criminal Police deals with the criminal 'underclass' (Hegel's 'rabble'), those who have fallen from indigence into crime. The Municipal Police is there to prevent the class of poverty from falling into indigence. The overall project of the science of police is to identify and implement the mechanisms necessary to prevent the poverty-stricken class from falling into indigence and from there into crime. 'The great desideratum, therefore, is to prop up *poverty* by judicious arrangements at those critical periods when it is in danger of descending into indigence. The barrier between these two conditions in society is often slender, and the public interest requires that it should be narrowly guarded.'[44] The key to prevention is thus not directly preventing crime, but preventing the class of poverty – the working class – from falling into indigence. Not for nothing do later editions of the *Treatise on Police* include a section called 'The Origin of Crimes: State of the Poor' and the *Treatise on Indigence* a section on 'A Board of General and Internal Police'; and not for nothing did Colquhoun earlier describe the 'Board of General and Internal Police' as 'Commissioners of the Poor'.[45] The Board of General and Internal Police is to 'embrace all objects in any degree connected with the casualties of life or a retrograde state of morals, producing *indigence, vagrancy*, or *criminal offences*'. It is in fact part of the system of police to 'relieve the indigent requiring assistance [and] to prop up the industrious poor ready to descend into indigence'. This is not an optional extra of police but its very essence, for it would have the effect of 'returning to police its genuine character, unmixed with those judicial powers which lead to punishment, and properly belong to magistracy alone'.[46] It has been said that 'if Adam Smith had shown the power of labour as a cause of wealth, Malthus thought he had shown the power of poverty as a cause of labour'.[47] We can add that Colquhoun thought he had shown the power of indigence as a cause of crime and disorder. In this sense the poor law becomes a form of municipal police, and we shall explore the implications of this point more fully in the next chapter.

For Colquhoun, then, the major police problem is the tendency to idleness, immorality and depravity among the indigent working class. This problem was already being overcome inside the factory through the discipline brought about by the division of labour and specialization. One of Adam Smith's complaints in the *Wealth of Nations* was that workers had a tendency to saunter, both inside and outside the workplace.

> A man commonly saunters a little in turning his hand from one sort of employment to another... The habit of sauntering and of indolent careless application, which is naturally, or rather necessarily acquired by every country workman who is obliged to change his work and his tools every half hour, and to apply his hand in twenty different ways almost every day of his life; renders him almost always slothful and lazy.[48]

The solution to the indolence brought about by sauntering inside the factory was, of course, the division of labour: 'riveting each worker to a single fraction of the work...compels each one of them to spend no more than the necessary time. This creates a continuity, a uniformity, a regularity, an order.'[49] Colquhoun's interest lay in the problem of idleness outside the factory. The task of police is to employ a whole panoply of measures and techniques to manage idleness, extending well beyond the administration of relief into the morality, profligacy and propriety of the working class. The working class need to be taught the morality of work and thus the immorality of idleness and related activities such as drinking, gambling, cohabitation, prostitution, political subversion, trade unionism and, a point which will become important in the following chapter, appropriation of property from the workplace, as well as 'crime' more generally. The range of mechanisms to be subsumed under the police project therefore include limiting, regulating and persistently checking public houses and what takes place in them, restricting gambling, introducing a moral code to be implemented in pawn shops so that the money gained there is wisely spent, placing in the *Police Gazette* short essays, articles and selections from the more moral sections of statutes to teach 'the labouring people a strong sense of moral virtue, loyalty and love of their country', and making sure the clergy and educational system are geared to moralizing the working class by teaching the poor about 'the rank they are destined to fill in society' and how to avoid 'those vices and temptations to which their situations, particularly in large cities, expose them'.[50] The general idea, then, is to put the poor to labour, to make the working class work.[51] 'Indigence' is merely coda for any attempt to avoid wage labour, to refuse exploitation. As Peter Linebaugh has noted, if a single individual could be said to have been the planner and theorist of class struggle in the metropolis it would be Colquhoun.[52] This is a point developed in Chapter 4, where Colquhoun's arguments for the role of police in the fabrication of the wage form will be discussed. For the moment, however, we need to further explore Colquhoun's views on the political economy of police.

Political economy and social police

Like most writers on police, it is crime against property that so concerns Colquhoun, and as the distinction between poverty and indigence is sharpened so his account of property is also refined. In doing so it comes to focus on the general *public* effect of crimes and the damage done to the state or community *as a whole* by crime. Significant here is the change in title between the earlier and later editions of his *Treatise on Police*. In the title of the earlier edition Colquhoun fails to mention property at all: it is presented as *A Treatise on the Police of the Metropolis, explaining the various crimes and misdemeanours Which at present are felt as a Pressure on the Community; and suggesting remedies for their prevention*. By the seventh edition ten years later property not only dominates the discussion, but its importance as a question of *public* concern has also become central. The work had therefore become *A Treatise on the Police of the Metropolis; containing a detail of the various crimes and misdemeanours by which Public and Private Property and Security are, at present, injured and endangered: and suggesting remedies for their prevention*. And it is for this reason that in trying to show that theft is a serious matter he gives figures for the total loss to the community and not just to any single individual or group of individuals. Much eighteenth-century legal theory had distinguished between public and private wrongs.[53] In his arguments regarding the necessity of police Colquhoun helped challenge such distinctions. It is for this reason that his discussions of crimes against property centre on the general *public* effect – 'all depredations on property are *public wrongs*, in the suppression of which every member of the community is called upon to lend his assistance' – and why he consistently refers to the damage done to the state or community *as a whole* by crime.[54] In doing so his argument rests on a set of claims about the political economy of the wealth of nations.

Since the labour of the class of poverty is clearly central to the wealth of the nation, and since this wealth is also understood as consisting in property, Colquhoun presents his vision of police as a contribution to political economy: 'police...is quite a new science in political economy'.[55] Colquhoun's work is indicative of the continued links between police science and political economy, and his distinction between poverty and indigence is in fact the crux of his contribution to both these modes of discourse. Since for Colquhoun the acceleration of wealth can only be achieved 'by establishing a correct system of police', political economy must concern itself with this. Yet the science of wealth has failed to grasp this point. 'In all the branches of the Science of Political Oeconomy, there is none which requires so much skill and knowledge of men and manners, as that which relates to this particular object [the poor].' Thus the main concern of his proposal for a Pauper Police Institution and a Board of General Internal Police should be seen as his contribution to the political economy of the wealth of nations, and the set of measures which Colquhoun subsumes under the police idea should also be seen as, in a roundabout way, his contribution to the science of political economy, but *in the form of a science of police*.[56] This in turn consists in showing not just the necessity of police to the prevention of indigence and thus crime, but to the security of property: 'where Property is exposed, a preventive Police must be resorted to, in order to be secure'.[57] Far from the discourse of police being displaced by the discourse of political economy and the system of natural liberty, in Colquhoun's work 'police' and 'political economy' are two sides of the same discursive coin. Police is a *complement* to the political economy of commercial society, rather than its opposite. The very same point can be made about Hegel, whose appropriation of political economy is similar to Colquhoun's: he appropriates it in order to point to its limitations, to develop a complementary argument concerning the limitations of the market as a spontaneous and self-regulating mechanism, and to subsume the whole problem under the police.

The originality of Colquhoun and Hegel should not be missed here. In breaking with the increasingly dominant liberal understanding of police they were not merely reiterating the central claims of cameralism. As was suggested in the previous chapters, the police theorists of the cameralist tradition found themselves unable to commit to a commercial society of the sort envisaged by Smith, Kant and others because it would have undermined the notion of police with which they worked. Thus writers who tried to develop the police idea in the late eighteenth century were often unable to theorize this in relation to a modern commercial society. In the British context, whereas Jonas Hanway looks back to an earlier age before the growth of commerce and an 'unattached' poor,[58] Colquhoun situates police within the modern system of commerce; whereas the language used by the Fieldings has an archaic tone – talk of 'thieftakers', 'highway robberies' and the 'hue and cry' – the language used by Colquhoun is quintessentially modern, not least in its focus on the growth of commodities and merchandise, international and national trade, and the expansion of commerce and industry.

Both Colquhoun and Hegel develop the account of the police of the poor as a fundamental part of a modern commercial market system within 'civil society'. Colquhoun and Hegel look forward to the expansion of modern commerce and industry across the face of society – 'a new aera in the world seems to have commenced'[59] – founded on wealth and private property. Since this new era *requires* the existence of a class of labouring poor, Colquhoun's objective (along with the major political economists of the period) was the fabrication of a 'free market' economy and, concomitantly, the commodification of labour. I shall develop this point more fully in the following chapter. The point here is that this cannot be achieved without a police mechanism enforced by the state. 'Police [is] the constant and never-failing attendant on the accumulation of Wealth.'[60] The police, on this score, both administers the disciplinary nature of the market and steps in where that discipline fails. It is not so much that no one before had suggested that the relief of the poor should come within the province of police, as Radzinowicz suggests,[61] but that no one before Colquhoun and Hegel had suggested that the administration of the poor within a modern market-driven civil society should come within the province of police.

Now, David Garland has commented that to refer to Colquhoun's 'criminology' would be to use an anachronism.[62] Given that the relief of poverty and regulations concerning the living conditions of citizens tends to be subsumed under the heading of 'social policy' rather than 'police', a better anachronism would perhaps be to refer to Colquhoun's 'social policy'. In other words, Colquhoun's conception of prevention has as much to do with what we now call 'social policy' as police; the same is true of Hegel's notion of police (hence the translations of 'police' as 'public authority'). I am arguing, in effect, that since the heart of Colquhoun's proposals is the overseeing of the condition of labour through the political management of poverty, he should be remembered for being a forerunner of the new poor law as much as a forerunner of the new police, a forerunner of preventive *social policy* as well as preventive *criminal policing*.[63] Those figures and institutions which emerged following the 'birth of the welfare state' and which became central to social policy – poor law and social security officers, social workers, probation officers and 'official' administrators of policy, and the public health system – are on this view as much a part of the policing of the system as uniformed police officers. This is entirely consistent with the links between police and policy identified in Chapter 1 and will be developed in the chapters to come. Here I will just suggest that, given Colquhoun's attempt to capture these activities under the heading of 'police', the term *social police* may be more appropriate.[64] To make sense of the reasons why, we must return to the question of security.

Towards social security

Colin Gordon has commented that in general Marxism credits non-Marxist thought with little share of the unease and uncertainty identified by Marx and Engels in *The Communist Manifesto* as one of the defining characteristics of the bourgeois epoch.[65] Colquhoun and Hegel would be good examples of the kind of non-Marxist thought in question, for their joint sublation of liberal property theory rests on their recognition that the need for security rests not just on the protection of individuals and their property, but on the inherent insecurity of the system of private property as a whole. When Colquhoun writes about security it is because of its importance to the trade of a commercial society as a system – it is for this reason that the term 'security' becomes important enough to warrant entering the full title of later editions of the *Treatise on Police*, in connection with the idea of order. The introduction of police would involve 'extending security to Commercial Property' as a whole. 'Wherever a proper Police attaches', he states categorically, 'good order and security will prevail.' The same point applies to Hegel's work: 'What the police provides for in the first instance is the actualization and preservation of the universal which is contained within the particularity of civil society, [and it does so] as *an external order and arrangement* for the protection and security of the masses of particular ends and interests.'[66]

Colquhoun's and Hegel's joint commitment to a modern commercial system and the domination of the system of needs by the demands of private property, a commitment, that is, to a market-driven civil society, is shot through with their fundamental insight – and fear – that as a system private property is fundamentally insecure. As part of its very foundation, private property requires and generates insecurity.[67] The market rests on the insecurity of economic actors, is founded on the insecurity of a class of poverty forever on the edge of falling into the state of indigence and becoming a rabble (or, as some would later come to argue, consciously opting for the assistance provided of the state rather than the wage provided by capital) and, finally, is rendered insecure by generating political enemies. It is for this reason that both writers rely heavily on the notion of security in their accounts of police. But their version of security sublates the liberal concept. Committed to a system of private property, Hegel and Colquhoun share the liberal vision of politics as a 'technique of security' in the sense that this applies to individual liberty, but recognize that because the foundation of the modern system of liberty is itself insecure it requires state power. On this reading the police of the poor is a mechanism for *securing the insecure*.

Michael Dillon has noted that modern politics is a security project in the widest possible sense of the term. One can see this in the way 'security' saturates the language of modern politics, resonating through the philosophical and political discourse of modernity: state security, national security, political security, global security, regional security, territorial security, economic security, financial security, individual security, collective security, personal security, physical security, psychological security, sexual security, environmental security, and so on.[68] Yet there is something peculiar about the notion of 'security' as it has been studied within academia and used by politicians. On the one hand, 'security studies' has been developed almost entirely within international relations where the focus has been on militarization as a means of securing national frontiers and the identification of the security of citizens with that of the state system. On the other hand, social and public policy have tended to turn the question of security into a technical discussion regarding the details of welfare provision. Furthermore, within police studies the notion of security is central and yet is hardly ever discussed at any length; it is assumed that 'security' simply refers to the implementation of law as a means of protecting individuals. The argument partly made so far in this chapter, continued in what remains of it, and developed in the two remaining chapters, is an attempt to shift discussions of security beyond these three 'disciplines'. In contrast to international relations, the argument focuses on the penetration of civil society by the state, a penetration which secures *internal* rather than external order and, as well as identifying citizens with the state, operates as a means of identifying citizens with the prevalent property system. In contrast to social and public policy, the argument attempts to spell out the police dimension to the security-based assumptions of the welfare system. And in contrast to police studies, the argument seeks to break the obsession with security as law-enforcement.

The *Oxford English Dictionary* organizes the entry for 'security' under three sections, each highly revealing. The first two sections reveal that 'security', like 'police', is both a noun and verb. 'Security' in the first section refers to a condition (of being secure or protected), a state (of freedom from care or doubt), or a quality (of being securely fixed). But, secondly, it also refers to a *means* of being secure and thus a *process* (of making safe, of securing something). The third meaning is financial – in the sense of security bonds – revealing that as with 'capital', 'security' is a key term for both bourgeois economics and law. The fact that 'security' is both noun and verb reveals that as much as one might talk about the *condition* of security, one must also address the substantive and active *process* of securing. As Dillon puts it, security is not just a noun that names something, but a principle of formation that does things.[69]

The definitions also reveal the connection between security and insecurity: all security is defined in relation to insecurity. Not only must any appeal to security involve a specification of the fear which engenders it (as in Hobbes), but this fear (insecurity) demands the counter-measures (security) to neutralize, eliminate or constrain the person, group, object or condition which engenders fear. Securing is therefore what is done to a condition that is insecure. It is only because it is shaped by insecurity that security can secure.[70] This is what James Der Derian describes as the paradox of security: in security we find insecurity; any argument for security contains a strong trace of insecurity within it. And yet 'originating in the contingency of life and the certainty of mortality, the history of security reads as a denial, a resentment, and finally a transcendence of this paradox. In brief, the history is one of individuals seeking an impossible security from the most radical "other" of life, the terror of death.'[71] One can apply this argument to civil society and the state in general: the terror of death can be thought of as a terror of *social* death – the death of civil society itself. The history of security is a history of the state seeking an impossible security from the terror of the death of civil society. Civil society, after all, generates its own enemies; the bourgeoisie produces its own gravediggers. In class terms this means that police is necessary because capital, as the modern master, is forever at risk of losing control of the class of which it is master. The economic inactivity of the class of poverty is the heart of the insecurity of the system, the resistance of this class to the social domination of private property is its next step, and the political mobilization of the class its highest form. Thus security involves not just the prevention and detection of crime but, more importantly, the imposition of a form of social police. The history of police as a security project is a history of private property's fear of its most radical 'other' (communism).

'Security' is thus far from merely a by-word for 'freedom' or 'liberty', as liberalism would have it, but refers to the process through which attempts are made to render the insecure secure. It is for this reason that security is the supreme concept of bourgeois society, one of the principal ideological mechanisms underpinning the order of property. As a policy-oriented discourse 'security' has frequently worked to constitute order which, in practice, means no more than the securing of civil society by the state. Far from being a spontaneous order of the kind found in liberal mythology, civil society is the security project par excellence. The demand for security is inevitably a demand for the greater exercise of state power – witness the way 'national security' essentially equates the political status quo with the desirable order and gives the state virtually *carte blanche* powers to protect it,[72] or the way that it is security which requires that civil

society be calculable and knowable, a project of knowledge and calculation in the services of state power.[73] The police project involves nothing
less than securing the system of social domination: the imposition of
social security.

4
Ordering Insecurity II:
On Social Security

What *is* social security? One assumption implicit within social policy and echoed in much popular belief is that social security is a response to poverty in the form of financial assistance: 'social security systems relate to transactions by government (or agencies approved by government) which increase individual money incomes in certain specific circumstances of income loss or need for income protection'.[1] But this is a very narrow conception of the notion. More generally, social security is seen in terms of the welfare system as a whole. The Laroque Report (1984) published by the International Labour Office argues that social security should be seen as 'the response to an aspiration for security in its widest sense...This involves not just meeting needs as and when they arise but also preventing risks from arising in the first place...Thus social security requires not only cash but also a wide range of health and social services.' Social security therefore 'has wider aims than the prevention or relief of poverty...It is the guarantee of security that matters most of all.' Far from being limited to cash payments for particular needs, social security is a combination of three trends: economic policy aimed at full employment, medical policy, and income policy aimed at modifying the clash of economic forces.[2] As William Jowitt, Minister for Social Insurance, put it in 1944, 'economic justice, political justice, justice everywhere, full employment, organisation of the health services, maintenance of a stable price level, a satisfactory housing policy – these things and many others are all necessary ingredients in a policy of social security'.[3] In that sense the system of social security is to all intents and purposes the same as the system of social insurance[4] and the welfare state in general. Indeed, 'in the end social security becomes another grandiose term for social and economic policy'.[5]

In this chapter I shall suggest that the fact that the welfare system and social policy share the same fundamental concept as police – the concept of security – is no coincidence. That the origins of social security lie in the 'birth of the welfare state', and that this birth is in turn traditionally traced to the 'revolution in British government' generally and the new poor law in particular, tells us something important about the nature of social security, especially its links with police, not least because of the birth of the new police alongside the new poor law. Implicit in the argument is the assumption that there is a conceptual continuity between the early use of the concept of security in its links with the transformation of the police idea and the twentieth-century notion of social security. The aim of 'social security' is less the security of the individual citizen, assured of a safety net in place to help him or her in times of need, and more to do with the security of the social system, achieved through the project of social police. The concept of *social security* emerged and exists as a way of dealing with *economic insecurity*, an insecurity rooted in the nature of a system founded on private property. 'Social security' is thus a vision of economic security in a system founded on insecurity.

This will enable me to provide a connecting thread between state power, police and the condition of the poor. In one of his accounts of the shifting dynamics of crime and the law in England in the nineteenth century, V.A.C. Gatrell comments that while it is clear that the police have never liked political dissidents, the real challenge for any argument concerning police is to show why they have never trusted the poor either.[6] The general assumption in police studies is that the new police that emerged in 1829 had a much narrower mandate than earlier police, and that the focus of this mandate was crime. It has been easy for commentators to claim that the new police emerged as, finally, the long sought after rational solution to a 'crime problem' which had disturbed Britain throughout the eighteenth century and into the nineteenth. Their evidence for this lies in the fact that the official instructions given to the Metropolitan Police in 1829 opened with the claim that 'It should be understood, at the outset, that the principal object to be attained is the Prevention of Crime. To this great end every effort of the Police is to be directed.' The point was reiterated to those joining the provincial forces later.[7] The view that the primary rationale of policing is the prevention and detection of crimes has been widely accepted as the foundation of police and has become the commonsense of police studies. Indeed, this discipline has tended to treat the new police as 'new' and 'modern' not only because it was finally a properly constituted police force, with uniforms, rules and procedures, but also because it was said to have a fairly clear mandate to prevent crimes and disorder. To give but one example: 'London's Metropolitan Police...was the first modern police force in a nation with representative government. Its modernity rested on its role as "preventive police", which could control crime by preventing it from occurring.'[8] As we shall see in this chapter and the next, the question of crime has served as a convenient obfuscation and assisted the police in its desire for ever greater powers. The point to note first, however, is that the condition of poverty – that is, the state of the working class – remained central to all police mechanisms even after 1829; hence Gatrell's challenge. For all the talk of the 'new' and 'modern' nature of the new police forces which emerged in the nineteenth century, the police retained the defining characteristic of the term as it had developed historically. Far from being some kind of radical break with older forms of police, the 'new police' in fact represent an institutional elaboration of the old police idea.[9] The argument will show how and why the 'first principles of the police' identified in Chapter 1 remained the core of the police project and, relatedly, why those other state institutions with the poor as their object should be thought of as a form of policing.

In developing the argument I shall be building on the account of political administration in *Administering Civil Society*, in which I argued that one of the functions of political administration is to actively constitute and shape the working class through the administration of the poor law. This chapter and the one which follows will argue that police acts as a form of political administration. The present chapter will first identify the common ideological presuppositions behind the new poor law and the new police, before moving on to explore the police role in the fabrication of wage labour and thus the making of the working class. In making this argument I will also challenge the view that the police merely defend the status quo. It has been said that 'it is not the mandate of the police to produce a new order' and that for this reason one can best see the police as upholders of the staus quo, as *reproducers* of order.[10] In fact I shall argue that the police did indeed come to play a crucial role in the fabrication of a new order of bourgeois rule. The original project of mastering the masterless had been turned into the project of constituting the previously masterless as subject to a new master – capital – consolidating the power of private property. Part of the point is to argue that not only are both police and social policy ranged against the same group – the nascent working class – but that they both emerged to *shape* this very group in the first place as part of the coordinated attempt by the state to *fashion the market* and thus consolidate the fabrication of a truly bourgeois order. A discussion of a further key feature of social security – public health and cleanliness – will then draw out the connections between this and order, police, property and poverty.

The question of treating police as a form of administration will then be dealt with in Chapter 5.

The fabrication of wage labour

To take up Gatrell's challenge then: why have the police never trusted the poor? Why is it wrong to narrow the police function down to the prevention of crime and ignore the more pressing question of poverty? Edwin Chadwick argued that 'the views generally taken of a Police force have always appeared to me extremely narrow. Popularly they are for the most part viewed as a mere agency for the apprehension of criminals.' In fact, he argued, the new police should also be engaged in an extensive range of 'collateral services' and, most importantly, should also be closely connected with the new poor law. 'The complete operation of the principles of the poor law Amendment Act is largely dependent on the aid of a rural Police whose chief functions would necessarily be clearly connected with the poor law business of a Board of Guardians.'[11] In one sense the close links between new police and new poor law were merely to ensure that the law was enforced. Those behind the new poor law and those resisting it all recognized that the law would need a police to crush any anti-poor law disturbances. Chadwick was clear that an effective police force was needed 'for the suppression of tumults connected with the administration of relief', while *The Herald* noted in 1839 that 'The Centralized Police Bill is a *pendant* to the New Poor Law. The object of the Centralized Police Bill is amongst other things to create a force that shall be available at any point for the enforcement of the odious Malthusian Act...the Centralized Police Bill will render it impossible for the labourer to struggle against the tendencies of the New Poor Law System.'[12] But the role of police went beyond merely enforcing the poor law. The central Poor Law Board sanctioned the use of police as poor law relieving officers in 1848, as Chadwick recommended, and the Select Committee on Police of 1853 noted that the new police constables were acting as assistant relieving officers under the poor law: between 1857 and 1880 some 35 counties in England employed their police as assistant poor law relieving officers. Key figures such as Major William Cartwright, chairman of the Brackley Poor Law Union in 1835 and also one of the first of Her Majesty's Inspectors of Constabulary, were also keen to encourage the police to act as relieving officers, and many Chief Constables, following the encouragement from Cartwright and the Poor Law Board, arranged for their men to act in this capacity. In 1887 Police Commissioner Warren tried to appease public criticisms over his handling of unemployment riots by opening a register of the unemployed in each of his districts, while in 1904 police inspectors and superintendents reported confidentially to Scotland Yard on the extent of the hardship during the winter.[13]

This conjunction of new poor law and new police was not peculiar to Britain. So central was the question of poverty in discussions surrounding the emergence and development of the police forces in nineteenth-century Europe that it would be no exaggeration to say that the forces were for the most part seen as an extension to the emerging machinery for managing the poor. In the case of the Italian city of Bologna, for example, Steven Hughes writes that 'whether employing idle workers or subsidizing victims of fraud, the police obviously sat at the center of the city's welfare system. They did so in part because they offered the most organized mechanism of distribution. Also, as the government's information agency, they could identify and judge possible welfare recipients. Above all, however, the police understood the many connections between public security and poverty.'[14] A similar claim has been made for the development of policing in virtually all nineteenth-century western states.[15]

Part of the reason for this conjunction lay in the concern over vagrancy. The Vagrancy Act (1824) gave the new police extensive street powers for the control of vagrants, and the extension of the police to the boroughs in the County and Borough Police Act of 1856 was justified by the need to suppress vagrancy. Having the police aimed directly at vagrancy allowed the state to label any group as vagrant (or at least potentially so), and thus bring them directly under police rule. The so-called *sus* law in which the police exercised its powers over the streets in Britain until almost the twenty-first century had its origins in the Vagrancy Act, section 4 of which gave to police the power to treat as a potential offender 'every suspected person or reputed thief, frequenting any river, canal, or navigable stream, dock, or basin, or any quay, wharf, or warehouse near or adjoining thereto, or any street, highway, or avenue leading thereto, or any place of public resort, or any avenue leading thereto, or any street (or any highway or any place adjacent to a street or highway) with intent to commit (an arrestable offence)'.[16] In the 1850s statutes dealing with the education of pauper children incidentally defined destitute children as vagrants, and in 1868 and again in 1872 the description of vagrant was extended to any person found gaming in a public place.[17] Much of the discussion in the 1853 Select Committee on Police focused on the value of professional county constabularies in the suppression of vagrancy. Following the line espoused by Colquhoun, Chadwick and many others – that crime was often perpetrated by itinerants who preferred an idle life of vagrancy and theft to one of useful toil, and that a properly organized constabulary force would solve the problem – the Committee believed that the new constabularies had contributed to a decline in vagrancy as well as a better 'maintenance of order, and the improved habits of the population'. The understanding was that since vagrants were potential criminals, relieving the casual poor was a key policing mechanism. Vagrants were required to report to the police station, from where the respectable were sent on to the overseers while the 'criminal' were retained. The practice of building a tramp ward next to the police station was developed in the 1860s, the period in which there was a strong move for handing the entire supervision of the vagrant poor over to the police. Well into the twentieth century leading politicians and police officers clung to the notion that the vagrant was a probable criminal – during the Depression the police found themselves responsible for the issue of Vagrancy Way Tickets.[18]

The links between new police and new poor law can be partly seen in the significant cross-fertilization of ideas and information between the institutions and dominant personnel of new police and new poor law, which was so extensive that the main presuppositions underline both the *Report on the Constabulary Force* (1839) and the official documents on the poor law from a few years earlier.[19] The principle of less-eligibility had a prominent part in both reports, and both reports involved a conscious attempt to dissociate poverty from pauperism and criminality. Just as the *Poor Law Report* insisted on the sharpest distinction between pauperism and poverty, so the *Report on the Constabulary Force* distinguished between crime and poverty. And as the first proposed a solution which was intended to deal with pauperism while leaving poverty alone (indeed, poverty was explicitly said to be not a social problem), so the problem of crime was defined in terms of its relationship to pauperism rather than poverty. Much of the evidence of the 1839 *Report on the Constabulary Force* was obtained through the Poor Law Commission (and the later *Select Committee on Police* of 1853 also based its judgements partly on the basis of reports from Poor Law inspectors). Indeed, the cross-fertilization was so strong that some of the reports from witnesses on the poor law in the early 1830s made their way into the *Report on the Constabulary Force*. The Poor Law Commissioners in 1833 cite Mr Wontner. Asked 'of the criminals who came under your care, what proportion...were by the *immediate presure of want* impelled to the commission of crime? By want is meant, the absence of the means of subsistence, and not the want arising from indolence and an impatience of steady labour?' Wontner replied only one-eighth. And they cite a Mr Chesterton who commented on the fact that he could not identify one prisoner out of 60 that appeared to have been urged by want to commit theft. The very same passages are reproduced in the *Report on the Constabulary Force*.[20]

That the new poor law and the new police shared the same conceptual foundation and ideological presuppositions, and that the institutions of the new police and new poor law overlapped enormously, is not in doubt. The point to be made, however, is that the new police and new poor emerged at the same historical moment as part of the fabrication of a new industrial capitalist order, and for this to be achieved the making of a working class appropriate to this order was required. To show this must involve more than just identifying some conceptual and practical links. Marx comments that:

> the process...which creates the capital-relation can be nothing other than the process which divorces the worker from the ownership of his own labour; it is a process which operates two transformations, whereby the social means of subsistence and production are turned into capital, and the immediate producers are turned into wage-labourers.[21]

The argument here is that the second of these transformations took the form of a massive police operation – that the transformation in question remained at the core of the police project well into its third stage. The forms of policing being traced here were a political force for the making of the working class in that the ultimate aim of the police project was the commodification of labour through the consolidation of the wage form. As such, the project of social police has historically been central to the function of political administration in fashioning the market.

In terms of the new poor law, the argument has been made at greater length before,[22] so I shall merely remind the reader of the main point. The new poor law was explicitly designed to enforce wage-labour on the working population by disallowing out-relief to all but the truly destitute. It was against the undifferentiated idea of poverty that the report objected to when it complained of 'the mischievous ambiguity of the word *poor*'.[23] The ambiguity was mischievous because it failed to differentiate between the poor labourer and the pauper, a failure the *Report* believed was exemplified most clearly in the Speenhamland system, which was believed to have had the effect of 'pauperizing the poor'. The underlying principle of the *Poor Law Report* was to distinguish between the poor and the indigent, and to bring the indigent alone within the province of the poor law. The purpose of the poor law was to remove that ambiguity by making clear that as the labouring class the poor are expected to obtain subsistence within the market through the wage. The *Report* noted that:

> In no part of Europe except England has it been thought fit that the provision, whether compulsory or voluntary, should it be applied to

more than the relief of *indigence*, the state of a person unable to labour, or unable to obtain, in return for his labour, the means of subsistence. It has never been deemed expedient that the provision should extend to the relief of *poverty*; that is, the state of one, who in order to obtain a mere subsistence, is forced to have recourse to labour.[24]

This was a point we have seen made by Colquhoun. It was reiterated by Chadwick writing independently of the Commissioners: 'Poverty...is the natural, the primitive, the general, and the unchangeable state of man; ... as labour is the source of wealth, so is poverty of labour. Banish poverty, you banish wealth', he claimed, adding that 'indigence, therefore, and not poverty, is the evil, the removal of which is the proper object of the Poor Laws'.[25] Conventional historiography's highlighting of the new workhouses introduced by the Act has obscured the fact that the new poor law was as much concerned with those outside the workhouse as those within. The strategy of the new poor law was 'the repression of pauperism' (Chadwick) by making indoor relief thoroughly unattractive and outdoor relief unobtainable for able-bodied men. The new poor law was the first attempt to draw a clear line of demarcation between the poor on the one hand and the indigent/vagrant/pauper on the other in order to prevent 'all but uninsurable cases of pauperism'.[26] The new centralized authority overseeing the workhouses was an administrative mechanism for making people work outside the workhouse as much as disciplining those inside. A strategy, in other words, of creating a class of wage labour.

Concomitantly, the parallel new police was explicitly designed to end the appropriation of any means of subsistence other than the wage. Where the new poor law denied assistance outside the workhouse to those unwilling to participate in the market and be disciplined by the power of capital, thereby closing off to all but the most desperate of the poor the access to any means of subsistence provided by the state, the contribution of the new police was to coercively close off any access to any means of subsistence other than the wage. To make sense of this we need to return briefly to the status of labour and wages in the eighteenth century.

In the eighteenth century, many workers were paid partly in money wages and partly in kind; as such, the worker was not yet fully tied to the money wage. Payment in kind was often understood in terms of ancient entitlements. The thresher was partly paid with part of the harvest, the coal worker by part of the coal he handled. In the docks the ships' carpenters were still entitled to some of the spare timber, dock workers generally claimed to be entitled to any sugar or other commodities that were spilt, and cloth workers received the scraps of material known as 'cabbage'. Many were often paid almost entirely in kind. T.S. Ashton notes that:

> Both the coal-hewers of the north and the coal-meters of the Thames received by custom an allowance of fuel; and ironworks and other establishments that used coal often supplied it on special terms to their workers. The mates of the West Indiamen had a right to the sweepings of sugar and coffee from the hold of the ship; the gangsmen and coopers established a claim to the drainings of molasses and spilt sugar on the floor of the warehouse; and the labourers in the corn ships believed themselves to be similarly entitled to the grain that had been removed as samples. At the Royal Yards, the shipwrights were allowed to take for firewood the chips that fell from the axe, and their womenfolk were permitted to do the gleaning.[27]

Though not a part of the actual wage, such customary rights, or 'perquisites', formed an important part of a labourer's income.[28]

As part of these irregular 'payments' and 'ancient entitlements' workers also tended to appropriate whatever they could, as part of their share of the product of their labour; 'the workers saw to it that the crumbs from the master's table were ample', as Ashton puts it. In such conditions the line between established rights and theft was difficult to draw, since the legal status of such items was uncertain (or at least was regarded by many as uncertain). It is partly this issue that spurred the young Marx into the study of political economy as he tried to make sense of the shifting legal status of particular forms of property. As he noted, 'All customary rights of the poor were based on the fact that certain forms of property were indeterminate in character, for they were not definitely private property, but neither were they definitely common property, being a mixture of private and public right, such as we find in all the institutions of the Middle Ages.'[29] From the mid-century many of these non-monetary forms of 'payment' were coming within the criminal sanction, yet the deeply embedded notion of customary right was so entrenched that the moral sanction against such 'crimes' was lacking.[30] Towards the end of the eighteenth and into the nineteenth century employers therefore began a more concerted attempt to enforce the moral sanction against such perks and to ensure that such activities were properly criminalized. To give just four examples: the Worsted Committee was established by legislation in 1777 in order to limit workplace appropriation in the textile industries of Yorkshire, Lancashire and Cheshire; the naval authorities increasingly began to treat chips as an illegal form of appropriation in the 1770s, and by the 1790s had begun to use the courts to restrict those entitled to chips; in 1790 the West India merchants introduced regulations prohibiting the allowance of sweepings or molasses to the Gangsmen, repeating their less successful attempt to do so some thirty years previously; and farmers generally began to use the courts to cut down on the amount of gleaning (collecting scattered grain left after the harvest had been gathered). More generally, statutes were passed to govern property rights in some fifteen industries, including, wool, silk, linen, cotton, hemp, flax, leather, iron, fur.[31] The increasingly dominant bourgeois class felt that the customary rights in question jarred with the fundamental purpose of labour, which was to earn a wage, and raised a fundamental question: are those who labour entitled to appropriate the products of their own labour, other than through the wage received? The answer given by capital was increasingly a firm 'no'. What had previously been seen as custom was gradually being reconceptualized as crime. The historical process paralleled that of the enclosures movement, as Jason Ditton has noted.[32] Just as the enclosures involved the gradual translation of 'rights' (held in common) into 'property' or 'capital' (held in particular), so the attack on customary perquisites involved the gradual translation of 'rights' (held by custom) into 'crimes' (against property). Thus despite the fact that well into the nineteenth century the working class still saw such 'thefts' as traditional 'perks' – in 1832 in Walsall the charging of five men for stealing iron led to a three-day riot which was only suppressed after the Riot Act had been read twice and a number arrested, many workers still defended themselves in court on the grounds that their moral claim was higher than the criminal law, and as late as 1877 complaints were still being made concerning the problem of pilferage – the increased prosecution for such 'thefts' in the nineteenth century 'mark an offensive by the employers designed to eliminate popular ideas about the legitimate taking of property, which the employers now wanted to be clearly defined as unlawful and liable to be punished'.[33] Moreover, it was an attempt to stamp out crimes which were taking place at the very heart of the circuit of capital.

Resistance to the attempt to criminalize the customary rights of labour meant that the historical tension between customary usage and the money wage could only be settled by a massive police operation.[34] Significant here is Colquhoun's first practical success in introducing a police for the Thames. This event has been understood as merely a limited precursor of the more widespread introduction of police forces from 1829, or as a pointer to the tension between 'private' and 'public' policing in the period, but these ways of understanding it have obscured the fact that the introduction of this force was deliberately designed not only to prevent commercial losses on the river and docks, but to consolidate the money wage for dock workers. London was then one of the world's largest ports. Unsurprisingly, it also held one of the largest concentrations of workers, and was therefore the site for the realization of a wide range of customary rights. But for Colquhoun there was little difference between customary right and crime, since the former merely encouraged the latter. 'The transition from innocence to acts of turpitude...is easy and obvious', he notes.

> An indulgent Master, at first, grants the privilege of a few samples or a trifling quantity of foul Corn, on the solicitation of an industrious serv-ant, under the pretence of feeding a pig, or a few poultry. The stock of poultry or pigs is increased, and additional quantities of grain become necessary. The indulgence of the Master in a few instances is, at length, construed into a sanction to appropriate Sweepings of foul Grain. These Sweepings are presently increased by previous concert among the Labourers. Corn becomes foul, which might have been preserved in a clean and Merchantable state.

This process is then extended to other commodities and industries.[35]

> What was at first considered as the wages of turpitude, at length assumes the form, and is viewed in the light of a fair perquisite of office...Cus-tom and example sanction the greatest enormities: which at length become fortified by immemorial and progressive usage: it is no won-der, therefore, that the superior Officers find it an Herculean labour to cleanse the Augean stable.[36]

It is because of such 'customs', Colquhoun argues, that workers agree to work without wages, on the grounds that this would provide them with opportu-nities for workplace appropriation: they would agree 'to be admitted to work...without any pay, trusting to the chance of Plunder for remunera-tion'.[37]

The major task of the new preventive police envisaged by Colquhoun was to therefore break the workers' notion that the appropriation of goods on which they laboured was 'sanctioned by custom'. The reason for the introduction of the river police was thus a deliberate attack on 'wastage' and 'loss' previously seen as customary. Obliterating the distinction between custom and crime, or, rather, engaging in a concerted effort to redefine custom as crime, was thus a key part of the police project. This then became the basis of the regularization of the wage. Such decisions were consolidated in 1798 with the issuing of a public notice of a new

'Marine Police Establishment...under the sanction of Government', by the West India merchants, which was soon followed by similar police forces in Bristol and Liverpool. Its fourth part – the 'Discharging Department', but which Colquhoun described as an 'Establishment for Protection and Labour' – was charged with controlling dock labour, especially of the lumpers.[38] Eight hundred and twenty lumpers were enlisted to perform their duties in accordance with instructions issued by the Marine Police. Master lumpers were appointed to restrain the lumpers from pillage and wilful breakage, and to regularly search them. Not only was the unloading of ships overseen by the Marine Police, but rates of pay were set by it too. The intention here was to instil the discipline of the wage. Colquhoun was clear that to police workers' customary perquisites out of existence, employers would have to both increase and regularize wages. 'On the abolition of this perquisite [chips]...a liberal increase of wages should be made to the Artificers in lieu thereof.'[39] The force designed to protect property was also at the heart of imposing the money wage on private property's most important component. While the river police has long been seen as a milestone in policing, it should in fact also be seen as a milestone in the history of the wage form, the political fabrication and cultural construction of one of the central categories of bourgeois society. The net effect of the first preventive police system was thus not just a *defence* of property, but the creation of a social order founded on private property via the consolidation of the money wage and commodification of labour.

This pattern was followed in the development of policing elsewhere in the nineteenth century. It is clear from Philips's study of crime in the Black Country that there was a concerted effort on the part of industrial capital, police and magistrates to impose the money wage on the worker class, while in Liverpool merchants complained of the way the 'secondary economy of the streets' threatened the power of private property and money, not just in creating alternative points of sale but also in draining the wages and time of those who should more properly be engaged in wage labour. As Mike Brogden has argued:

The secondary economy that served the lower classes featured low costs, low overheads, and irregular hours of provision. It was the domain of the street hawker, the street market, the pawnshop, the fence, and included betting shops, beer houses, common lodging houses and brothels...City merchants complained vociferously of the spill-over of pedlars and beggars from city slum to residential park, of the extent of thieving of goods (to disappear in the maze of fences, receivers, and pawnshops) from warehouse and from quay, and of the way the secondary economy appeared to drain the wages and time of the casual labourer, distracting the latter from the disciplined expectations of wage labour.[40]

While in some ways functionally useful for the bourgeois class, the form of this economic activity was undermining the imposition of the wage.

This sheds greater light on an aspect of policing that has for some time been the focus of police studies, namely, the policing of the working class on the streets. Begging, of course, was severely curtailed, but customs and common rights in general all became subject to the police power and eventually eliminated. The Sunday Observance Act (1677) prohibited the exposure of goods for sale on a Sunday and gave police powers to seize such goods; the Vagrancy Act (1824) could be used against suspicious characters, beggars, prostitutes and people selling or sleeping in public places; the Highways Act (1835) established penalties for obstructing the footpath; and the Metropolitan Police Act (1839) gave the London police extensive legal powers over street activities with its provision of broad stop-and-search powers. The 1839 Act also defined a range of activities as offences, including causing public obstruction with animals or vehicles, rolling tubs, hops and wheels, sticking bills, writing on walls, using noisy instruments in the process of begging, selling or entertaining.[41] Such legislation and subsequent police action put into operation a concerted attempt on the part of the state to criminalize traditional activities which were either recreational or rooted in an alternative economic mode of life and which centred on the street – the 'proletarian public sphere'. As Alf Lüdtke notes, 'policing inevitably became preoccupied with controlling that sphere of communal life which, for the propertyless...represented virtually the only social space within which they could pursue their social interests and material needs'.[42] In particular, the police necessarily became involved in removing the possibility of obtaining non-wage subsistence. Traditional activities which labour used to eke out an existence – casual labour for payment in kind, grazing cattle on public byways, pilfering wood, picking fruit and vegetables for either consumption or sale, poaching, fishing from rivers without licence, hawking, peddling and street selling – all became targets for police action. As Carson puts it, 'policing was extremely consequential in suppressing subsistence practices antithetical to the development of new forms and relations of production, in closing off access to the means by which a substantially dispossessed population might obtain subsistence other than through the sale of its labour'.[43] In other words, one should see the street powers granted to the police as an expression of the state's contribution to class *formation* as well as class domination. The new forms of police operation coming into existence were fundamental to the imposition of the money wage as a means of making the working class, and thus need to be seen in the broader context of the role of police in the fabrication of a new, bourgeois, order.[44] The attack on the non-monetary form of the wage and its transformation into a fully-fledged money form meant criminalizing a range of traditional working-class activities, bringing them into the orbit of police power and thus legitimizing their oppression, a project designed to stamp the authority of private property over the living conditions of the majority of the population and confirm the power of capital as the new master. In other words, the order of the new industrial workplace was brought about in part by the ordering power of police.

It is for this reason that crimes against property were and have remained at the heart of the law in bourgeois society, and why the solution to the 'crime problem' was and is considered to be work. Ever since Peel announced his reform of the criminal law in 1826 by stating that he would begin with felony on the grounds that he considered 'the crime of theft to constitute the most important class of crime', official document after official document has revealed that crimes against property were and are dealt with harshly because they raise the possibility of a form of subsistence beyond wage labour. To give but one example: the *Report from the Departmental Committee on Prisons* noted in 1895 that the tendency to punish property offences more severely than offences involving violence against the person but no theft 'arises simply from the fact that offences against property are those by which a person can gain his living'.[45] The *Poor Law Report* explicitly challenged the assumption that 'poverty is the mother of crime'. The Commission approvingly cite the comments by one witness to the committee who, asked whether crime is linked to pauperism, replied that they invariably go together, but asked whether 'poverty – meaning unavoidable and irreproachable poverty – and crime go together', replied that in the whole of his experience of 25 years he could remember but one solitary instance of a poor but industrious man out of employment stealing anything.[46] Thus 'whatever impels any class into courses of sustained industry must necessarily diminish crime; and we find that one characteristic of the dispauperized parishes is the comparative absence of crime'. In his essay on the new poor law, Chadwick claims that 'whatever impels a man into a course of steady industry must of necessity diminish crime. If a man be driven to work hard during the day, it is no small security that he will not be habitually upon the prowl as a pilferer or as a poacher during the night.'[47] In other words, the key to reducing crime is to stop the poverty-stricken class from falling into pauperism. Thus the key to ending crime is 'dispauperizing the able-bodied'.[48] Likewise, a central claim of the 1839 *Report on the Constabulary Force* is that crime is committed by the indigent, by those seeking to avoid poverty without working. It makes great show of citing the confessions of known and convicted criminals that crime freed them from the obligation to labour: 'I gave up all labour and supported myself entirely by thieving, about three years ago. I have not worked since'; 'I never did much work; while I did work in the day I thieved at night; I only worked for two or three weeks at once'; 'sometimes I worked for two or three months, and then went on to thieving for some months, and then go to work again'; 'as an honest labourer, for factory work I got 11s to 13s; while I was boating I have made 50s in one trip, by taking goods out of packages'.[49] The *Report* therefore claims that the problem of crime is that it enables criminals to 'obtain more money with less labour than is obtainable by means of honest industry by a large proportion of labourers'. 'We have investigated the origin of the great mass of crimes committed...and we find [them] ascribable to one common cause, namely, the temptations of the profit of a career of depradation, as compared with the profits of honest and even well paid industry...The notion that any considerable proportion of the crimes against property are caused by blameless poverty or destitution we find disproved at every step.' The *Report* therefore sums up with an identical argument to that behind the new poor law. 'Having investigated the general causes of depradation, of vagrancy, and mendicancy...we find that in scarcely any cases is it [crime] ascribable to the pressure of unavoidable want or destitution; and that in the great mass of cases it arises from the temptation of obtaining property with a less degree of labour than by regular industry.' The problem is thus not just to use the police to *prevent* crime, but that crime is committed as a means of earning a living without succumbing to wage labour.[50] The way to prevent crime is thus to enforce wage labour. On the one hand, then, the new police institution that was emerging as the nineteenth century progressed was part and parcel of the new mechanisms for the prevention of pauperism (and thus the preservation of poverty and property). On the other hand, although the new mechanisms of state power introduced to administer the class of poverty, such as the new poor law, were later thought of under the label of 'welfare' and 'social security', they were in fact part and parcel of the new mechanism for policing the working class. As such the new poor and new police were integral parts of the same system, operating alongside each other towards the constitution of labour power as a commodity. The new poor law was itself a central mechanism of social police.

Once one understands the importance of money and the wage to the police project one can re-read other crucial issues concerning the emergence of the police, such as its role in crushing disturbances within civil society. Many commentators have argued that a major spur to innovation in policing in the early nineteenth century was the threat of working-class struggle. Radzinowicz, for example, notes that in its first six years the Metropolitan Police found that its most urgent challenge was keeping the peace rather than halting crime, and Stanley Palmer has at great length shown that a major impetus to innovations in the police in the 1830s was the threat of working-class radicalism and unrest.[51] The point to note, however, is that this was intimately connected to the consolidation of a new order founded on private property. The conventional form of mass protest in the eighteenth century – riots – could be put down with military force. Besides, the ruling class could live with such flashes of disorder, serving as they did as a form of communication between classes.[52] The ascendant bourgeois class realized that a more efficient force was needed to check the possibility of such disorders breaking out in the first place. The consolidation of bourgeois property relations in the nineteenth century created a social order far more troubled by collective disorder than the eighteenth century. 'The market system was more allergic to rioting than any other economic system', comments Karl Polanyi.[53] In particular, the market's sensitivity to violence as sparks of a more long-term instability meant that riots could no longer be allowed to flare up and then either die down or be savagely repressed. As one anonymous American commentator observed in 1854, 'men will go with reluctance to make money in a city where pestilence or violence renders life unsafe'.[54] The insecurity of stocks meant that 'a shooting affray in the streets of the metropolis might destroy a substantial part of the nominal capital...Under a market economy otherwise harmless interruptions of public order and trading habits might constitute a lethal threat since they could cause the breakdown of the economic regime upon which society depended.'[55] The military was and remains ill-equipped to police a market order, alternating as it does between no intervention and the most drastic and violent procedures. The newly emerging police, in contrast, could penetrate civil society in a way impossible for military formations, less to crush disorder in the form of riots and collective resistance (though it also came to do that of course) and more to fabricate an order in which such disorder did not occur.[56] When writers talk about the fact that the new police emerged as a means of maintaining 'public order', the argument generally rests on a narrow and somewhat misleading vision of disorder (the typical example is riots). 'Order' should be understood not just as the absence of riots or generalized peace and quiet on the streets, but as the acceptance of the capital–labour relation, the domination of capital over the working class.

Border patrols: classes, criminals and claimants

In the light of the links between the new police and the new poor law, some have argued that poverty came to be regarded as equivalent to crime. Disraeli, for example, remarked that the Poor Law Act 'announces to the world that in England poverty is a crime' and some recent radical commentators have made similar claims – as in Carolyn Steedman's suggestion that 'poverty was united with crime'.[57] In fact, the issue is more subtle than this, and teasing out some of its subtleties tells us something important about the conception of order and its links to police in the nineteenth century. 'Crime' has always been a loose and slippery category. More to the point, crime has always been the repository of a range of diverse and ambiguous fears, investing crime with an important social and political significance; the way a society thinks about crime tells us a great deal about that society's fears and, in particular, a great deal about how a society's fears about change and disorder are displaced on to 'criminals'.[58] In this sense discussions of 'crime' are frequently barely veiled discussions of disorder, a point to which we shall return in the following chapter. It was only with the development of the new police and bourgeois order that 'crime' acquired the kind of meaning which it had only dimly possessed in the eighteenth century but which it has possessed ever since. One of the major historical achievements of the bourgeois class was to simultaneously incorporate the working class as part of the new bourgeois conception of order and impose an ideological separation on the class by distinguishing the working class from the 'criminal class' on the one hand and 'claimant class' on the other. Here we need to once again return briefly to the eighteenth century.

Writing about the Black Act (1723), E.P. Thompson notes that commentators on the Act and on eighteenth-century 'crime' more generally make frequent reference to 'gangs of criminals', 'criminal subculture' and the like. He writes that:

> Eighteenth-century class prejudice unites here with the anchronistic employment of the (inadequate) terminology of some twentieth-century criminology. Thus [one account] cites the Ordinary of Newgate's account of the seven hanged Hampshire Blacks as 'an unusually full picture of the criminal subculture of Georgian England'. The lamentable thing about this account – and many other accounts of the hanged by the Ordinary – is that they are nothing of the sort; they are simply accounts of the commonplace, mundane culture of plebian England – notes on the lives of unremarkable people, distinguished from their fellows by

little else except the fact that by bad luck or worse judgement they got caught up in the toils of the law. In the Hampshire case in question we have two carters, a publican who was perhaps a receiver of venison, an ostler who may have had a 'criminal record', a farm servant, a shoemaker's apprentice and a seventeen-year-old servant (a tailor's son)...If this is a 'criminal subculture' then the whole of plebeian England falls within the category.[59]

Thompson's point is a crucial one. In eighteenth-century England the line between a 'criminal class' and the 'plebian class' was an impossible one to draw. This was partly because the 'line' between criminal activity and other activities performed by those across the social spectrum was also difficult to draw. That one highwayman became Attorney-General and pirates could be knighted is indicative of the real structural and social affinities between the organizations which incorporated legitimate and illegitimate enterprises and the mobility between the legal and illegal centres of power: Jonathan Wild, the principal thief-taker of the eighteenth century, notoriously describes himself as a 'factor' journeying between the worlds of crime and power. Thief-takers were in essence in a position to establish an *imperium in imperio*, a concentration of power over criminal activity acknowledged by the state. Receivers of stolen property themselves, thief-takers were nonetheless called upon to regulate and provide access to the world of crime. Wild, for example, was asked for his advice by the Privy Council concerned with ways of reducing the number of highway robberies.[60] By the time Fielding published *Jonathan Wild* (1743), the analogy between the 'criminal and man of power' Wild and the 'man of power and criminal' Walpole was almost universally recognized. But this was not just a link between the political-cum-criminal styles of two individuals. As Thompson notes, the Walpole–Wild analogy is symptomatic of the way in which 'the "subculture" of Hanoverian Whig and the "subculture" of Jonathan Wild were mirror-images of each other'.[61] The general point is that individuals fell into and out of whatever activities they needed to engage in to eke out a living. Clear-cut oppositions between crime and 'good citizenship', or between morality and criminal immorality, had not yet been separated out. As Juliet Mitchell puts it in her commentary on Defoe's *Moll Flanders* (1722): whether Moll is a criminal or not is a difficult question to answer. Moll sometimes steals and at other times is a 'good citizen'; is sometimes a good wife and sometimes a prostitute; is sometimes an honest moneymaker and sometimes a thief.[62] The truth is, Moll does whatever she needs to do to survive. Moll is *both* criminal *and* plebian, and no one at the time thought this odd because there was no categorical distinction between a 'working class' and a 'criminal class'.

Yet the distinction between a 'criminal class' on the one hand and the rest of the population on the other became increasingly commonplace in the nineteenth century. Indeed, the distinction as it developed focused almost entirely on separating the 'criminal class' out from the 'poor but respectable' working class. This is not to say that such a distinction *was* clear, for there is abundant evidence to show that it was not. As one 17-year-old confessed in 1839: 'Sometimes I worked for three months and then went to thieving for some months, and then go to work again', illustrating what Stuart Hall and his co-writers describe as 'that dialectic of work-poverty-unemployment-crime which [was] the defining matrix of working-class London throughout most of the century'.[63] Despite this reality, the myth of a 'criminal class' gained currency in the nineteenth century, conveniently serving a bourgeois state increasingly interested in demarcating boundaries within the working class, to both fragment and police it accordingly.

The new system of social police that emerged in the second quarter of the nineteenth century announced to the world not that poverty was equivalent to crime, but that pauperism was; it was the 'pauper-claimant' and the criminal that were treated as equivalents. 'A line was drawn', as Chadwick puts it.[64] Just as the poor law came to separate out the 'claimant class' (scroungers, feckless, wasters, parasites) from the 'respectable classes', so the police served to separate out the 'criminal class' (dishonest, threat, disease) from the respectable classes. But the key issue in each case is how the distinction in question is related to the working class.[65] Both criminal and claimant are understood as engaged in the refusal of wage labour – the criminal steals and the claimant claims in order to avoid work – and both claimant and criminal are viewed through the lens of idleness. This is a constant feature of bourgeois order – witness the way the trope of the 'underclass' has come to the fore in the late twentieth century, for example. Just as 'criminality became one of the mechanisms of power',[66] so too did the claimant. But both criminal and claimant became one of the mechanisms of power by virtue of being an ideological by-product of the wage as a mechanism of power. The making of the working class was simultaneously the *making of a claimant class* and *making of a criminal class*. Both claimant and criminal have failed to achieve the dizzy heights of respectability by failing to be a bona fide proletarian; as such, they fall outside of the social pact. In both cases, the threat to the order of property is apparent; and for much of the time, the bourgeois class cannot even distinguish between the two 'threats'.[67]

Recent sociology of the police has developed the notion of 'police property' to describe 'any category of citizens who lack power in the major institutions of their society...A category becomes police property when the dominant powers of society (in the economy, polity, etc.) leave the problems of social control of that category to the police.'[68] Given the expanded definition of police being developed here, one might also say that the 'pauper-claimant' also becomes police property, in the sense that they are left to the control mechanisms of the institutions of social police (the poor law). In this sense social police is in some sense a form of border patrol – the policing of the borders of citizenship; the borders, that is, of the categories defining those who are to come under the greater control, surveillance and administration by the state. And it is by removing the individual from the category 'citizen' and placing them in the category 'claimant' or 'criminal' that the case can be made for granting the claimant/ suspect fewer rights.

But such differentiation has a paradoxical effect. As Gertrude Himmelfarb has noted, the sharper the differentiation between the subgroup and the larger group and the more dramatic the image of the former in contrast to the latter, the more inevitable it is that the dramatic image will be transposed to the larger group.[69] The image of 'pauperization' and 'criminalization' was so dramatic that it spilled over to the image of poverty itself, and thus the image of the working class. In the case of pauperism, the poor become saddled with the worst attributes of the pauper; as such they are always *potentially the pauper-claimant*. In the case of criminality, the working class get saddled with the worst attributes of the criminal; as such they are always *potentially criminal*. It is for this reason that discussions of crime are often barely veiled discussions of class. The point is not that any particular group *is* police property, however true that may be, but that because it is workers who are always seen to be on the verge of becoming criminal or claimant (or both), it is the working class which is the object of police power. The military metaphors within which both criminal and claimant are conceptualized within the bourgeois mentality – the perpetual 'war on crime' mirrored in the equally perpetual 'war on scroungers' – disguise the social characteristics of the enemy in question, which if revealed would show the battle to be no more than coda for the permanent low-intensity warfare against the working class. And it should be added that this is a war which the state cannot win, for to win it would mean abolishing the condition of private property that gives rise to it, and thus abolishing itself as a state.

The fact that the 'criminal class' is intimately connected to the working class in the bourgeois ideology is shown in the way that crimes committed by capital in pursuit of ever greater rates of accumulation have never been treated with the same seriousness as crimes committed against property. As it eliminated the customary rights of the working class by treating them as new forms of criminality targeted at the sanctity of property, capital reserved for itself a new set of 'rights' allowing it to circumvent any suggestion of illegality on its part. For all its talk of the equality embedded in the rule of law (a topic we shall have reason to discuss more fully in the following chapter), bourgeois law has always treated capital and labour (and thus members of the bourgeoisie and proletariat) very differently. The Master and Servant Act of 1823 identified breach of contract as very different kinds of offences if committed by worker or employer: where the former was liable to criminal prosecution, the latter could only by prosecuted in civil law,[70] and from the first Factory Act of 1833 onwards crimes committed by capital and its representatives have never been thought of as 'real' crime. As Foucault notes, the bourgeoisie reserved for itself

> the possibility of getting round its own regulations and its own laws, of ensuring for itself an immense sector of economic circulation by a skillful manipulation of gaps in the law – gaps which were foreseen by its silences, or opened up by *de facto* tolerance. And this great redistribution of illegalities was even to be expressed through a specialization of the legal circuits: for illegalities of property – for theft – there were the ordinary courts and punishments; for the illegalities of rights – fraud, tax evasion, irregular commercial operations – special legal institutions applied with transactions, accommodations, reduced fines, etc.[71]

In fact, one could argue that the institutions of the criminal justice system are geared to *conceal* rather than reveal the crimes of the powerful, and this despite the much higher cost, in both human and financial terms, of corporate crime. Such 'costing' would have to take into account the following: first, the phenomenal scale of income tax fraud compared to the fraud perpetrated by social security benefit claimants. Taking one year as an example, 'there were only 17 prosecutions for false income-tax returns (as against some 80,000 cases settled without prosecution). But there were 12,000 prosecutions over that period by the Department of Health and Social Security for fraudulent claims by its (largely working-class) clients. The amount recovered in these 12,000 cases amounted to less than 15 per cent of the amount recovered by the Inland Revenue in its seventeen income tax prosecutions.'[72] Second, the deliberate cost-cutting measures ignoring health and safety standards at work, resulting in the injuries and deaths – some in 'accidents', some over a prolonged period of poisoning – of countless numbers of workers. As Engels commented in 1845, a social order which allows companies to place workers in such a position that they inevitably meet an early and unnatural death should be considered to have committed the deed of murder just as much as murder may be the deed of the individual – 'disguised, malicious murder against which none can defend himself, which does not seem what it is, because no man sees the murderer, because the death of the victim seems a natural one, since the offence is more one of omission than of commission. But murder it remains.'[73] And third, the placing of products on the market which are known to be dangerous. To give but one example: in 1970 Ford released their new Pinto car, which tests had shown would explode from a rear-end collision. A cost–benefit analysis told them that installing the appropriate safety measures would cost $135 million, while prospective law-suits resulting from fatalities and injuries would be unlikely to top $50 million. It is estimated that between 500 and 900 people lost their lives as a result. The indictment for reckless homicide in 1978 failed.[74]

By treating corporate 'crime' as mere failure to follow regulations and procedures and thus not 'crime' at all, the ruling class has defined itself as beyond incrimination. Those with social power by definition cannot be members of the criminal class. Being *for* the order of private property, the ruling class is by definition on the *right side of the law*.

The metaphysics of the proper: medical police, pigs and social dirt

I shall return to the question of law in the following chapter. For the moment I wish to address one further aspect of social security: the question of health and hygiene. In Chapter 2 I suggested that although the terms are now usually treated separately, property was once intimately linked with propriety, and had explicit connotations of hierarchy and order. The terms 'property' and 'propriety' have their roots in the notion of the proper and are thus connected to the complex of terms related to the proper. While the *Oxford English Dictionary* defines 'proper' as 'belonging to oneself', 'owned as property' and 'that which is one's own', it also makes reference to 'proper' as 'conformity with social ethics, or with the demands or usages of polite society; becoming decent, decorous, respectable, genteel and correct'. This complex of terms gives rise to what Jacques Derrida refers to as the 'metaphysics of the proper', where *le propre* = self-possession, propriety, property and cleanliness. There is an intimate connection between property, propriety, order and a range of terms which Derrida subsumes under the notion of cleanliness (decency, correctness, respectability).[75] That property is intimately connected to cleanliness is illustrated by the converse assumption that poverty is intimately connected to dirt and disease. Given the place of health and hygiene in social security, it is worth exploring the connections between dirt, disease, police and order.

We know from the first two chapters that the clearing of refuse was traditionally the task of police, and that even Adam Smith's initial definition of police included within it the provision of cleanliness. Smith's comment that the provision of cleanliness is 'too trifling' to be considered a branch of jurisprudence should not detract from the importance of dirt to the police of good order. The period we have been dealing with in this chapter is the period in which the metaphors of pollution and moral contagion became the standard form of expression in social commentary. It was also the period in which the question of sanitation, especially of the city, was at the forefront of commentators' minds. 'The residuum was considered dangerous', argues Gareth Stedman Jones, 'not only because of its degenerate nature but also because its very existence served to contaminate the classes immediately above it.'[76] Dirt was a central theme of Chadwick's *Report on the Sanitary Condition of the Labouring Population of Great Britain*, for example. His principal concern was with the open cesspools, garbage and excrement in the streets and the filth and scum floating in the river, and in particular the 'miasma' emanating from them. The background to this was the cholera epidemic that spread through Europe in the 1820s and 1830s and the three rival theories used to explain the epidemic. Both the germ theory of infection and the belief that cholera was produced by spontaneous chemical combustion within the blood were generally dismissed. It was the 'pythogenic' or 'atmospheric' theory which was more widely believed, especially by several key sanitary reformers such as Chadwick and Florence Nightingale. This view held that the atmosphere became charged with an epidemic influence which turned malignant when combined with the effluvia of organic decomposition. The resulting miasma produced disease; hence it was also sometimes known as the 'miasmatic' approach.[77] Scientifically, the focus of the miasmatic approach was the 'fetid effluvia' and 'poisonous exhalations' that constituted the miasma; socially and politically, the fetid effluvia and poisonous exhalations were taken to denote something about the class which lived in such conditions. This was the period in which smell itself was taken to be a form of disease, and sanitary reformers more generally had started to use tactics creating a clear distinction between the deodorized bourgeoisie and the foul-smelling masses. For Chadwick, bad odours belong to the undisciplined and untrained world, the world of the disorderly. Thus he devised a simple doctrine: 'all smell is, if it be intense, immediate acute disease, and eventually we may say that by depressing the system and making it susceptible to the action of other causes, all smell is disease'. Miasma thus supposedly justified a concern with the 'secretions of poverty'.[78] More importantly, for many writers it was the effluvia exhaled by the lower orders – 'human miasms'

Chadwick dubs them – that was more poisonous than the miasma created by decomposing matter. 'It is my decided opinion', Chadwick approvingly cites one reformer as saying, 'that the vitiation of the atmosphere by the living is much more injurious to the constitution than its impregnation with the effluvia from dead organic matter.'[79]

Norbert Elias has suggested that civilization be considered as a transformation of human behaviour in which new forms of social technology increasingly come to mediate between the physical productions of the body and interactions with others. The buffer provided by these forms of technology – such as the handkerchief and fork – were thus first and foremost a means of social differentiation and, as such, a means of denying humanity to others. These others could then be thought of in terms of 'dirt', 'garbage', 'scum', 'waste', 'slag' and so on.[80] Now, Gertrude Himmelfarb has noted that the same words – 'residuum', 'refuse', 'offal' – were used to denote the sewage waste that constituted the sanitary problem and the human waste that constituted the social problem. In this sense there is a correspondence between the 'sanitary condition' and the condition of the working class. The word 'residuum' referred to the excrement and waste which constituted the sanitary problem and to the lowest layer of society that constituted the social and political problem.[81] In other words, the miasma theory pointed to human agents of infection, concentrated in the class of poverty and based in urban areas. The logic was that the task of cleaning dirt and filth from the street was the task of cleaning moral filth and social dirt from those same streets; the ideal city is not only physically clean, but socially clean too. Just as the sewer appeared to speak to the nineteenth century about its dangerous moral and material condition – the ever-present possibility of contagion and contamination – so as sewage the working class could be seen as the source of disease (through infection), waste (since even human sewage could in fact be put to good use – Flinn notes that 'to Chadwick the emptying of sewers into rivers anywhere seemed like pouring away liquid gold'), and the subversion of all order (since the sewer on occasion erupts, flows on to the streets and reminds the whole of the city of its dangerous refuse).[82]

'Dirt is matter in the wrong place', Freud notes.[83] As matter out of place, dirt is essentially disorder. Dirt presupposes system, since it is the by-product of a systematic ordering and classification of matter. Indeed, dirt is an *offence* against order, evidence of imperfection and a constant reminder of change and decay. Eliminating it is thus an attempt to organize and stabilize the environment.[84] As crime came to be one of the strongest reminders of disorder, so it came to be thought of in terms of dirt and garbage. The dirt – that is, the crime – needs to be removed in order to deny the disorder which it produces. The removal of the dirt/crime is a reimposition of order, a re-placement of matter into an ordered system.

The movement for sanitary reform should therefore be seen as part of the concerted attempt to impose order on civil society by the state, embodying a faith in the reordering capacities of the state over the population. 'If sanitary reform could induce men to abandon anarchy in an area of their lives prized most highly as theirs to rule as they alone willed, they could then be led to learn many other orderly ways of behaving.'[85] The water closet and the sewer do not ensure the end of crime or, for that matter, laziness. Their contribution to order lies in the way they underpin and strengthen the new industrial discipline in a wider environment. In the context of the consolidation of industrial capitalism this meant making workers learn ways of behaving which they would repeat on a daily basis without thinking. Thus Chadwick's hidden agenda in the *Sanitary Report* was identical with the agenda behind his work on police and the poor law: the creation of a well-ordered working population within the rising industrial system; that is, a disciplined working class. He reports that improved ventilation and sanitation for the labouring population have major 'manufacturing advantages': 'the improved health of the workspeople [is] attended by more energy and better labour; by less of lassitude and waste from relaxed attention; by fewer interruptions from sickness, and fewer spare hands to ensure the completion of work'. Indeed, such improved discipline also helps bring about a reduction of trade union activity and strikes.[86]

It is worth noting here that ex-police officers report that the police see the criminal and potential criminal as 'social dirt' – forms of 'slag' or 'scum'. An affront to cleanliness and purity and possessing the danger of the contagious and impure, the criminal and potential criminal needs to be removed from public vision. Police officers constantly wash their hands after touching the suspect or his belongings, and the permanent dislike of long hair, beards, and pierced body parts by the police is because such things are indicative of dirt and must be cleaned up and purified. It is because of the equation of crime with dirt that police officers constantly refer to themselves as 'refuse collectors, sweeping up the human dross'.[87] Incidentally, this means that the English use of the term 'pig' to refer to the police is in fact structurally correct, as Malcolm Young has noted. The pig is an interstitial animal, situated between the domestic world and the wild. The 'house-pig' was a common part of the Victorian domestic world even in the towns, and was used to clear up the dross and refuse. It became a family animal, treated almost as a pet, and yet was always destined to be killed and eaten by those who gave it such a peculiar structural place in domestic society. The term 'pig' as a slang reference for police officers became increasingly common in the nineteenth century. In many ways, the 'police-pig' occupied a position similar to the 'house-pig': situated between ordered domestic society and the wild criminal and expected to clear up the dirt and refuse identified as such by its masters.[88] Indeed, when the prevalence of 'pig' as a term of abuse for police officers became widespread, the police defended themselves in terms of the pig's greater propensity for cleanliness than the filthy criminal or semi-criminal. In 1970 *Police* magazine responded to the 'Pig of the Month' column in the underground magazine *Frendz* in the following way: 'Should we be upset? Not at all. The pig has made a notable contribution to our national well-being over the centuries. As such, it has a great advantage over hippy squatters...whose concepts of sanitation are far more primitive than its own.'[89]

   Given the centrality of policing to the fabrication of order, it is significant that many writers regarded the search for order through sanitary reform as a form of medical police. As Foucault notes, questions of health and hygiene relate as much to the police as to the field of medicine.[90] The term 'medical police' was first used in 1764 by Wolfgang Thomas Rau to describe the creation and implementation of a state medical policy through administrative regulation of the population. The idea was popularized by Johann Peter Frank's *System einer vollständigen medicinischen Polizey* (the first volume of which was published in 1779, the sixth and last volume in 1817). Frank placed medical police within the context of police science generally: 'The internal security of the state is the subject of a general police science. A very considerable part of this science is to apply certain principles for the health care of people living in society.'[91] Thus part of the police project was the health of the people, 'from cradle to grave' as one writer on medical police put it.[92] Frank's *Medicinischen Polizey* was of fundamental importance in spreading the idea of medical police beyond Germany.[93] In Britain, the idea caught on in the context of the discussion and implementation of a 'new police' and the growing focus on the health and sanitary conditions of the population – Chadwick's *Report* on the sanitary condition of the working class was heavily indebted to Continental sources, especially German authorities on medical police. Robert Cowan, Professor of Medical Jurisprudence and Police at the University of Glasgow, clearly writing with one eye on the emergence of a more narrowly defined 'criminal police', argued that 'besides the criminal police of the district a sanitary police is also requisite, and for this purpose much more extensive powers should be invested in the police than they at present possess. Powers should be given to remove filth of every description daily...and proper conveniences, constructed of durable materials and under the charge of the police, should be erected in the localities occupied by the working classes.'[94] And in reviewing a series of books on medicine, hygiene and the principles of population *The British and Foreign Medical Review* commented in 1842 that 'state-medicine' and 'medical police' are terms 'which have been used synonymously to express the art or science which has for its object the application of the principles of medicine to securing the well-being and amelioration of society'.[95] Other articles of the period can be found on devising a national medical police. W. Strange, writing in the *London Medical Gazette*, commented on 'the intention of the legislature to provide for the establishment of a more or less complete system of medical police'. By this he meant nothing more than that every large town have a public health officer.[96] The first medical officers in Scotland were known as 'medical police', and local authorities there thought highly of the 'cholera police'.[97] Conversely, Police Acts for the city of Glasgow in 1800 and 1807 and Edinburgh in 1805 contained provisions regarding cleaning dirt from the pavements and removing dung, while in Edinburgh Police Acts during the cholera epidemic of 1832 established the removal of dung and the cleaning of common areas as police activities.

Finally on this score, one should note that the notion of medical police was frequently connected to the question of poverty. Motard's *Essai d'Hygiène générale* (1841), one of the texts reviewed by *The British and Foreign Medical Review*, recommended a system of medical police on the grounds that one of its strengths is to stem the growth of indigence: 'It is in protecting extreme indigence from the necessities to which it would otherwise be compelled to submit, and in enforcing police regulations – important alike to the health, the manners, and the morals of the lower orders – that the power of government is most beneficially exerted. Like the laws of quarantine or of public cleanliness, such regulations are necessary to enforce those salutary rules, which...indigence [is] too often unwilling to obey.' And Cowan believed that the prevalence of epidemic disease depended on a variety of causes, 'but the most influential of all is poverty and destitution'.[98]

Towards the legal reconstruction of police work

In 1902, 86 Southampton policemen petitioned against the borough council's instructions that the police should turn off gas and water in public urinals at night, on the grounds that it was degrading and not in fact a police duty. They were backed by the watch committee, and the Home Office ruled that it was not competent to override the committee.[99] The case is representative of what appears to be a trend within policing in which what

were previously widely understood as police functions were slowly transformed into other institutions of state. From its very inception the new
police had found itself engaged in a broad range of 'collateral services', as
we have seen with the poor law. The Superintendent of the York City Force,
for example, found that he was expected to serve as Inspector of Nuisances,
attend meetings of the local Board of Health, implement public health regulations, inspect lodging houses, supervise the city's scavengers and the sale
of manure, while elsewhere officers were inspecting weights and measures, collecting rates and taxes, acting as postmen and road surveyors,
taking the votes for the election of Poor Law guardians, assisting the
Inland Revenue in checking the duties on stage carriages, and delivering
and collecting the Census papers.[100] The reason the 'collateral services'
remained central to police work in the nineteenth century lies in the fact
that the original legislation establishing the new police was an enabling
measure prescribing no plan of organization or specification of duties but
imposing instead a general catch-all function. The wide administrative
functions for the ordering of civil society were allocated to police simply
because they constituted a reservoir of state bureaucracy and power which
was available to carry out tasks in lieu of other agencies to which they
could be assigned.[101]

Gradually, however, such collateral services came to be carried out by the
local state under the auspices of the relevant Department of central government. Thus during the late nineteenth and early twentieth centuries
functions and activities previously subsumed under the police idea – refuse,
road cleansing, welfare, health and the administration of poverty – were
separated off from the notion of police and managed by other state bodies.
For example, in the course of the nineteenth century the notion of 'medical
police' was increasingly seen to be bound up with obsolete eighteenth-
century forms of rule and therefore out of place in a world of bourgeois
order, capitalist enterprise and parliamentary constitutionalism, supposedly
the antithesis of absolutist ideals.[102] It was not that the idea of administering
the health of the population disappeared (quite the opposite, of course), but
that this was *no longer thought of as a police practice*. As the tasks of 'medical
police' were gradually removed from the police and placed in the hands of
other municipal institutions, so the idea of medical police gave way in
intellectual and political circles to designations such as 'public health' or
'hygiene'. In the twentieth century this would become the medical arm of
social security: 'from medical police to social medicine' Rosen comments,[103]
and from there to the National Health Service and public health officers, we
can add. Likewise, the police of poverty was gradually placed under the
notion of 'welfare'. The name changes, but the function remains the same.

On the one hand, one could view this as part of the *narrowing* of the function of police down to a concern with crime and law, as many have. On the other hand, rather than buy into such a liberal re-reading of police, it makes more sense to see these other emergent 'services' and 'departments' as part of what Mike Brogden has called the functional differentiation of the police project, within which the *expansive* nature of the police function remained, but was carried out by services and institutions which increasingly went under different names.[104] In many cases, that name was 'social security'. It is not that policing was narrowed down to the prevention and detection of crime, but that police work was passed over to other administrative agencies dedicated to ordering the lives of citizens, notably those of the working class who might not work willingly, be 'decent' ('proper') in public and 'orderly' at all other times.

There are two issues here which feed into the next chapter. First, what had changed was partly the legal construction of police work: the ideological presentation of the prime concern of policing being essentially 'legal' belied the continued police concern with questions of order way beyond the juridical. The relevant changes in legal form disguised the persistent social reality of policing.[105] Second, 'social security' is frequently understood as a set of administrative processes. To describe social security as a police project would seem to imply that policing is a form of administration, an implication which jars with the central assumption concerning the police function – that in abandoning the 'collateral services' it has been reconstructed as a project concerned essentially with law. These two issues touch at the heart of the police function, for they raise the question of the relationship between law and administration and thus the nature of state power.

5
Law, Order, Political Administration

One of the central assumptions made about 'modern' policing is that it is concerned first and foremost with law. On this assumption the task of police is the prevention of crime through the enforcement of law. There are a number of good reasons why this belief exists. As we have seen, the new police from 1829 onwards was indeed charged with the task of preventing crime. The formal bureaucratic organization of the police reinforces the view that the police are primarily dedicated to criminal law enforcement. Police training emphasizes things criminal – criminal law, criminal statistics, crime prevention – and the internal administration of police authority tends to reflect formal criminal enforcement specializations, for example in the way that key units are named after specific offences, or the way record keeping is of crimes. The criminal process is almost always set in motion by the police and the work of a certain number of police activities is determined by the provisions of the penal code. Moreover, the image of the police as the vanguard fighter in a protracted war on crime is propagated by the police, politicians and the media.[1]

Many commentators have accepted this view at face value and it has dominated commonsense understanding of the police and political debates about 'what is to be done about law and order'. But, as Gatrell has rightly argued, the idea that the police are concerned first and foremost with crime is in fact a self-serving and convenient obfuscation.[2] It is a myth – a convenient legitimizing myth, but a myth nevertheless – which panders to the law and order lobby by mystifying the real issues which underline the police project. Moreover, critiques of policing have been undermined by the Left's collusion in the myth.[3] Left critiques of policing have tended to get bogged down on the very terrain occupied by politicians: that of crime, crime figures, the causes of crime, and so on. This has had deleterious consequences for the Left: not only has it failed to understand the police institution and policing in general, but it has also lost sight of how to use the police concept in the attempt to make sense of social and political power generally.

For a start, both the 'law and order' lobby and its Left critics have failed to take on board the implications of a mass of research on the police which has shown that criminal law enforcement is something that most police officers do with the frequency located somewhere between virtually never and very rarely. The overwhelming majority of calls for police assistance are 'service' rather than crime related: in an average year only 15 to 20 per cent of all the calls to the police are about crime, and what is initially reported by the public as a crime is often found to be not a crime by the responding police officer. Studies have shown that less than a third of time spent on duty is on crime-related work; that approximately eight out of ten incidents handled by patrols by a range of different police departments are regarded by the police themselves as non-criminal matters; that the percentage of police effort devoted to traditional criminal law matters probably does not exceed 10 per cent; that as little as 6 per cent of a patrol officer's time is spent on incidents finally defined as 'criminal'; and that only a very small number of criminal offences are discovered by the police themselves. Moreover, most of the time the police do not use the criminal law to restore order. In the USA police officers make an average of one arrest every two weeks; one study found that among 156 officers assigned to a high-crime area of New York City, 40 per cent did not make a single felony arrest in a year. In Canada a police officer on average records one indictable crime occurrence a week, makes one indictable crime arrest every three weeks, and secures one indictable crime conviction every nine months.[4]

The point, however, is not just that the historical and sociological evidence has made clear that crime fighting never has been the prime activity of the police, but that it *could not* be the prime activity of the police, as Robert Reiner has noted.[5] Despite the functional differentiation of the police project discussed at the end of the previous chapter, the original enabling legislation establishing the new police has never been lost. As Egon Bittner has argued, 'no human problem exists, or is imaginable, about which it would be said with finality that this certainly could not become the proper business of police'.[6] It is partly for this reason that we need an expanded concept of police. All institutions concerned with the order and behaviour of citizens have a close relationship with the police and frequently operate in tandem with the police as part of a more generalized police project. Hence whenever an ill-defined emergency arises, from transporting medical supplies, providing initial support for a spouse bereaved in a traffic accident, to clearing animals which have wandered on to the motorway, the police institution is the first to respond. The police institution intersects with all other major institutions, concerning anything from driving licences, the mentally ill,[7] to school truants.[8] It provides physical assistance to other departments of state, such as Housing Departments and Court Bailiffs in the eviction of tenants, information to Social Security investigators, and acts as an agency of last resort in handling the 'hot potato' cases rejected by other agencies.[9]

Many have responded to the 'discovery' that much police time is spent not on crime but on 'ancillary services' by arguing that this is indeed how police should be thought of and developed. In other words, since the police are *de facto* social workers – a 'secret social service' in one commentator's words – they should be better trained in this way.[10] This is the basis of the debate between whether the state should provide a police *force* or a police *service*. Those who argue that the police should be a 'service' work on the assumption that this would merely formalize what they do anyway. In contrast this is challenged by those who feel that such a 'service culture' is a poor reflection of the 'real' tasks in enforcing the law. This latter point can work both ways: on the one hand, it is a position held by those, often officers themselves, who believe that policing is about the 'hard' job of enforcing the law rather than the 'softer' welfare tasks. On the other hand, in recent years radical criminologists and 'new left realists' have advocated a 'minimalist' policing strategy: police should only intervene when there is clear evidence of law-breaking. Only in this way, they claim, can the police be made accountable to law and civil liberties be properly protected. But as Reiner points out, the service/force debate rests on a false dichotomy. Insofar as the two roles are distinguishable, they are interdependent. In truth, both 'service' and 'force' roles derive from the mandate of *order maintenance*.[11]

The reason that the myth of police as crime fighters is so pervasive is because of a parallel myth concerning the police and law. Given the links perpetually drawn between 'law' and 'order', policing is considered to be related to order via law: the police maintain order by enforcing the law. In this chapter I shall argue that the way in which the police institution is consistently collapsed into 'law' is fundamentally misleading. If we are to think of policing as a form of political administration, as we started to do in Chapter 4, then we need to consider at greater length the administrative nature of police power. In some ways this will take us back to the account of the early stages of police dealt with in Chapter 1, in which it was argued that historically policing was an exercise of administrative power as much as anything else. The present chapter will therefore also argue that despite the immensely complex legal relation surrounding the police (brought about in part by a hegemonic liberalism as the core ideology of bourgeois society), the police function should be seen through the lens of administration as much as law. Given the integral links between law and administration in the exercise of modern state power, the lens in question should be the law-and-administration continuum. This is because it is through the continuum of law and administration that the state administers civil society politically as part of the fabrication of social order. Incorporating the police into this argument will help develop the theory of the state which places political administration at its core.

Arrest and police 'illegality'

One of the essential justifications of the liberal democratic state is its foundation in legality – in the rule of law. This foundation implies both obedience to the laws on the part of citizens and to limits imposed on state power. It insists that the citizen is protected from the institutions of the state by having these controlled by law. In particular, the rule of law is said to constrain and inhibit the discretionary powers of agents of the executive. Thus power is exercised within the contraints of law. 'Due process' is said to prioritize the liberties of the individual citizen over the coercive powers of police. This model is distinguished from the 'crime control' model in which crime prevention is the most important police function and to which other issues, such as individual liberties, can be regarded as of secondary importance. While I have little to say about this distinction, 'due process' can be thought of as the application of the rule of law to the practices of police.[12]

   A key aspect of the rule of law is that citizens be free from arbitrary arrest or imprisonment and that when in custody any suspect be treated fairly. Until the Police and Criminal Evidence Act (PACE) of 1984 the main guidelines concerning arrest and interrogation of suspects in Britain lay in the Judges' Rules, drawn up originally in 1912 (on the request of the police) and amended in 1918, 1930 and 1964. The Rules defined the line between police powers and civil rights according to the criterion of voluntariness. Confessions or statements could only be used as evidence if they were given voluntarily. The Judges' Rules accepted police interrogation in custody so long as it did not force or induce a confession against a suspect's will. They forbade the use of threats and inducements and stipulated, among other things, that persons under arrest could not be questioned without being cautioned and that they should be informed of the right to consult privately with a solicitor.

In many ways this was a reiteration of the common law principle surrounding questioning in general, with an attempt to apply it to questioning in custody. Arrest was originally a mechanism for bringing suspects before the magistrates so that they could decide whether a prosecution should take place or not; that is, arrest was originally the culmination of the criminal investigation rather than the start of it. That arrest required a warrant reflected the judicial control of prosections and the idea that the police act purely on the authority of law. As such, the police function was to bring arrested suspects before a magistrate, a common law principle confirmed in *Wright* v. *Court* (1825). This was consistent with the view that questioning in custody was per se coercive, contrary to the concept of voluntariness, and therefore unlawful. This meant that in effect police were legally unable to arrest for the purposes of investigation, or for the questioning of suspects. In *R.* v. *Gavin* (1885) the court stated that 'when a person is in custody, the police have no right to ask him questions', confirming Lord Brampton's view, in his influential 1882 Preface to *Vincent's Police Code*, that the constable's duty 'is simply to arrest and detain him [the accused] in safe custody...For a constable to press any accused person to say anything with reference to the crime of which he is accused is very wrong.' This finding fed into the Judges' Rules, and as late as 1970 Lord Devlin was criticizing the police for making 'the mistake of arresting before questioning'. In a parallel development, however, the new police in the nineteenth century gradually took control of prosecutions: by the mid-nineteenth century the police were the prosecuting body in the vast majority of prosecutions, despite their lack of statutory or common law power to carry out prosecutions. The police thus not only apprehended the offender but also prepared the case against him. With an increasing interest in a successful conviction, the police began to engage in practices designed to improve the possibility of conviction, arresting on suspicion and in order to question suspects in the hope that enough evidence could be secured to prosecute. As David Dixon notes, 'practices evolved of police taking arrested suspects to stations for questioning and charging before their presentation to magistrates', adding that 'no provision was made in law for this enormously significant change in practice'. Thus key concepts such as arrest and charge became ambiguous.[13]

Thus it soon became clear that despite the legal requirement that police do not question suspects before presenting them before the judges, the police were doing precisely that. The Royal Commission on Police Powers and Procedure reported in 1929 that detention for questioning was a 'practice followed not infrequently in the Metropolitan Police' and occasionally in a few large provincial towns, even though the Report reiterated that 'no questioning of a person in custody, about any crime or offence with which he is or may be charged, should be permitted' and pointed to Lord Brampton's advice as reflecting 'best practice'. In fact, the Metropolitan Police had freely admitted in its evidence to the Commission that they used arrest as a means for detaining supects at the police station for further questioning, going so far as to 'round up the usual suspects' for questioning after a serious crime. Despite the fact that the Commissioners thought these practices illegal, they nonetheless continued. In *Houghton and Franciosy* the police were criticized for their 'flagrant disregard' of the Judges' Rules in detaining a suspect for five days incommunicado; on hearing the case in 1979 the Court of Appeal found it neccessary to once again reiterate that 'police officers can only arrest for offences...They have no power...to arrest anyone so that they can make enquiries about him.'[14] But despite this 'official' and supposedly 'legal' position, the divergence between the theory and practice was apparent: it was clear that questioning by police was commonplace. A tension thus existed between the Judges' Rules and statements of the official position on the legality of questioning on the one hand, and police practice on the other. This tension surrounded virtually all of the other major police practices. Yet, crucially, this tension has always ultimately been resolved on the side of the police practice. As Satnam Choong has shown, the general trend concerning police arrest and questioning shows that the police tightened their grip on the suspect by simply assuming powers that the law denied them. Successive police chiefs have openly admitted that the police have merely assumed the powers that they felt were necessary. Sir Robert Mark once felt comfortable in stating that there was a 'moral justification for getting round the rules', while another Commissioner, Sir David McNee, openly flaunted the flagrant disregard of the rules by the police in front of Royal Commissioners, arguing that since a range of powers outside the law and the Judges' Rules were exercised by the police *de facto*, these powers should be granted to them *de jure*. In effect, the police ignored the judicial demands that the rule of law be followed, and it is indicative of the prestige and power of the police that Mark and McNee's admission of potentially unconstitutional and lawless behaviour should be accepted with equanimity in a liberal democratic society.[15] The process of expanding their powers by engaging in unauthorized practices was accompanied by a coordinated effort on the part of the police to legitimate their actions by persuading judges, politicians and the public that what they were doing was necessary to curb crime – research suggests that most officers believe that to fully impose the rule of law on police work would render it impossible.

As it became clear that police practice was at odds with the rule of law as understood in Britain, two ways of dealing with it emerged. In both cases, police practice won out. In the first case, the judiciary simply deferred to the police. As Choong notes, there is not one reported case in which the Court of Appeal quashed a conviction on the grounds that the judge should have refused to admit a confession because no caution had been given. Neither is there a case in which the Court of Appeal quashed a conviction because of unlawful refusal of access to a solicitor. Despite its vehement criticism of the police's flagrant disregard of the Judges' Rules in *Houghton and Franciosy*, the Court of Appeal nonetheless agreed with the trial judge that the confession obtained when the suspect was held be admissible.

The second way of dealing with it has been for the law to be transformed as an effect of police practice, first through a change in the Judges' Rules, then through important judicial findings, and finally in new legislation. As such, the police have constantly extended the boundaries of 'legal' behaviour to the point where the law itself has been transformed. A few examples will suffice: at one time arrest was only lawful if backed by a judicial warrant, as we have seen, but it is now rare for police to seek approval for an arrest – the Criminal Law Act (1967) created the concept of an 'arrestable offence' for which the police may arrest without a warrant, a situation since re-enacted in PACE; the new Judges' Rules which emerged in 1964 gave explicit approval to the questioning of arrested suspects before charge, a situation now formalized with PACE (section 37 of which allows arrest and detention for the purposes of investigation); the unlawful act of detention for the purpose of interrogating in a fashion likely to secure conviction was legitimated by the Judges' Rules and then transformed into lawful practice (in *Holgate-Mohammed* v. *Duke* [1984], followed by PACE); the rules on search and seizure of evidence in the absence of a warrant were extended on the basis of reasonableness as spelled out by Lord Denning in *Ghani* v. *Jones* (1970) and then in *Garfinkel* v. *Metropolitan Police Commissioner* (1972); the unlawful practice of officers preparing evidence together instead of separately continued until they had a special rule for them which legalized the practices (*Bass*, 1953); the police illegally searched houses until they were given legal sanction to do so, first by the judiciary (*Ghani* v. *Jones*) and then with Parliamentary approval (in PACE). Thus rather than police carrying out law as made by Parliament, Parliament has made laws which have legitimized existing police practice. 'Law reform' is often little more than a product and legitimation of police operational practices.[16] The law has been formally rewritten to suit the exercise of police power. And in being rewritten to suit police practice, the law has mystified, legitimized and rationalized the exercise of police power, a point to which I return below.

Now, some have argued that since the general trend concerning police procedures shows that the police simply assumed powers that the law denied them and systematically ignored the legal rights of suspects, it is meaningful to talk of police 'illegality' or to describe the police as 'beyond the law'.[17] Many on the Left have argued that the solution is to impose the rule of law more firmly on the police, a point I shall take up below. But while it may be true to say that police officers are rarely inhibited by 'due process' from doing what they want to do and that 'the rule of law does not, in general, operate in relation to police powers'[18] their behaviour can usually be classified as lawful. As Sanders and Young write, this situation arises because either the law is a *product* of state agencies (and the police in particular, as we have seen), or because the law is *sufficiently flexible* to accommodate what the police want to do.[19] The following two sections deal with these points respectively.

Administration and the rationality of police: discretion

It is widely accepted that discretion is a key feature of police power. Rowan and Mayne built discretion into the General Instructions given to new constables from 1829, stating that 'something must necessarily be left to the intelligence and discretion of individuals', while key figures such as Chadwick defended the discretionary powers of the new authority. More recently, Lord Scarman has pointed out that 'the exercise of discretion lies at the heart of the policing function'.[20] For much of the nineteenth and twentieth centuries the question of discretionary police powers was generally ignored, presumably because it was assumed that the police merely act according to the rule of law and within the framework of 'legal' restraints. Yet it is now clear that one cannot understand the police function without understanding the place of discretion in the police role. First, because 'the discretion of law enforcement agencies is near absolute'.[21] Second, because according to the doctrine of 'constabulary independence', individual police officers have the legal right and duty to enforce the law as they see fit, including whether to arrest, interrogate and prosecute, regardless of the orders of their superiors. 'The irony', Mike Brogden notes, 'is that the lowest of the low – the street constable, unlike in other "professional" occupations, is the one who can exercise the maximum discretion at work.'[22] And third, because identifying the issues surrounding discretion reveals some of the key features of police power.

Many on the Left have rightly pointed to the way that discretion leads to discrimination; both words share a common root referring to the act of separating, distinguishing and judging. By definition the exercise of police discretion defines who is deviant in any social context and how that deviance is controlled. Some laws may be enforced more strictly against some groups than others, while at other times certain techniques of maintaining order will be utilized for different groups. There is ample evidence that the discretionary values in operation are congruent with those of the ruling class. Historically, and consistent with the police mandate, police discretionary power discriminated against the working class, whom policemen were more likely to consider 'disorderly'. The various Police Acts, the legislation of 1869–71 concerning 'habitual' criminals, various by-laws and, most notoriously, the Vagrancy Act of 1824 gave police immense discretionary powers. As mentioned in the previous chapter, the Vagrancy Act gave police the power to arrest on the basis of loitering with intent, while the Habitual Criminals Act 1869 and the Prevention of Crimes Act 1871 gave police the power to arrest a person merely on the grounds that they had been convicted of more than one offence before (and were therefore 'habitual criminals' – in other words, members of the 'criminal class'). As Gatrell comments, in application discretion was group specific and was intended to be so. Early police orders made it quite clear which groups were to be the targets of such powers, focusing police attention on the working class.[23] More recently an enormous amount of research has revealed the racial dynamics inherent in the exercise of police discretion, with young blacks statistically far more likely to be stopped than any other group. Conversely, where some discretion leads to discrimination via an over-enforcement of laws against certain groups, the systematic under-enforcement of other laws simultaneously fails to protect other groups. The most obvious example involves police decisions not to intervene, arrest, charge and prosecute in the vast majority of cases of male violence against women in the household.[24] Either way, 'discretion' in practice involves discrimination in the form of selective law-enforcement and order maintenance.

To say that 'the police enforce the law' fails to recognize the enormous range of police discretion which, far more than legal codes, shapes the way the police behave.[25] In the case of arrest, for example, it is clear that suspects can be stopped and searched on the street or arrested and taken to a police station; outside of arrest with a warrant the power to arrest relies solely on the discretion of a police officer. Moreover, the police have discretion to take control of the body and property of the suspect to the utmost degree. The police have powers over whether or not to search property, to keep the suspect incarcerated at the station for up to 36 hours, control the speed with which the case is dealt with, interrogate suspects without permission, relieve them of their personal belongings, remove their clothes, search their bodily orifices, forcibly take fingerprints, pluck their hair, take swabs from their mouth and scrape substances from under the nails; the police can also refuse exercise, blankets, cigarettes and food and drink.[26] To be sure, the correct procedures must be followed by the police in carrying out such acts, but the acts nonetheless emphasize that the power resides almost entirely with the state and is exercised through the body of the police. Since discretion can involve any form of behaviour from ignoring a crime altogether to the most vicious and brutal acts, even the kind of beating meted out to Rodney King in Los Angeles can be justified according to the discretionary powers of police.[27]

The discriminatory nature of discretion therefore has its foundation in the permissive structure of law and the powers given to the police to preserve order.[28]

> The citizen who is deemed to be suspect stands stripped of his canopy of rights, and the police can lawfully take control over and work on his body and mind. The law does not recognise suspects as having a right not to be stopped, searched, arrested or detained without charge or trial. The law does not proclaim that suspects have an absolute right not to answer police questions, or that they have a right not to be man-handled by the police once arrested. Instead the law speaks primarily in terms of what the police *can* do to the suspect.[29]

The fact that discretion is so integral to the exercise of police powers tells us something important about the police and its relation to state power, for discretion is a key feature of state power generally. Unsurprisingly, it has therefore become one of the most debated issues concerning the institutions of the modern liberal welfare state in general and the institutions of political administration in particular. While liberal jurisprudence tends to treat discretion entirely in terms of its place in judicial decisions,[30] police discretion can in fact be understood only by considering policing less as a form of juridical power and more as a form of political administration. For the exercise of discretion is as much an *executive* function as it is a judicial one. In *Shaaban Bin Hussein* v. *Chong Fook Kam* (1970), Lord Devlin argued that 'To give power to arrest on reasonable suspicion does not mean that it is always or even ordinarily to be exercised. It means that there is an executive discretion.' This allows us to subsume police discretion under the concept of administration generally. In *Holgate-Mohammed* v. *Duke* (1984) the Lords confirmed that the power of arrest was an executive discretion and that the exercise of discretion by the police (in this case concerning a claim of wrongful arrest) is no different from that exercised by other administrative officials. The constable was held to have exercised 'an executive discretion' under the statute (section 2 (4) of the Criminal Law Act 1967, and now section 24 (6) of PACE), and thus his actions were governed by the principles of unreasonableness as applied to administrative acts. As Lustgarten notes, the officer was here being treated as an executive officer, subject to the same legal analysis as any wielder of discretionary power. Rather than see the police constable as merely the citizen in uniform enforcing the law, he needs to be recognized for what he is: a state official exercising administrative or executive powers – a form of 'street-level administration'.[31] And to retrace our steps momentarily, the point about the police activities discussed earlier is not that some police actions were technically illegal and then made legal, but that the actions in question were regulated according to administrative rules and procedures. The Judges' Rules were *not* law, but principles of administrative guidance approved by the judiciary and the executive, as the judges themselves always knew.[32] The kind of changes brought about by police practice amounting to major changes in criminal procedure therefore involved extraordinary use of administrative rule-making power.

Thus while discretion is *structurally provided* by legal powers, the way to understand it is in the context of *administrative law* in particular. In *Holgate-Mohammed* v. *Duke* Lord Diplock commented that as an executive function, discretion should be exercised in accordance with the key principle of administrative law that discretion be exercised reasonably. Now, the exercise of police discretion has not been seen as obviously subject to administrative law, not least because the courts have been reluctant to encroach on operational freedom. But as Kenneth Culp Davis argued some time ago in his classic account of discretionary power, while traditional legal classifications such as 'administrative law' and 'administrative agencies' have customarily excluded the police institution, given that the greatest concentration of discretionary power lies in the hands of police officers, they should in fact be understood according to the principles of administrative law.[33] Police discretion differs from the exercise of discretion by other public officials only in the specific character of the human relations element and the places in which it is exercised, and not because it is somehow a more 'legal' process.

The legal uncertainties surrounding discretion are not anomalous but a product of the vagaries of administrative law. The law is sufficiently flexible to allow the police extensive discretionary powers under the rule of 'reasonable suspicion' – arrest and stop and search powers, for example, are controlled by no more than the 'reasonable suspicion' standard. Yet there is no definition in either statute or case law of 'reasonable suspicion'. Instead the notion of 'reasonableness' is understood according to the 'Wednesbury rules' established in *Associated Provincial Picture Houses*

v. *Wednesbury Corporation* (1948), assessed according to the standards applicable to executive officers and measured by basic principles of administrative law.[34] This gives the police virtually *carte blanche* powers: 'unreasonableness' has been said to apply 'to a decision which is so outrageous in its defiance of logic or of accepted moral standards that no sensible person who had applied his mind...could have arrived at it'.[35] Unsurprisingly therefore, there are few grounds for a defendant to challenge the 'reasonable grounds for suspicion' if being held under stop and search powers: one major study found that the reasonable suspicion criteria included both 'moving quickly' and 'moving slowly'.[36] Like other categories under which police act on the citizen, such as 'helping police with their enquiries', 'obstruction' and 'resisting arrest', 'reasonable suspicion' is merely one more euphemism for the exercise of police power, offering vast discretionary powers to enable the police to structure a particular encounter. Far from being weak points in the system, such factors are in fact sources of operational strength, for it means that rather than search for particular infringements of particular laws, the police use law as part of the general mandate of order maintenance.[37] Discretion allows the exercise of power with law standing at arm's length, deferring to the power of administration but using its own symbolic and political significance to confirm that same power.

This is entirely consistent with the role of discretion within the other institutions of social security. The emergence and development of forms of political administration from 1834 has meant a proliferation of discretionary powers vested in a wide range of authorities and officials, of which the police is just one such authority. Discretionary powers have been integral to the new political forms for administering the unemployed in the twentieth century, for example. I have argued elsewhere that the creation in 1934 of an Unemployment Assistance Board (UAB) was part of the attempt to take unemployment relief 'out of politics', to subsume working-class struggle under a new administrative form, and to bypass the courts by producing an appeals machinery with a quasi-judicial form.[38] By 1934 it was clear that the Unemployment Insurance Scheme of 1911 was inadequate during periods of recession and that there was massive inconsistency in 'transitional payments'. At the same time, the government was determined to bring expenditure under firm control. The application of a means test involved discretionary decisions over individual cases, and the discretionary powers granted by the *Unemployment Assistance Regulations 1934* were wide.[39] The changes show how the discretion of a body seemingly independent from executive control – the UAB was created as a corporate body with executive functions not under the control of a minister, yet the Minister of Labour was able to vary UAB regulations and had to approve the rules for operating the means test – created the image of a body operating at arm's length from state power more generally. The existence of discretion allows the state in general and government in particular to appear to stand at arm's length from the processes of administration, and thus the policing of civil society. Discretion encourages the idea that administration and policing are somehow outside politics. Any criticism of or challenge to the system can thus be focused on particular instances of the exercise of discretion rather than the more fundamental existence of state power behind the institutions in question. Thus criticism of and challenges to the welfare system become focused on questions of maladministration in the exercise of discretionary power, while criticisms of and challenges to the police are turned into debates about individual acts of individual officers and whether they used their discretion in the most 'reasonable' way.

It is important to recognize that as it developed with the rise of the administrative state, 'administrative law' came to refer not just to laws concerning the powers of administration, but to bodies of law developed within and applied *by* the administration. This created a *law and administration continuum*. One aspect of this continuum is that political administration can function in a quasi-legislative and quasi-judicial manner. Quasi-legislation operates through delegated legislation or through government departmental pronouncements; quasi-judicial action operates in tribunals, which either exercise judicial functions or administrative functions in a judicial form. The development of quasi-legislative and quasi-judicial administration occurred from 1834, blurring the line between the judicial and the administrative in the policing of civil society.[40] The argument here is that this has a direct parallel in the development of the police institution: as a form of political administration the police also act in a quasi-judicial manner. More decisions of a judicial type, in the form of interpreting and determining the rule of law, are made by the police than by the judiciary and courts. Police judicial power is employed in several major forms. Discretionary decisions to enforce and not to enforce particular laws are, in effect, judicial decisions, and recognized as such by the state: the Donoughmore Committee on Ministers' Powers in 1932 argued that there was a distinction between a judicial and a quasi-judicial function, which lay in the element of discretion which they thought resided only in the latter. And whereas the process of arrest followed by prosecution was once part of the judicial process, it is now part of the executive process with quasi-judicial aspects. The choice of enforcement – by caution or prosecution – also falls outside the liberal democratic conception of the separation of powers and of the autonomy of the judiciary, while the selection of charge is also a form of judicial decision. And one judge has noted that in terms of police investigation, 'the police have a duty to make enquiries in a quasi-judicial spirit', implying that police enquiries are expected to be conducted with the spirit of judicial fairness, even if they are not part of the judicial process.[41] Moreover, the police institution quickly came to exercise quasi-judicial functions under certain statutes such as section 4 of the 1824 Vagrancy Act and the 'stop-and-search powers' enshrined in certain Local Corporation Acts. The police powers under these Acts reversed the traditional assumption of innocence on the part of the accused – police officers determine the guilt of the suspect under these statutes, and the onus is on the suspect to prove his or her innocence. Given that most street encounters are structured by stop-and-search legislation and fall way outside any systematic legal regulation, this grants police considerable quasi-judicial autonomy. Finally, the law is very much a police product, as we have seen.[42]

The standard retort to this from the position which stresses the rule of law is that ultimately the courts have the power of judicial review over the police, a claim which mirrors the view that ultimately the courts have the power of judicial review over administration. The assumption is that the judiciary can reassert the rule of law as a matter of course and that therefore the law has ultimate power over administration/police. But in both cases the courts have consistently deferred to the power of administration and the police. The effect produced by the quasi-judicial nature of police action is similar to the effect produced by the quasi-judicial nature of many of the other institutions of political administration, such as administrative tribunals. The fact that they are quasi-*judicial* provides what Jeffrey Jowell describes as 'symbolic reassurance'.[43] The affirmation that the processes in question are *in some way* legal, combined with the deference of the courts themselves to the policing practices engaged in by the institutions in question, invokes the myths and symbols surrounding law and achieves the quiescence of oppositional forces.

That the police are as much an administrative as judicial body is consistent with the fact that its position in the liberal democratic separation of powers has also never been clear. The original legislation bringing the modern police into existence in Britain failed to specify the legal position of the new police officers; neither did it specify the source of their powers. In one sense then, the legal status of the police was left in an ambiguous void. The first Commissioners of Police in London were sworn in not as police officers but as Justices of the Peace; in other words, those in charge of the police were judicial officers. But the Metropolitan Police Act of 1829 simultaneously subordinated the Commissioners to the executive (the

Home Secretary), and from the very outset the Home Office admitted that 'the police are under the control of the Home Department'.[44] Although they were judicial officers their judicial powers were never clear, nor was the role they were expected to play vis-a-vis either executive or judiciary.[45] While the British police and politicians propagate the myth of police independence from executive control, at the end of the day it is clear that the exercise of police power takes place according to the guidelines, decisions and interests of the executive arm of the state. Lustgarten notes that the extension in 1919 of the Home Secretary's power of making regulations for all forces concerning pay, terms and conditions of employment, promotion and discipline has meant that the Home Office 'achieved unprecedented legal power and administrative capability to influence the evolution of policing throughout England and Wales'.[46] It is also quite clear that in operational terms the executive plays a key role in police activities, especially concerning the policing of the organized struggles of the working class. The policing of industrial conflict has more than anything else shown how closely the Home Office is involved in operational matters concerning police action across different police authorities. Home Secretaries have consistently used the Association of Chief Police Officers (ACPO) as a mechanism for coordinating police activities across forces. The liberal myth that a national force is inherently totalitarian has merely masked the *de facto* even if not *de jure* national control of the police by the Home Office, as the range of 'national' police units – National Reporting Centre, National Computer, National Identification Bureau, and so on – testifies.[47]

The reason it is difficult to 'place' the police within the institutions of the state is not due to the peculiarly British fusion rather than separation of powers, for the dual patronage of the police by the executive and the judiciary is characteristic for all liberal democracies.[48] Far from sitting uncomfortably in both judicial and executive spheres, the police institution straddles the boundary between these spheres *naturally*, operating most comfortably in the 'open border' between the spheres of state power and giving the police an aura of independence which no other institution of the state appears to have.

'Wonderful and marvellous things': the mythology of modern law and order

A number of writers on the police have responded to the problems identified above by demanding a 'return to legality' and the imposition of a properly functioning rule of law, not just on the police but on all administrative practices of the modern state. In terms of discretion, for example, the debate concerning its exercise in both welfare bureaucracy and the police institution is remarkably similar. In both cases the central issue concerns the question as to whether the exercise of discretionary powers lies somehow 'outside' or 'beyond' the law, and thus whether there should be greater legal control over such powers. Discretion is treated as a problem, as something that gets in the way of rights. The issue has therefore been understood as a contest between the potentially arbitrary exercise of executive power – often but not solely via the exercise of discretion – versus the formal equality of the rule of law: the option of 'discretion or rights' in the words of one writer, and 'discretion or legalism' in the words of another.[49] Discretion *as administration* appears to undermine rights *as law*. In the case of social policy, the rights are understood as social rights; in the case of police, the rights are the legal rights entrenched in the rule of law. On the other hand, some have argued that discretion is at least inhibited or restricted by law. Galligan, for example, comments that 'the rule of law has been a powerful basis for condemning the use of discretionary powers, and so for limiting the activities of the state'.[50] One might argue that this issue has dominated debates around both social policy and the police in the last decades of the twentieth century. But whichever 'side' one is on, the general assumption is that there is some sharp divide between discretion, as the exercise of power on an everyday level, and the rule of law. This assumption has wider resonance within social and political thought. Liberals have long held that the rule of law and discretion are contradictory. A.V. Dicey, for example, claims that 'the rule of law is contrasted with every system of government based on the exercise by persons in authority of wide, arbitrary, or discretionary powers', while F.A. Hayek defines the legal limits of administrative discretion as 'the crucial issue' in the constitution of liberty and notes a radical disjuncture between the rule of law and discretion: 'the principle of the rule of law, in effect, means that the administrative authorities should have no discretionary powers'. From a different political position, Bob Jessop has noted that 'the rule of law is replaced in the interventionist state by administrative discretion'.[51]

The broad theoretical background to this is in fact a misplaced assumption about the rule of law, an assumption that is intimately connected to a confusion over the legal foundation of the police relation. The problem with the argument that all that is needed is a reassertion of the rule of law and a return to legality – the achievement of good law as opposed to bad laws – is that it buys into what might be described as legal fetishism (Balbus) or a pathology of legalism (Titmuss),[52] in which law becomes a mystical answer to the problems posed by power. In the process, the problems inherent in law are ignored. Law is treated as an 'independent' or 'autonomous' reality, explained according to its own dynamics, a subject in itself whose very existence requires that individuals and institutions 'objectify' themselves before it. This produces the illusion that Law has a life of its own. I shall develop this argument through a short discussion of a claim made by E.P. Thompson.

Towards the end of his account of the origin of the Black Act and the role of law in shaping an oppressive set of social relations in the eighteenth century, Thompson comments that the rule of law is 'a cultural achievement of universal significance...an unqualified human good'.[53] In one sense, all Thompson means by this is that rule by law is undoubtedly better than authoritarian rule (although as Bob Fine points out, the rule of law does not have to be an unqualified human good for it to be better than authoritarianism).[54] But in a wider sense Thompson's claim – a common one on the Left – simply assumes that the rule of law is the best form of rule there is. In doing so, however, it buys into an essentially liberal understanding of the rule of law, fetishizes law, and ignores a fundamental part of the reality of the rule of law. As we saw in Chapter 2, while the rule of law developed as part of the liberal attack on arbitrary and excessive state power, its flip side was that it was used as part of the ideological attack on the power that lay in 'the mob', that is, the working class. As much as the rule of law has been used against state power, it is also in the name of the 'rule of law' that the authoritarianism of the state and the power of capital have been deepened and strengthened.[55] To see the rule of law as an unqualified human good, or even as of a fundamentally different order to the practices of executive power, discretionary acts and police decisions, is to abstract the rule of law from its origins in class domination and oppression and obscure the ideological mystification of these processes in the liberal trumpeting of the rule of law.

Moreover, arguments such as Thompson's assume that when the law does act in class terms this is a deviation from its ideal standards. 'The law when considered as an institution (the courts, with their class theatre and class procedures) or as personnel (the judges, the lawyers, the Justices of the Peace) may very well be assimilated to those of the ruling class', but for Thompson this is a problem of the institution or personnel rather than the law as such.

> All that is entailed in 'the law' is not subsumed in these institutions. The law may also be seen as ideology, or as particular rules and sanctions which stand in a definite and active relationship (often a field of conflict) to social norms; and, finally, it may be seen in terms of its own logic, rules and procedures – that is, simply *as law*.[56]

On this view law *as law* has a logic independent of social process (a 'logic of equity', Thompson calls it). A logic, that is, independent of class domination. Thus in serving a certain kind of class domination the Black Act was merely a *bad* law, in the sense that it failed to live up to the logic of equity which Law in general should contain. 'If I judge the Black Act to be atrocious, this is not only from some standpoint in natural justice, and not only from the standpoint of those whom the Act oppressed, but also according to some ideal notion of the standards to which "the law", as regulator of human conflicts of interest, ought to attain.'[57] If there is something wrong with the system of law, then, the problem lies in its administration, personnel or simply the passing of bad laws, and not with Law itself. It is precisely this sort of assumption which lies at the heart of much of the debate concerning the nature of policing and police powers (and state power generally), for the legal fetishism in question is magnified dramatically when it comes to police. As Doreen McBarnet has noted, in many studies of police some vague notion of 'law' is there as a background assumption, operating as an ambiguous standard from which the police, as 'law-enforcers', are assumed to deviate.

> The assumption has been in effect that the law incorporates rights for the accused, and the problem has been simply to ask why and how the police and courts subvert, negate or abuse them...In conventional sociological studies of criminal justice then, 'law' stands merely as a supposed standard from which the enforcers of law routinely deviate; legal procedures are simply *assumed* to incorporate civil rights. The 'law in action' is scrutinised but what the 'law in the books' actually says is simply taken as read; it remains unproblematic and unexplored.[58]

It is because of such assumptions that many consider the central policing issue is how to make policing more consistent with the rule of law.

John Baxter has noted that an important shift takes place between 'law and order' in the enforcement sense and 'law and order' in the qualitative sense (the latter being another term for the rule of law).[59] The slippage plays a crucial ideological role, for it allows the myth of police *enforcement* of law (and *maintenance* of order) to be presented and understood as a *defence* of the rule of law. It is a short step from the belief that police enforce *laws* to the assumption that the police enforce *the law*, leading to the even more misguided notion that 'police' = 'law'.[60] The effect is a collapsing of the categories 'police' and 'law' into each other. (Not for nothing do working-class youth often refer to the police as 'The Law'.) Such claims represent, in effect, the triumph of liberalism over the definition of the police concept, for they buy into the liberal recoding of the police concept. In Chapter 2 I cited Eduard Lasker's comment in the mid-nineteenth century that rule of law and rule of police are two different ways to which history points, two methods of development between which a people must choose. To suggest a distinction between the rule of law and the rule of police now sounds inconsistent with everything we are told about the police, since the dominant ideological claim regarding the police is that it is the bastion of democratic state, on the grounds that in defending law and order the police is the prime defence of the rule of law. Liberalism's attempt to make law – bourgeois law, the rule of law – triumph over the state meant transforming 'police' into a usable liberal term, which meant *equating* it with 'law' and *separating* it from 'state' (apart, that is, from the negative category 'police state', to which I shall return briefly towards the end of this chapter). The genius of the ruling class was to use this liberal recoding to gradually collapse the distinction between the rule of law and the rule of police. Police came to *represent* Law. Conversely, the dominant ideology insists that the police is in turn ruled by law.[61] In other words, part of the triumph of the liberal recoding of the police concept was not only to make the police appear consistent with the rule of law, but also to transform the police into the thin blue line between the rule of law on the one hand and widespread disobedience (lawlessness and disorder) on the other. The thin blue line, in other words, between order and chaos. The outcome was even further encouragement to equate police with 'Law' in its most general, abstract and mystified terms.

One reason why legal fetishism is so widespread is because many have succumbed to the liberal myth that Law is the foundation of justice. Any order founded on the rule of law is thus presented as just. But in bourgeois society justice has never been the *primary* value to which law devotes itself. The primary value to which all law has been dedicated has been order. To maintain the rule of law at all costs is to therefore defend the permanence of this order and to resist political novelty, change and transformation – to say 'not yet' to revolution.[62] Since the rule of law is taken to imply justice, and since police is taken to be equivalent to law, 'justice' and 'police' are drawn so closely together that it is assumed that for justice to exist (i.e. for a just order to exist) police is necessary. The assumptions present in legal fetishism – that the legal order is necessary for social order and that law is a unique phenomenon, the solution to all problems – are thereby replicated in a *fetishism of police*. What Peter Manning has described[63] as the sense of sacredness or awesome power that the police convey is intimately connected with the sacredness and awesome power contained in the rule of law. The sacred canopy is drawn over both police and Law. Together, as we shall see, this canopy is intimately connected to the general *fetishism of the state*.

That one needs to analytically separate police from law is clear. As Walter Benjamin notes,

> The assertion that the ends of police...are always identical or even con-
> nected to those of general law is entirely untrue. Rather, the 'law' of the
> police really marks the point at which the state, whether from impo-
> tence or because of the immanent connections within any legal system,
> can no longer guarantee through the legal system the empirical ends
> that it desires at any price to attain. Therefore the police intervene 'for
> security reasons' in countless cases where no clear legal situation exists,
> when they are not merely, without the slightest relation to legal ends,
> accompanying the citizen as a brutal encumbrance through a life regu-
> lated by ordinances, or simply supervising him.[64]

Yet the reason it is so difficult to analytically separate them lies in the paradoxical unity of law and order that runs through the political discourse of
modernity. Order, as we know, is regularly, almost universally, connected
with the notion of law; 'law and order' is often said as though it were one
word. It has certainly been claimed that law and order is one word in the
consciousness of the police, and in much political rhetoric law and order
are treated as synonymous.[65] 'Law' comes to represent all that is most
impartial and independent, to the point of being above the field of politics. Since the rule of law comes to stand for social *order*, any challenge to
it is a sign of social disintegration – of social *disorder*. It is for this reason
that the bourgeois class tend to dismiss as 'illegal' all forms of order which
appear to pose a threat to class society. As Lukács comments on the bourgeois response to the Soviet revolution: 'with the same naive complacency
with which it [the bourgeoisie] formerly contemplated the legality of its
own system of law it now dismisses as illegal the order imposed by the
proletariat'.[66]

This view of law as the supreme guarantor of order is never stronger
than in respect of the laws which protect the security of the state itself. As
Gatrell notes,

> the special vehemence of the judicial retaliation against treason, sedi-
> tion, etc., derives from the conviction that these acts challenge the
> paramount social value of *order* – paramount because every other value
> (justice and liberty included) is conditional upon it...The industrialis-
> ing State was guaranteed its stability by its laws against sedition and by

the military and judicial machinery which enforced them. These were the front-line defences against disorder.[67]

But it is the 'secondary' defences which law provides that most condition the daily lives of the population through the penal sanctions attached to the commission of even the most trivial of offences against property and public order: since crime is a symbol of a *lawless* condition, even the most petty of crimes is treated as symbolic of *disorder*.

Since, as we have seen, law-enforcement is merely an incidental and derivative part of police work, and since, as Lustgarten has noted, the police invariably under-enforce the law, the equation of policing with law-enforcement is clearly untenable.[68] The police enforce the law because it falls within the scope of their larger duties of regulating order which, in an ideological loop of remarkable ingenuity, is then justified in terms of crime control and the need to 'uphold the law'. In other words, law-enforcement becomes part of police work to the same extent as anything else in which the exercise of force for the maintenance of order may have to be used, and only to that extent. Police practices are designed to conform to and prioritize not law, but order, as the judges and police have long known.[69] Law-enforcement is therefore a means to an end rather than an end in itself, as witnessed by the fact that, for example, police often prefer to establish order without arrest. The assumption central to the rule of law that people should not take the law into 'their own hands' reminds us not only that the law is meant to be used and controlled by chosen hands, as Bauman puts it,[70] but that police do in fact *handle* rather than enforce the law. The law is a resource for dealing with problems of disorder rather than a set of rules to be followed and enforced. The kind of police behaviour which offends the sensibilities of civil libertarians or which seems at odds with the assumptions in the liberal democratic conception of the rule of law in fact turns out to be within the law and exercised according to the need to deal with things considered disorderly. The police follow rules, but these are *police* rules rather than legal rules. Thus when exercising discretion, the police are never quite using it to enforce the law, as one might be led to believe. Rather, officers decide what they want to do and then fit their legal powers around that decision. Hence the main 'Act' which police officers purport to enforce is the 'Ways and Means Act', a set of mythical powers which they use to mystify and confuse suspects, and the question of whether an officer should detain a suspect on legal grounds is displaced by the question 'which legal reason shall I use to justify detaining this person'. Exercised according to police criteria rather than specific legal criteria, the rules are rules for the abolition of disorder, exercised by the police and *enabled* by law; vaguely defined offences such as being 'drunk and disorderly' speak to the very heart of the police function. 'If you know what you are doing', one serving police officer has commented, 'if you know the law well enough...you can make it do wonderful and marvellous things.'[71] The criminal law therefore becomes just one resource among many which a police officer uses, one means among many to achieve a well-ordered civil society, proving that the exercise of state power in a liberal democracy is less a form of government of law, as liberal mythology would have it, and more a form of government by men who *use* law to legitimize the exercise of power.[72] The constable is an officer of order rather than an officer of the law.

'We fear the policeman' then, as Slavoj Žižek comments, 'insofar as he is not just himself, a person like us, since his acts are the acts of power, that is to say, insofar as he is experienced as the stand-in for the big Other, for the social order.'[73] And it is because the police officer is the stand-in for social order that order is the central trope around which even the smallest police act is conducted. As a number of ex-police officers have testified, the police themselves are obsessed with order, being institutionalized to achieve order at all times and in all contexts. Malcolm Young has commented on how one folder containing a record of the Orders by a range of senior officers reveals 'how everything in this world had an ordained place and could therefore be controlled, ordered, disciplined, checked, scrutinized'. Likewise ex-police sergeant Simon Holdaway has pointed to the way prisoners are treated as 'visible evidence of disorder'. Needing to detect and end disorder among citizens, the police cannot cope with ambiguity in any way.[74] In dealing with any particular situation a police officer makes a decision about what, if anything, is out of order and then makes a decision about how to overcome it. Because each individual officer is institutionalized to achieve order at all times the police institution must have a strong sense of the order they are there to reproduce, reflected in the activities they are taught to pursue, the techniques they use in pursuit, and compounded by a unitary and absolutist view of human behaviour and social organization.[75] So for example, failure to display deference to an officer significantly increases the probability of arrest, for it is understood as a failure to display deference to an officer's demand for order. Any hostility directed to them is treated as an attack on their authority and power to order, and thus an attack on authority and order in general, mediated by a supposed hostility to the Law. Antagonistic behaviour is a symbolic rejection of their authoritative attempt to reconstitute order out of a disorderly situation; it is this which may result in more formal (i.e. legal) methods of control.[76] Regardless of the legal issues pertinent to the situation, the failure to display deference is therefore likely to make one an *object of the law* as an arrested person as a *means* of *reproducing order*.

Being preoccupied with (dis)order means the police make a major contribution to the mythology of modern order. The police institution is now a key mechanism for the masking over of the fact that however orderly modern society is, it is founded on the profound insecurities and forms of stratification produced by a system founded on private property and the cash nexus. The condition of fear, insecurity, disorder and threat at the heart of civil society is the permanent state of emergency over which the police must preside.[77] Yet the disorder and insecurity of civil society is masked over ideologically by its presentation as *the* highest form of order. By treating civil society as an orderly state of affairs to be maintained, the police, like the state generally, essentially disavows the contradictions endemic to liberal capitalist society.[78] The whole police system is geared towards 'consensus' – the ideological precondition of bourgeois society – while denying the fact that such consensus by definition cannot exist. The police world, like the bourgeois world of which it is part, is a world in which conflict and disorder is necessarily present, and yet is treated as dysfunctional and therefore something to be eradicated.

This is because the preoccupation with 'disorder' serves a specific ideological function which masks over the hierarchical nature of order. Disavowing the earlier openly admitted bias against the working class, the police defence of 'order' is intended to operate as a defence of 'society' and the 'common good'. But to emphasize police as the demand for order in civil society, as Allan Silver has rightly done,[79] requires us to also recognize the hierarchical divisions operative within civil society. The concept of order is now so heavily indebted to bourgeois liberal assumptions that its connotations of unity and homogeneity have come to conceal underlying antagonisms and contradictions. The 'equality' supposedly embodied in the rule of law is always already undermined by the hierarchical nature of the order that the police are expected to defend. Behind the 'common good' there remains a particular interest: for all its talk of the universal desire for order, police protects the *imaginary* universality of particular interests within this order.[80] The demand for order in civil society is thus *a demand for class order*. Conversely, the permanent fear of 'disorder' acts as a convenient metaphor for the social tensions which attend the continual reproduction of class society, and the underlying preoccupation of the 'law and order' refrain is a set of heavily overdetermined concerns about the fabrication of consent and orderly behaviour among the working class.[81] The main threat of 'disorder' is thus almost always considered to come from those either reluctant to succumb to the discipline of wage labour, or from those who challenge the order of capital and the state: in class society 'the content of the word "Order" always indicates repression'.[82]

Formless power and ghostly presence: the state of the police

In 1929 the Royal Commission on Police Powers and Procedure claimed that 'the Police have never been recognised, either in law or in tradition, as a force distinct from the general body of citizens...a policeman possesses few powers not enjoyed by the ordinary citizen...A policeman...is only "a person paid to perform, as a matter of duty, acts which if he was so minded he might have done voluntarily".' And in 1962 the Royal Commission on the Police reiterated the principle 'that police powers are mostly grounded in the common law and differ little from those of ordinary citizens'.[83] Like the medieval constable, the modern professional police are said to practise forms of arrest and prosecution as citizens-in-uniform. Official reports and orthodox conservative accounts of police like to portray police power as citizen power writ large.

Not only does such an identification ignore the legal reality and material practice of police work in Britain (while citizens can make arrests and instigate prosecutions, the police officer possesses rights granted by statute, such as being able to break into dwellings, as well as extensive powers to stop, search and arrest citizens with a reasonable belief that a felony has been committed; unlike citizens, police are expected to take an active rather than passive approach to law-enforcement, and for this reason don a uniform marking them out as officers of the police; they also carry objects which would count as offensive weapons if carried by ordinary citizens) it also acts as a crucial legitimating device, helping to sustain the 'historic tradition that the police are the public and that the public are the police'.[84] And by identifying police with the public, the police institution is in turn treated as synonymous with civil society, rather than the state. The outcome is that 'police' and 'state' are kept at a safe distance, implying that in liberal democracies the state and the police have no real connection. This is related to a further key feature of liberal mythology surrounding the police, which is that 'police and 'state' can only be thought together in terms of totalitarian (and thus non-liberal) regimes.

A cursory glance at the reasons why certain regimes are classed as 'police states' suggests that there are severe problems with the category. One of the most common reasons rests on the assumption that in a police state the rule of law is not operative and that the police are not answerable to the law – the 1962 Royal Commission held that 'the criterion of a police state...is whether the police are answerable to the law'. But as we have seen, it is far from clear that the police are subject to the rule of law in the way that liberal democratic theory assumes. And the criteria provided by Brian Chapman for measuring the applicability of the police state model – centralization, politicization, penetration, determination, and militarization – remind us as much of the *similarities* between police powers in liberal democracies and other regimes as the differences. In terms of penetration, for example, Chapman notes that in the police state this involves the

> encroachment by the police apparat, under one pretext or another, on the general police powers of other state institutions, and in particular those of the civil service for licensing, inspecting and controlling trade, the professions, education, the communications media, social security agencies, and government agencies with overseas interests. This encroachment is matched by inroads into the judicial domain, the police apparat obtaining powers of arrest, supervision and detention, and a right to inflict penal sanctions outside the control of the normal judicial machinery.[85]

Yet this is no more than a description of the police powers of a liberal democracy. That this applies to all regimes should not surprise us, since the construction of order through the varied forms of law and administration is a central feature of all states.

My point here should not be misconstrued as implying that there is no difference between liberal democratic and other states. It is, however, to say: first, that we have categories to understand these other states – 'fascist' or 'stalinist', for example – and that one cannot understand the differences between different state forms by simply describing some of them as 'police states' and leaving it at that. Second, that the twentieth-century concept 'police state' leads one away from the other forms of power present in the states said to belong under that title, not least the power of capital – describing fascist regimes as 'police states' picks up on their attack on civil liberties but fails to register the continued social power of capital within the regime.[86] And third, that to draw these two concepts together for only non-liberal democratic regimes will lead us to understand neither police nor state.

The problems with the category 'police state' arise from the liberal recoding of the police concept. Part of liberalism's need to develop the concept of the police state in the twentieth century was rooted in the desire to conceptually differentiate between the welfare mechanisms of liberal democracies and those of either the eighteenth-century *Polizeistaat* or twentieth-century 'police states'. To distinguish, that is, between the positive (liberal) and negative (anti-liberal) ways in which 'social security' might be achieved. Given the historic links between welfare and police, and welfare *as* police, identified in Chapter 1, this was always an impossible task. The logic of this argument suggests that the twentieth-century idea of the 'police state' – generated by liberal ideological delusion and sustained by cold-war hysteria – is one of the most misleading categories of political thought. Misleading because it fails to grasp the intimate connection in practice between state power and police power, and thus obliterates the need to grapple with this connection theoretically. For example, liberalism's insistence that the police be 'non-political' rests on a very narrow conception of 'political'. As Reiner, notes, the persistent claim to the political neutrality of the police in liberal democracies is a reference to their supposed ability to stand above the party political fray.[87] This in itself may be doubted, since there is ample evidence of the tendency for the police both as an institution and as a collection of individual officers to lean to the Right. But as soon as one works with an expanded concept of the political which includes the institutions of political administration and is connected to the exercise of state power in general it is impossible to see the police in liberal democracies as somehow 'depoliticized'. The police institution is inherently and inescapably political because it is at the heart of the state's functioning.[88] The police is political in the sense that it is a creature of the state, brought into being by the state and used by the state for purposes of social ordering. Hannah Arendt's comment that under totalitarian rule 'the police dreams that one look at the gigantic map on the office wall should suffice at any given moment to establish who is related to whom and in what degree of intimacy', is the police dream in a liberal democracy too. It is no more than the dream of state power.[89] In one sense this merely takes us back to the original police mandate, which drew its power not from law, and certainly not from the liberal rule of law, but from the state and its attempt to fabricate social order. Because the state has empowered the police institution to secure order in ways apparently beyond the law, the liberal attempt to make 'law' triumph over 'state' has never been completely successful, and this is why 'due process' has never been able to fully determine and delimit police power.[90]

Policing in the most general sense of the term – through both the criminal law and through the more generalized mechanisms of political administration – is the most direct way in which the power of the state manifests itself to its subjects, the way in which the state constitutes and 'secures' civil society politically.[91] It is for this reason that the police encroaches on the exercise of power by the other institutions aiming to achieve social security, forming a unified social police. Bittner's comment noted above, that no human problem exists, or is imaginable, about which it would be said with finality that this certainly could not become the proper business of police, in fact should be that no human problem exists, or is imaginable, about which it would be said that this certainly could not become *the proper business of the state*. This is partly because the police institution generally, but especially in times of crisis, provides the coercive power and information to support the activity of other organs of state. The order mandate is useless unless combined with the potential use of coercion and it is the police institution that has inherited part of the monopoly of the means of violence possessed by the state. Whereas the military uses its part of this inheritance externally (though not only externally of course, as the history of industrial disputes shows), the police use it internally, within civil society. The ultimate truth of the police is that it deals in and dispenses violence in protection of the interests of the state.[92] In class society, this means no more than the police dispense violence on behalf of the bourgeois class.

To argue, as I have done, that state power is geared towards the political administration of civil society is to argue that bourgeois order is constituted politically by the state. To make sense of the constitutive practices of order, one cannot do without the police concept. Just as all roads lead to property in the bourgeois concept of order, so all roads lead to the state in the concept of police. Benjamin's comment that 'a consideration of the police institution encounters nothing essential at all. Its power is formless, like its nowhere tangible, all-pervasive, ghostly presence in the life of civilized states'[93] in fact captures the tangible, all-pervasive and ghostly presence of the state in general. The logic of this argument is that it is impossible to make sense of the police concept without aligning it to the concept of the state and, conversely, one can only really make sense of state power by thinking about the ways in which this power is used to police civil society.

Notes

Preface

1. Paul Rock, 'The Present State of Criminology in Britain', *British Journal of Criminology*, Vol. 28, No. 2, 1988, pp. 188–99.
2. Douglas Hay, 'Property, Authority and the Criminal Law', in Douglas Hay et al., *Albion's Fatal Tree: Crime and Society in Eighteenth-century England* (Harmondsworth: Penguin, 1975), p. 24.
3. The work most highly regarded among the Foucauldians is Jacques Donzelot, *The Policing of Families: Welfare Versus the State*, trans. Richard Hurley (London: Hutchinson, 1979) which, despite its title, contains only a handful of references to 'police'. Also see Graham Burchell, Colin Gordon and Peter Miller (eds), *The Foucault Effect: Studies in Governmentality* (London: Harvester, 1991); Andrew Barry, Thomas Osborne and Nikolas Rose (eds), *Foucault and Political Reason: Liberalism, Neo-liberalism and Rationalities of Government* (London: UCL Press, 1996); Mitchell Dean, *Governmentality: Power and Rule in Modern Society* (London: Sage, 1999). The journal *Economy and Society* has become the intellectual home of the Foucauldians, and many of their uses of 'police' can be found there. Also see Neil Websdale, 'Discipling the Non-disciplinary Spaces: The Rise of Policing as an Aspect of Governmentality in 19th Century Eugene, Oregon', *Policing and Society*, Vol. 2, 1991, pp. 89–115.
4. The recent exception to this is Richard V. Ericson and Kevin D. Haggerty, *Policing the Risk Society* (Oxford: Clarendon Press, 1997); but also see Roger Grimshaw and Tony Jefferson, *Interpreting Policework: Policy and Practice in Forms of Beat Policing* (London: Allen and Unwin, 1987).
5. See, for example, Simon Watney, *Policing Desire: Aids, Pornography and the Media*, Third edition (London: Cassell, 1997); Sue Lees, *Ruling Passions: Sexual Violence, Reputation and the Law* (Buckingham: Open University Press, 1997), pp. 17–37; Maureen Cain (ed.), *Growing Up Good: Policing the Behaviour of Girls in Europe* (London: Sage, 1989); Deborah Lynn Steinberg, Debbie Epstein and Richard Johnsen (eds), *Border Patrols: Policing the Boundaries of Heterosexuality* (London: Cassell, 1997). Also see Anita Phillips, *A Defence of Masochism* (London: Faber, 1998), p. 90.
6. David Dixon, *Law in Policing: Legal Regulation and Police Practices* (Oxford: Clarendon Press, 1997), p. 28.
7. Egon Bittner, *The Functions of the Police in Modern Society: A Review of Background Factors, Current Practices, and Possible Role Models* (New York: Jason Aronson, 1975), p. 15.
8. Kit Carson and Hilary Idzikowska, 'The Social Production of Scottish Policing 1795–1900', in Douglas Hay and Francis Snyder (eds), *Policing and Prosecution in Britain 1750–1850* (Oxford: Clarendon Press, 1989), p. 270.
9. See Jeffrey Minson, *Genealogies of Morals: Nietzsche, Foucault, Donzelot and the Eccentricity of Ethics* (London: Macmillan, 1985), p. 105; Alan Williams, *The Police of Paris 1718–1789* (Baton Rouge: Louisiana State University Press, 1979), p. 6; Ericson and Haggerty, *Policing the Risk Society*, p. 3.

10. See Christopher Tomlins, *Law, Labor and Ideology in the Early American Republic* (Cambridge: Cambridge University Press, 1993), p. 38.
11. Ian Taylor, Paul Walton and Jock Young, *The New Criminology: For a Social Theory of Deviance* (London: Routledge, 1973). For arguments along these lines see Robert Reiner, 'British Criminology and the State', *British Journal of Criminology*, Vol. 28, No. 2, 1988, pp. 268–88; and Stuart Hall, Chas Crichter, Tony Jefferson, John Clarke and Brian Roberts, *Policing the Crisis: Mugging, the State, and Law and Order* (London: Macmillan, 1978), p. 194.
12. My phrase here is taken from Jürgen Habermas, *The Structural Transformation of the Public Sphere: An Inquiry into a Category of Bourgeois Society* (1962), trans. Thomas Burger (Cambridge: Polity, 1989).
13. As examples see James O'Connor, 'Productive and Unproductive Labor', *Politics and Society*, Vol. 5, No. 3, 1975, pp. 297–336; Center for Research on Criminal Justice, *The Iron Fist and the Velvet Glove: An Analysis of the US Police* (Berkeley, CA: Center for Research on Criminal Justice, 1977), p. 16; Otwin Marenin, 'Parking Tickets and Class Repression: The Concept of Policing in Critical Theories of Criminal Justice', *Contemporary Crises*, 6, 1982, pp. 241–66; Cyril D. Robinson and Richard Scaglion, 'The Origin and Evolution of the Police Function in Society: Notes Toward a Theory', *Law and Society Review*, Vol. 21, No. 1, 1987.
14. Evgeny Pashukanis, *Law and Marxism: A General Theory* (1924), trans. Barbara Einhorn (London: Ink Links, 1978), p. 173.
15. The *Oxford English Dictionary* tells us that the use of fabrication to describe 'the action or process of fabricating; construction, fashioning' is now rare. Given what some might take to be the rather anachronistic approach to police in this book, it seems appropriate to use this rare term. For similar uses of 'fabrication' to capture the productive capacities of power, see Richard Biernacki, *The Fabrication of Labor: Germany and Britain, 1640–1914* (Berkeley: University of California Press, 1995); and Robin Evans, *The Fabrication of Virtue: English Prison Architecture, 1750–1840* (Cambridge: Cambridge University Press, 1982). Both these texts also make clear that the fabrication in question was as much of the concept (of labour or virtue) as the material practice.
16. Paul Hirst, 'Marx and Engels on Law, Crime and Morality', in Ian Taylor, Paul Walton and Jock Young (eds), *Critical Criminology* (London: Routledge, 1975), pp. 203–4. Also see Dario Melossi, 'The Penal Question in *Capital*', *Crime and Social Justice*, Vol. 5, 1976, pp. 26–33.
17. It is pertinent to note that it was his attempt to deal with issues surrounding 'crime' in the very early stages of his career that pushed Marx into the study of law and state power more generally and from there into the critique of political economy (i.e., that pushed him into Marxism). This is the gist of the biographical sketch of the 1859 Preface. We shall briefly take up this point in Chapter 4.
18. Mark Neocleous, *Administering Civil Society: Towards a Theory of State Power* (London and New York: Macmillan/St. Martin's Press, 1996).
19. In general the present work is intended to be able to stand alone, but where necessary I have reminded the reader of the relevant part of the argument in the earlier book.
20. The phrase is from Albert O. Hirschman, *The Passions and Interests: Political Arguments for Capitalism before Its Triumph* (Princeton, NJ: Princeton University Press, 1977), p. 3.

21. Ben Agger, *Fast Capitalism: A Critical Theory of Significance* (Urbana: University of Illinois Press, 1989), p. 95. Compare George Steiner, *Real Presences: Is There Anything In What We Say?* (London: Faber, 1989), p. 39: 'In the worlds of interpretative and critical discourse, book...engenders book, essay breeds essay, article spawns article. The mechanics of interminability are those of the locust. Monograph feeds on monograph, vision on revision...Essay speaks to essay, article chatters to article in an endless gallery of querulous echo.'
22. Ben Agger, *The Decline of Discourse: Reading, Writing and Resistance in Postmodern Capitalism* (New York: The Falmer Press, 1990), p. 2. This is what Ben Watson, *Art, Class and Cleavage: Quantulumcunque Concerning Materialist Esthetix* (London: Quartet, 1998), p. 218, describes as 'the baton-passing of the academic jogging-crew'.
23. Roland Barthes, *Sade/Fourier/Loyola*, trans. Richard Miller (New York: Hill and Wang), p. 10; Judith Butler, 'Against Proper Objects', *Differences*, Vol. 6, Nos 2 & 3, 1994, pp. 1–26, p. 22.

Chapter 1

1. See Carl Friedrich, *Constitutional Government* (Cambridge: Cambridge University Press, 1982), p. 156; Marc Raeff, *The Well-Ordered Police State: Social and Institutional Change Through Law in the Germanies and Russia, 1600–1800* (New Haven: Yale University Press, 1983), p. 5; Arnold J. Heidenheimer, 'Politics, Policy and Policey as Concepts in English and Continental Languages: An Attempt to Explain Divergences', *Review of Politics*, Vol. 48, No. 1, 1986; Roland Axtmann, '"Police" and the Formation of the Modern State: Legal and Ideological Assumptions on State Capacity in the Austrian Lands of the Habsburg Empire, 1500–1800', *German History*, Vol. 10, No. 1, 1992, pp. 39–61. An alternative translation of 'well-ordered police state' is Steven Kaplan's notion of France as a 'well-policed state'. See Steven Kaplan, *Bread, Politics and Political Economy in the Reign of Louis XV* (The Hague: Martinus Nijhoff, 1976).
2. Perry Anderson, *Lineages of the Absolutist State* (London: New Left Books, 1974), p. 19; Catharina Lis and Hugo Soly, *Poverty and Capitalism in Pre-Industrial Europe* (Brighton: Harvester Press, 1979), p. 85.
3. Thomas Hobbes, *Leviathan* (1651), ed. Richard Tuck (Cambridge: Cambridge University Press, 1991), p. 128.
4. Franz-Ludwig Knemeyer, 'Polizei', *Economy and Society*, Vol. 9, No. 2, 1980, pp. 173–95; Gerhard Oestreich, *Neostoicism and the Early Modern State*, trans. David McLintock (Cambridge: Cambridge University Press, 1982), p. 158; Axtmann, '"Police" and the Formation of the Modern State', p. 42; Michel Foucault, '*Omnes et Singulatim*: Towards a Criticism of "Political Reason"', in S. McMurrin (ed.), *The Tanner Lectures on Human Values, Vol. II* (Cambridge: Cambridge University Press, 1981), p. 249; R.W. Scribner, 'Police and the Territorial State in Sixteenth-century Wurttemberg', in E.I. Kouri and Tom Scott (eds), *Politics and Society in Reformation Europe: Essays for Sir Geoffrey Elton on his Sixty-Fifth Birthday* (London: Macmillan, 1987).
5. Alan Williams, *The Police of Paris 1718–1789* (Baton Rouge: Louisiana State University Press, 1979), p. 211; Raeff, *Well-Ordered Police State*, pp. 85–7.

6. The police censorship reached such an extent that under Maria Theresa not only were some 5,000 items prohibited, but the index of prohibited books listing the 5,000 items was itself withheld to avoid whetting the public appetite. See Leslie Bodie, 'Enlightened Despotism and the Literature of Enlightenment', *German Life and Letters*, Vol. 22, pp. 324–32, p. 326.

7. Philip John Stead, *The Police of France* (London: Macmillan, 1983), p. 28; John LeDonne, *Absolutism and Ruling Class: The Formation of the Russian Political Order, 1700–1825* (Oxford: Oxford University Press, 1991), p. 164; also see Mack Walker, *German Home Towns: Community, State, and General Estate 1648–1871* (Ithaca: Cornell University Press, 1971), p. 165. The British police theorist Patrick Colquhoun, whose work I discuss at length in Chapter 3, liked to report that Sartines had perfected the surveillance of the population so well that he could inform Joseph II of where a criminal had stayed in Paris, the date he had left, and the address he could be found at in Vienna.

8. Cited in Pasquale Pasquino, 'Theatrum Politicum: The Genealogy of Capital – Police and the State of Prosperity', in Graham Burchell, Colin Gordon and Peter Miller (eds), *The Foucault Effect: Studies in Governmentality* (London: Harvester Wheatsheaf, 1991), p.109. Foucault, 'Omnes et Singulatim', p. 248, cites Turquet to the effect that 'it [police] branches out into all of the people's conditions, everything that they do or undertake...The Police's true object is man.'

9. Lemaire cited in Kaplan, *Bread, Politics and Political Economy*, p. 13; Sonnenfels cited in Albion Small, *The Cameralists: The Pioneers of German Social Polity* (Chicago: University of Chicago Press, 1909), p. 494.

10. Nicolas Delamare, *Traite de la police* (1722), (Second edition Amsterdam, 1729), p. 120. See Williams, *Police of Paris*, p. 37.

11. Knemeyer, 'Polizei', p. 177.

12. 'The Police begets good order and sound morality...It is the soul of citizenship and of orderly arrangements...and the basic support of human safety and comfort' – cited in Sidney Monas, *The Third Section: Police and Society in Russia under Nicholas I* (Cambridge, MA: Harvard University Press, 1961), p. 24. Compare the demand of the Parisian *lieutenance générale de police* in the 1660s that his range of functions embraced 'everything which treats of the public good'. Cited in Steven Kaplan, *Provisioning Paris: Merchants and Millers in the Grain and Flour Trade During the Eighteenth-century* (Ithaca: Cornell University Press, 1984), p. 36. Dedicating his *Traite de la Police* to Louis XIV, Delamare identified the need for police as the 'almost universal disorder' in France, in contrast to which police is 'the handsome order on which the happiness of states depends'. The French royal edict of December 1766 establishing the post of *lieutenant de police* for Paris summarized itself in the following way: 'Police...consists in ensuring the repose of the public and of individuals, purging the City of all that can cause disorders, bringing about abundance and making everyone live according to his condition and his duty.'

13. A range of writers have identified the first two stages, though in different ways. See Howard Caygill, *Art of Judgement* (Oxford: Blackwell, 1989), p. 105; Raeff, *Well-Ordered Police State*, pp. 14, 167–71; Axtmann, '"Police" and the Formation of the Modern State', p. 44. Williams, *Police of Paris*, identifies a shift in the nature of policing in France, but sees it as occurring slightly later and as involving a shift towards the city.

14. Raeff, *Well-Ordered Police State*, pp. 50, 149.
15. Mitchell Dean, *The Constitution of Poverty: Toward a Genealogy of Liberal Governance* (London: Routledge, 1991), pp. 58–60; Jeffrey Minson, *Genealogies of Morals: Nietzsche, Foucault, Donzelot and the Eccentricity of Ethics* (London: Macmillan, 1985), p. 103. Also see Mike Brogden and Ann Brogden, 'From Henry III to Liverpool 8: The Unity of Police Street Powers', *International Journal of the Sociology of Law*, Vol. 12, No. 1, 1984, pp. 37–58; and Cyril D. Robinson and Richard Scaglion, 'The Origin and Evolution of the Police Function in Society: Notes Toward a Theory', *Law and Society Review*, Vol. 21, No. 1, 1987, pp. 109–53.
16. St Thomas Aquinas, *Summa Contra Gentiles*, in *Selected Political Writings*, trans J.G. Dawson (Oxford: Basil Blackwell, 1954), p. 101.
17. William Shakespeare, *Troilus and Cressida*, Act I, Scene iii.
18. Stephen L. Collins, *From Divine Cosmos to Sovereign State: An Intellectual History of Consciousness and the Idea of Order in Renaissance England* (Oxford: Oxford University Press, 1989), pp. 14–28.
19. Richard Hooker, *Of the Laws of Ecclesiastical Polity* (1593–97), Book I, ch.x.4, ch.x.10, Book VIII, ch.ii.2; in *The Works, Vol. I*, Fifth edition, ed. Rev. John Keble (Oxford: Clarendon Press, 1865), pp. 242, 248, 341–2, emphasis added.
20. See for example 'Speech to Parliament of 31 March 1607', in King James VI and I, *Political Writings*, ed. Johann Sommerville (Cambridge: Cambridge University Press, 1994). For a similar argument in the same period see Sir Walter Raleigh, *Maxims of State*, and *The Cabinet Council: Containing the Chief Arts of Empire, and Mysteries of State*, both in *The Works of Sir Walter Ralegh* [sic] (London: R. Dodsley, 1751), pp. 1 and 138, on how the fact that Commonwealths change from order to disorder and back again means that order has to be imposed by the state: 'State, is the...set order of a Commonwealth.' For a French example see Loyseau's comment that his *Traité des ordres et simples dignités* deals with the question of 'bringing some order and good regulation to the confusion and disorder which today pervert the eutaxy and good arrangement of this state' – *A Treatise of Orders and Plain Dignitaries* (1610), trans. Howell A. Lloyd (Cambridge: Cambridge University Press, 1994), p. 3. This period ties in with the birth of what Foucault describes as the 'Classical age', to which the question of order became essential. See Michel Foucault, *The Order of Things: An Archaeology of the Human Sciences* (London: Routledge, 1970), pp. xxii, 57.
21. See here the conclusion to Collins, *From Divine Cosmos to Sovereign State*.
22. Knemeyer, 'Polizei', p. 29; Oestreich, *Neostoicism and the Early Modern State*, p. 161; Friedrich Meinecke, *Machiavellism: The Doctrine of Raison d'État and its Place in Modern History*, trans. Douglas Scott (London: Routledge, 1957).
23. Michel Foucault, *Discipline and Punish: The Birth of the Prison*, trans. Alan Sheridan (Harmondsworth: Penguin, 1977), pp. 213–16.
24. Brian Chapman, *Police State* (London: Macmillan, 1971), pp. 15–16; Rheinhold August Dorwart, *The Prussian Welfare State Before 1740* (Cambridge, MA: Harvard University Press, 1971), pp. 4, 14, 310–11. For similar points see Raeff, *Well-Ordered Police State*, p. 254; Hsi-Huey Liang, *The Rise of Modern Police and the European State System from Metternich to the Second World War* (Cambridge: Cambridge University Press, 1992), p. 12; Kenneth Dyson, *The State Tradition in Western Europe: A Study of an Idea and Institution* (Oxford: Martin Robertson,

124 The Fabrication of Social Order

1980), p. 118. Writers from very different political positions have used this to make points about the nature of twentieth-century welfare states. For example, compare E.P. Thompson's comment (*Writing By Candlelight* [London: Merlin, 1980], p. 165), that 'the dividing line between the Welfare State and the Police State became obscure', with Michael Oakeshott's suggestion in *On Human Conduct* (Oxford: Oxford University Press, 1975), p. 311, that 'the connection between Fabianism and Cameralism is unmistakable'. I return to this issue in Chapter 5.

25. Dyson, *State Tradition in Western Europe*, p. 118; Hubert Johnson, 'The Concept of Bureaucracy in Cameralism', *Political Science Quarterly*, Vol. 79, 1964, pp. 378–402.

26. Leibniz, for example, bought into the central themes of the police state in his attempt to develop a system of rational jurisprudence. Since society is 'a union of different men for a common purpose', the most perfect society is one in which the purpose is 'the general and supreme happiness'. Thus Leibniz proposes the state's care for the common good, expressed through the welfare of its subjects as the price of submission. His model for the mutual rights in such an exchange – an exchange which takes place on the grounds that the basic natural right is not a right to property but to happiness – is what he refers to as 'political' laws, a reference to police laws promoting the common welfare. G.W. Leibniz, 'On Natural Law', in *Political Writings*, trans. Patrick Riley (Cambridge: Cambridge University Press, 1988), pp. 77–80. As Caygill notes, in his classification of laws, the 'Systema Iuris', Leibniz uses '*ordinationes politicae*' and '*Polizeisachen*' synonymously. This view was developed by Leibniz's close intellectual colleague, Christian Wolff, in whose work the metaphysical conception of perfect good is associated with the 'common good' of police, and the rational society as the bureaucratic administration of welfare by the police. See Caygill, *Art of Judgement*, pp. 125–40, 401. I shall return to this issue briefly in Chapter 2.

27. Jeremy Bentham, *An Introduction to the Principles of Morals and Legislation* (1789), in *A Fragment on Government and An Introduction to the Principles of Morals and Legislation* (Oxford: Blackwell, 1960), p. 323.

28. Francis Bacon, *The Advancement of Learning* (1605), (London: Dent & Sons, 1915), Bk. I, Pt. II, sec. 3; Bk. I, Pt. VII, sec. 6. In the 1605 and 1629 editions 'policing' was spelt 'pollicing'; in the 1633 edition it was rendered 'pollishing'. The notion of polishing is especially useful given the connections between police and dirt, discussed in Chapter 4. James I, 'Speech to Parliament of 21 March 1610', in *Political Works*, p. 183; Raleigh, *Maxims of State*, p. 1.

29. John LeDonne, *Ruling Russia: Politics and Administration in the Age of Absolutism 1762–1796* (Princeton, NJ: Princeton University Press, 1984), p. 115. G.R. Elton, *Policy and Police: The Enforcement of the Reformation in the Age of Thomas Cromwell* (Cambridge: Cambridge University Press, 1972).

30. David Dixon, *Law in Policing: Legal Regulation and Police Practices* (Oxford: Clarendon Press, 1997), p. 50; cf. Clive Emsley, *Policing and its Context 1750–1870* (London: Macmillan, 1983), p. 30. The key institution here was the justice of the peace. Although this institution undoubtedly exemplifies the peculiarity of state formation in England compared with the Continent, it makes perfect sense to say that with the power to administer the poor law, regulate the conditions of work and relations between masters and servants, demand

good behaviour sureties and arrest, as well as try most crimes and commit to gaol, the justices were fulfilling a police as much as a judicial function.

31. Gerald Stourzh, '*Constitution*: Changing Meanings of the Term from the Early Seventeenth to the Late Eighteenth-century', in Terence Ball and J.G.A. Pocock (eds), *Conceptual Change and the Constitution* (Lawrence, Kan.: University of Kansas Press, 1988), pp. 35–54, pp. 35–6. The relevant passage is para. 1278b of the *Politics*.

32. Keith Tribe, 'Cameralism and the Science of Government', *Journal of Modern History*, Vol. 56, 1984, pp. 263–84; Keith Tribe, *Governing Economy: The Reformation of German Economic Discourse 1750–1840* (Cambridge: Cambridge University Press, 1988), pp. 53, 63–4.

33. Joseph von Sonnenfels, *Grundsatze der Policey, Handlung und Finanz* (1765) and Johann Heinrich Gottlob von Justi, *Staatswirthschaft* (1755), in Small, *Cameralists*, pp. 327, 490.

34. Oestreich, *Neostoicism*, pp. 259, 270; Dorwart, *Prussian Welfare State*, p. 26. Compare Isabel Hull, *Sexuality, State and Civil Society in Germany, 1700–1815* (Ithaca: Cornell University Press, 1997), pp. 54, 95, 141, 181. As Hull points out, even those writers who conceived of some form of private sphere did not do so in the modern liberal sense of the term. Justi, for example, appears very liberal in his claim that 'the police should absolutely least of all hinder the innocent amusement in private houses [*Privat-Hausern*]', but adds that 'as soon as things [in private houses] reach the point of public disturbance, seduction of young people and ruination of morals then it is their duty to put a stop to these excesses. Thus they must not permit gambling in either private or public houses; and if music and dancing are used to offer the services of loose wenches, or similar annoying things take place, then the police must destroy these houses of vice' (*Grundsatze der Policey-Wissenschaft*, cited in Hull, p. 195). Note how the shift is so easily made from 'private house' to 'house of vice', and thus to a 'public' (i.e. police) concern. As Hull notes, for Justi even the very 'private' behaviour of sex cries out for police surveillance.

35. Pasquino, 'Theatrum Politicum', p. 112; Hull, *Sexuality, State and Civil Society*, p. 155. Raeff, *Well-Ordered Police State*, p. 8, suggests that the body of police ordinances for the Germanies and Russia is so extensive that it is virtually impossible to find all the documents.

36. Justi, *Staatswirtschaft* and *Grundsatze der Policeywissenschaft*, both cited in Small, *Cameralists*, pp. 307, 366, 437.

37. The Chairs were at the Universities of Halle and Frankfurt-an-der-Oder respectively. Similar Chairs were instituted in Vienna (1752), Leipzig (1763), Würzburg (1764), Freiburg, Klagenfürth and Innsbrück (1768), Göttingen (1765) and Ingolstadt (1780). The teaching of police as a discipline in Universities was crucial to its spread, given how important the Universities were in training the bureaucrats and administrators of the European regimes. For this reason many works on police were 'training manuals' to be used to teach future servants of the state.

38. Tribe, 'Cameralism and the Science of Government', pp. 263–5, 267, 273. Also see Rosen, 'Cameralism and the Concept of Medical Police'; Small, *Cameralists*, pp. 19–20; and Mack Walker, 'Rights and Functions: the Social Categories of Eighteenth-Century German Jurists and Cameralists', *Journal of Modern History*, Vol. 50, 1978, pp. 234–51.

39. Eli Heckscher, *Mercantilism* (1931), trans. Mendel Shapiro (London: Routledge, 1994), p. 21; Max Weber, *General Economic History*, trans. Frank Knight (London: George Allen and Unwin, 1927), p. 347; Maurice Dobb, *Studies in the Development of Capitalism* (London: Routledge, 1946), p. 209; Anderson, *Lineages of the Absolutist State*, p. 36.

40. The index entry for cameralism in Immanuel Wallerstein, *The Modern World System II: Mercantilism and the Consolidation of the European World-Economy, 1600–1750* (New York: Academic Press, 1980), sums this up perfectly. It reads: 'Cameralism, *see* Mercantilism'. The same identification is found in Raeff, *Well-Ordered Police State*, p. 92; Raeff, 'The Well-Ordered Police State and the Development of Modernity in Seventeenth- and Eighteenth-Century Europe: An Attempt at a Comparative Approach', *The American Historical Review*, Vol. 80, No. 5, 1975, pp. 1221–43, p.1224; George Rosen, 'Cameralism and the Concept of Medical Police', *Bulletin of the History of Medicine*, Vol. 27, 1953, pp. 21–42; Louise Sommer, 'Cameralism', in Edwin Seligman (ed.), *Encyclopaedia of the Social Sciences*, (London: Macmillan, 1937), pp. 158–61; Leonard Krieger, *Kings and Philosophers, 1689–1789* (London: Weidenfeld and Nicolson, 1970), p. 64; Foucault, '*Omnes et Singulatim*', p. 249; Melchior Palyi, 'The Introduction of Adam Smith on the Continent', in John Clarke (ed.), *Adam Smith, 1776–1926* (Chicago: University of Chicago Press, 1928), p. 192. For a sense of the possible differences see Hans-Joachim Braun, 'Economic Theory and Policy in Germany 1750–1800', *Journal of European Economic History* Vol. 4, No. 2, 1975, pp. 301–22; Lars Magnusson, *Mercantilism: The Shaping of an Economic Language* (London: Routledge, 1994), pp. 175, 187; Hermann Rebel, 'Reimagining the *Oikos*: Austrian Cameralism and Its Social Formation', in Jay O'Brien and William Roseberry (eds), *Golden Ages, Dark Ages: Imagining the Past in Anthropology and History* (Berkeley: University of Califronia Press, 1991), pp. 57–60; Small, *Cameralists*, pp. 7–15, 456; Tribe, 'Cameralism and the Science of Government', pp. 265, 272; Tribe, *Governing Economy*, p. 66.

41. Justi, *Staatswirthschaft* and *Grundsatze der Policeywissenschaft*, both cited in Small, *Cameralists*, pp. 307, 459.

42. Hull, *Sexuality, State and Civil Society*, pp. 103–4, 161, 164.

43. See Kaplan, *Bread, Politics and Political Economy*, pp. 11, 14, 35, 66–70, 86; Kaplan, *Provisioning Paris*, pp. 23–40; Judith Miller, *Mastering the Market: The State and the Grain Trade in Northern France, 1700–1860* (Cambridge: Cambridge University Press, 1999), pp. 25–113; Charles Tilly, *Coercion, Capital, and European States, AD 990–1990* (Oxford: Blackwell, 1990), p. 119.

44. See Jonathan Knudsen, *Justus Möser and the German Enlightenment* (Cambridge: Cambridge University Press, 1986), pp. 114–19; Raeff, *Well-Ordered Police State*, pp. 95–8, 231–4; LeDonne, *Absolutism and Ruling Class*, pp. 148–51; LeDonne, *Ruling Russia*, pp. 119–22; Axtmann, '"Police" and the Formation of the Modern State', pp. 39–61.

45. Pasquino, 'Theatrum Politicum', p. 110; Dean, *Constitution of Poverty*, pp. 58–9.

46. Williams, *Police of Paris*, p. 206; Kaplan, *Bread, Politics and Political Economy*, p. 245.

47. Geoffrey Kay and James Mott, *Political Order and the Law of Labour* (London: Macmillan, 1982), p. 126.

48. Karl Marx, *Capital: A Critique of Political Economy, Vol. 1*, trans. Ben Fowkes (Harmondsworth: Penguin, in association with New Left Review, 1976), pp. 896, 905.

49. Robert M. Schwartz, *Policing the Poor in Eighteenth-century France* (Chapel Hill: University of North Carolina Press, 1988), pp. 1, 19.

50. Sonnenfels, *Der Mann ohne Vorurteil* (1765–7), cited in Robert Kann, *A Study in Austrian Intellectual History: From Late Baroque to Romanticism* (London: Thames and Hudson, 1960), p. 179.

51. Alan Hunt, *Governance of the Consuming Passions: A History of Sumptuary Law* (New York: St. Martin's Press, 1996), p. 275.

52. Cited in Lis and Soly, *Poverty and Capitalism*, p. 124. For Colbert's attention to the disciplinary potential of the manufacture see Charles Woolsey Cole, *Colbert and a Century of French Mercantilism, Vol. II* (New York: Columbia University Press, 1939), pp. 453–5.

53. The phrase was noted by the abbé Malvaux in one of the essays submitted for a prize in 1777. See Thomas McStay Adams, *Bureaucrats and Beggars: French Social Policy in the Age of Enlightenment* (Oxford: Oxford University Press, 1990), p. 240.

54. Sonnenfels, *Der Mann ohne Vorurteil*, cited in Kann, *Study in Austrian Intellectual History*, p. 179.

55. Michel Foucault, *Madness and Civilization: A History of Insanity in the Age of Reason*, trans. Richard Howard (London: Tavistock, 1967), p. 46.

56. On one campaign against beggars and vagrants in Lower Austria in 1721, the government deployed more than 1,000 cavalry and 400 infantry in addition to local forces – see Axtmann, '"Police" and the Formation of the Modern State', pp. 50–2.

57. Schwartz, *Policing the Poor*, pp. 1–2, 14–21, 241; Williams, *Police of Paris*, pp. 190–1. Olwen Hufton's claim, *The Poor of Eighteenth-Century France 1750–1789* (Oxford: Clarendon Press, 1974), p. 220, that 'the police proper did not regard beggars and vagrants as their concern unless they troubled public order', is difficult to sustain. As Hufton goes on to say, the main business of police was 'with the policing of markets, refuse-tipping, and street-cleaning'. But beggars and vagrants were a policing concern because of the need to ensure the state of prosperity. Just as the economy was always already political, so the class of the poor was always already a threat.

58. Oestreich, *Neostoicism and the Early Modern State*, pp. 265; Anderson, *Lineages of the Absolutist State*, pp. 15–42; 402–4.

59. Marx, *Capital*, p. 899.

60. Kristin Ross, *The Emergence of Social Space: Rimbaud and the Paris Commune* (London: Macmillan, 1988), p. 57; A. L. Beier, *Masterless Men: The Vagrancy Problem in England 1560–1640* (London: Methuen, 1985), pp. 4, 10, 146; Foucault, *Discipline and Punish*, p. 291.

61. 'One can observe', wrote Justi, 'how in those countries where commerce and manufacturing thrive, children in their earliest years are spurred to industry and diligence.' Both Maria Theresa and Frederick II claimed that their subjects 'must grow accustomed to diligence and hard work' and sought to devise ways of disciplining the children of the poor. See James Van Horn Melton, *Absolutism and the Eighteenth-Century Origins of Compulsory Schooling in Prussia and Austria* (Cambridge: Cambridge University Press, 1988), pp. 114–15, 131–2,

144–65; Kann, *Study in Austrian Intellectual History*, pp. 190–2; Williams, *Police of Paris*, pp. 218–20.

62. Sonnenfels, for example, carefully estimated how many labour-hours were lost through holidays and festivals. His arguments were put into practice by Maria Theresa. See van Horn Melton, *Absolutism and the Eighteenth-Century*, p. 128; Kann, *Study in Austrian Intellectual History*, p. 177.

63. Raeff, *Well-Ordered Police State*, pp.173–8, 253; also see Hull, *Sexuality*, p. 171.

Chapter 2

1. Vivienne Brown, *Adam Smith's Discourse: Canonicity, Commerce and Conscience* (London: Routledge, 1994), p. 154. This is an issue that has been barely touched on in commentaries on Smith. For exceptions see Knud Haakonssen, *The Science of a Legislator: The Natural Jurisprudence of David Hume and Adam Smith* (Cambridge: Cambridge University Press, 1981), p. 95; Istvan Hont and Michael Ignatieff, 'Needs and Justice in the *Wealth of Nations*', in Istvan Hont and Michael Ignatieff (eds), *Wealth and Virtue: The Shaping of Political Economy in the Scottish Enlightenment* (Cambridge: Cambridge University Press, 1983); L.J. Hume, *Bentham and Bureaucracy* (Cambridge: Cambridge University Press, 1981), pp. 35–6.

2. Adam Smith, *Lectures on Jurisprudence*, ed. R.L. Meek, D.D. Raphael and P.G. Stein (Indianapolis: Liberty Fund, 1982), pp. 5–6, 331, 333, 398, 486.

3. Smith, *Lectures*, pp. 332–3, 487.

4. Howard Caygill, *Art of Judgement* (Oxford: Blackwell, 1989), pp. 103, 400.

5. Adam Smith, *Inquiry into the Nature and Causes of the Wealth of Nations*, ed. R.H. Campbell, A.S. Skinner and W.B. Todd (Indianapolis: Liberty Fund, 1979), pp. 77, 79, 80, 137, 265, 541, 729, 730; also see 151, 679, 681.

6. Brown, *Adam Smith's Discourse*, p. 155.

7. Smith, *Lectures*, pp. 5, 398.

8. Smith, *Wealth of Nations*, pp. 37, 456, 540, 687–8; *The Theory of Moral Sentiments*, ed. D.D. Raphael and A.L. Macfie (Indianapolis: Liberty Fund, 1982), pp. 184–5.

9. Duncan Forbes, 'Introduction', to Adam Ferguson, *An Essay on the History of Civil Society* (1767) (Edinburgh: Edinburgh University Press, 1966), p. xxiv.

10. Ian Simpson Ross, *The Life of Adam Smith* (Oxford: Clarendon Press, 1995), pp. 195–220. That the title of one of the *Lectures* is 'Report of 1766' is the result of an earlier editorial decision. For the background and explanation see the Editors's 'Introduction' to Smith, *Lectures*, pp. 5–13.

11. Steven Kaplan, *Bread, Politics and Political Economy in the Reign of Louis XV* (The Hague: Martinus Nijhoff, 1976), pp. 90–163; Judith Miller, *Mastering the Market: The State and the Grain Trade in Northern France, 1700–1860* (Cambridge: Cambridge University Press, 1999), pp. 43–4, 60.

12. The term had of course been used before. Colbert, on asking the merchants of Lyons what he could do for them, famously received the answer: *laissez-nous faire*, and Petty had referred to the doctrine of *vadere sicut vult* ('let it go as it wills'). But only from the 1750s did it become a commonplace of economic discourse in France (and then in England in the nineteenth century). See Guy Routh, *The Origin of Economic Ideas* (London: Macmillan, 1975), p. 45; Edward

Kittrell, '"Laissez Faire" in English Classical Economics', *Journal of the History of Ideas*, Vol. 27, No. 4, 1966; Jacob Viner, *Essays on the Intellectual History of Ideas* (Princeton, NJ: Princeton University Press, 1991), pp. 200–25; Thomas McStay Adams, *Bureaucrats and Beggars: French Social Policy in the Age of Enlightenment* (Oxford: Oxford University Press, 1990), p. 34.

13. Smith, *Wealth of Nations*, pp. 199, 216; Letter to Lord Hailes, Jan. 1769, in *The Correspondence of Adam Smith*, ed. E. Campbell Mossner and I. Simpson Ross (Indianapolis: Liberty Press, 1987), p. 139.

14. Ross, *Life*, p. 210–17; see also Smith's letter to David Hume from Paris in July 1766, in *Correspondence*, p. 113.

15. Kaplan, *Bread, Politics and Political Economy*, pp. 74, 86.

16. Ferguson, *Essay on the History of Civil Society*, p. 144.

17. Kaplan, *Bread, Politics and Political Economy*, p. xxvi.

18. Smith, *Wealth of Nations*, p. 428.

19. Donald Winch, *Riches and Poverty: An Intellectual History of Political Economy in Britain, 1750–1834* (Cambridge: Cambridge University Press, 1996), pp. 21, 96; Peter N. Miller, *Defining the Common Good: Empire, Religion and Philosophy in Eighteenth-century Britain* (Cambridge: Cambridge University Press, 1994), p. 403. Also see Mary Poovey, *A History of the Modern Fact: Problems of Knowledge in the Sciences of Wealth and Society* (Chicago: University of Chicago Press, 1998), p. 237.

20. The phrases are from the *Theory of Moral Sentiments*, pp. 185–6. Compare Leon Radzinowicz, *A History of English Criminal Law and its Administration from 1750, Volume 2: The Clash between Private Initiative and Public Interest in the Enforcement of the Law* (London: Stevens and Sons, 1956), who suggests (p. 425) that Smith was 'fundamentally...hostile to the institution of police'.

21. J.G.A. Pocock, 'The Mobility of Property and the Rise of Eighteenth-century Sociology', in *Virtue, Commerce and History* (Cambridge: Cambridge University Press, 1985), p. 111.

22. Smith, *Wealth of Nations*, p. 664. On banking see pp. 312–14, 329; on the corn trade pp. 538–9; on liberal rewards for labour pp. 91, 98, 99, 565; on liberalism in the social realm pp. 794–6; on the liberal professions pp. 119, 12, 126, 143, 796, 866; on miscellaneous other issues on which Smith points to the superiority of liberal arrangements see pp. 53, 123, 163, 349, 402, 509, 516, 522, 525, 576, 619, 671, 771, 796, 803, 864.

23. Lasker cited in Leonard Krieger, *The German Idea of Freedom: History of a Political Tradition* (Boston: Beacon Press, 1957), p. 353.

24. Justi, *Staatswirthschaft*, in Albion Small, *The Cameralists: The Pioneers of German Social Polity* (Chicago: University of Chicago Press, 1909), pp. 310, 319, 364, 372, 441; see also James Van Horn Melton, *Absolutism and the Eighteenth-Century Origins of Compulsory Schooling in Prussia and Austria* (Cambridge: Cambridge University Press, 1988), p. 113. G.W. Leibniz, 'On Natural Law', in *Political Writings*, trans. Patrick Riley (Cambridge: Cambridge University Press, 1988), pp. 77–80. On happiness as the universal obsession of the eighteenth century see Paul Hazard, *European Thought in the Eighteenth Century: From Montesquieu to Lessing* (Gloucester, MA: Peter Smith, 1973), pp. 14–26.

25. Immanuel Kant, *Critique of Pure Reason* (1781), trans. Norman Kemp Smith (London: Macmillan, 1933), Preface to the Second Edition, p. 27; 'An Answer to the Question: "What is Enlightenment?"' (1784), 'On the Common Saying:

"This May be True in Theory, but it does not Apply in Practice"' (1793), and 'The Metaphysics of Morals' (1797), all in *Political Writings*, trans. H.B. Nisbet (Cambridge: Cambridge University Press, 1991), pp. 54–5, 73–5, 80–3. For a discussion of Kant's influence on the codification of the rule of law see Henry E. Strakosch, *State Absolutism and the Rule of Law: The Struggle for the Codification of Civil Law in Austria 1753–1811* (Sydney: Sydney University Press, 1967), pp. 195–215.

26. Wilhelm von Humboldt, *The Limits of State Action* (1792), ed. J.W. Burrow (Indianapolis: Liberty Fund, 1993), pp. 16–17, 86.

27. Christopher Tomlins, *Law, Labor and Ideology in the Early American Republic* (Cambridge: Cambridge University Press, 1993), pp. 36, 56, 88. Tomlins also usefully points out how the Chair is usually remembered as a Chair in Law, a 'remembering' which conveniently obliterates the importance of the police concept at this time.

28. Thomas Paine, *Common Sense* (1776), in *Rights of Man, Common Sense and Other Political Writings*, ed. Mark Philp (Oxford: Oxford University Press, 1995), p. 34; James Madison, Alexander Hamilton and John Jay, *The Federalist Papers* (1787–8), No. 49 (Harmondsworth: Penguin, 1987), p. 314. It is for this reason that Alexis de Tocqueville described the judiciary as the American aristocracy. See *Democracy in America, Vol. 1* (1835), ed. J.P. Mayer and Max Lerner (London: Fontana, 1968), p. 329.

29. Tomlins, *Law, Labor and Ideology*, pp. 21, 94.

30. William Novak, *The People's Welfare: Law and Regulation in Nineteenth-Century America* (Chapel Hill: University of North Carolina Press, 1996).

31. See David Lindenfeld, *The Practical Imagination: The German Sciences of State in the Nineteenth Century* (Chicago: University of Chicago Press, 1997).

32. The description is from Joseph Schumpeter, *History of Economic Analysis* (London: George Allen and Unwin, 1954), p. 179; also see Lars Magnusson, *Mercantilism: The Shaping of an Economic Language* (London: Routledge, 1994), p. 200.

33. Mack Walker, *German Home Towns: Community, State, and General Estate 1648–1871* (Ithaca: Cornell University Press, 1971), p. 330; Roland Axtmann, '"Police" and the Formation of the Modern State: Legal and Ideological Assumptions on State Capacity in the Austrian Lands of the Habsburg Empire, 1500–1800', *German History*, Vol. 10, No. 1, 1992, pp. 39–61.

34. Kaplan, *Bread, Politics and Political Economy*, pp. 14, 223; Paul Bernard, *From the Enlightenment to the Police State: The Public Life of Johann Anton Pergen* (Urbana and Chicago: University of Illinois Press, 1991), p.128; Axtmann, '"Police" and the Formation of the Modern State', p. 58.

35. Michael Shapiro, *Reading "Adam Smith": Desire, History and Value* (London: Sage, 1993), pp. 9–12, 53.

36. Wendy Motooka, *The Age of Reasons: Quixotism, Sentimentalism and Political Economy in Eighteenth-Century Britain* (London: Routledge, 1998), p. 203. The fact that Smith uses the metaphor of the hidden hand only once in the *Wealth of Nations* (p. 456) and once in the *Theory of Moral Sentiments* (p. 184) (and, for records' sake, once in his 'History of Astronomy'), is irrelevant. As Christopher Berry, *Social Theory of the Scottish Enlightenment* (Edinburgh: Edinburgh University Press, 1997), p. 44, notes, the phenomenon that the image captures pervades the whole of his work. And, as Motooka notes, it evades the most pressing question in his theory. The fact that two hundred years later liberals

were still celebrating Smith's account of the hidden hand, not only as the first description of a self-ordering process but also as the first *scientific* description, tells us a great deal about how little liberalism has advanced in two centuries. For such celebration see F.A. Hayek, *The Fatal Conceit: The Errors of Socialism* (London: Routledge, 1988), p. 148.

37. Perry Anderson, *Lineages of the Absolutist State* (London: New Left Books, 1974), p. 404; Colin Gordon, 'Governmental Rationality: An Introduction', in Graham Burchell, Colin Gordon and Peter Miller (eds), *The Foucault Effect: Studies in Governmentality* (Hemel Hempstead: Harvester Wheatsheaf, 1991), p. 26.
38. The phrase is from Siegfried Kracauer, *The Salaried Masses: Duty and Distraction in Weimar* (1930), trans. Quintin Hoare (London: Verso, 1998), p. 88.
39. See J.A.W. Gunn, *Politics and the Public Interest in the Seventeenth Century* (London: Routledge, 1969), pp. 42–3; also see his '"Interest Will Not Lie": A Seventeenth-Century Political Maxim', *Journal of the History of Ideas*, 29, 1968, pp. 551–64. Similarly, Felix Rabb, *The English Face of Machiavelli: A Changing Interpretation* (London: Routledge, 1964), p. 237.
40. Albert Hirschman, *The Passions and the Interests: Political Arguments for Capitalism before Its Triumph* (Princeton, NJ: Princeton University Press, 1977), pp. 40–1.
41. Smith, *Wealth of Nations*, p. 27; also *Lectures*, p. 493.
42. Herbert, *Essai*, cited in Kaplan, *Bread, Politics and Political Economy*, pp. 102–3.
43. Smith, *Wealth of Nations*, p. 80.
44. Kant, 'On the Common Saying', pp. 74–8; 'Metaphysics of Morals', pp. 139–40.
45. See Nancy Fraser, *Justice Interruptus: Critical Reflections on the 'Postsocialist' Condition* (London: Routledge, 1997), pp. 121–49.
46. Geoffrey Kay and James Mott, *Political Order and the Law of Labour* (London: Macmillan, 1982), pp. 125–8.
47. Montesquieu, *The Spirit of the Laws* (1748), trans. Anne Cohler, Basia Miller and Harold Stone (Cambridge: Cambridge University Press, 1989), Pt 1, Book 5, Chap. 6.
48. Richard Hooker, *Of the Laws of Ecclesiastical Polity*, Book I, ch.x.4, ch.x.10, in *The Works, Vol. I*, Fifth Edition, ed. Rev. John Keble (Oxford: Clarendon Press, 1865), p. 341; Angel Rama, *The Lettered City*, trans. John Charles Chasteen (London: Duke University Press, 1996), p.14.
49. Smith, *Wealth of Nations*, p. 138; John Locke, *Two Treatises of Government* (1690), (Cambridge: Cambridge University Press, 1988), p. 287.
50. Karl Marx, *Capital, Vol. 1*, trans. Ben Fowkes (Harmondsworth: Penguin Books, 1976), pp. 280, 723, 899–901; *Grundrisse*, trans. Martin Nicolaus (Harmondsworth: Penguin, 1973), pp. 163–4; 'Economic and Philosophical Manuscripts', in *Early Writings*, trans. Rodney Livinstone and Gregory Benton (Harmondsworth: Penguin, 1975), p. 326; Smith, *Wealth of Nations*, pp. 37, 83.
51. Locke, *Two Treatises*, p. 289. William Blackstone, *Commentaries on the Laws of England*, Vol. 4 (1769) (London: Dawsons; Blackstone, 1966), p. 162, defines 'public police' as involving the citizens conforming to 'the rules of propriety, good neighbourhood, and good manners' and being 'decent, industrious, and inoffensive in their respective stations'. I return to this issue in the section on 'Medical Police, Pigs and Social Dirt' in Chapter 4, where it is given a slight Derridean twist.

52. See for example, Smith, *Lectures*, pp. 10, 21, 26.
53. This can be traced back to feudal law. Frederick Pollock and Frederic William Maitland, *The History of English Law Before the Time of Edward I*, Volume I (1895) (Cambridge: Cambridge University Press, 1968), p. 230, note that with its remnants in feudal law 'the same word *dominium* has to stand now for *ownership* and now for *lordship*'. For discussion see Morris Cohen, 'Property and Sovereignty' (1927), in C.B. Macpherson (ed.), *Property: Mainstream and Critical Positions* (Oxford: Blackwell, 1978), pp. 155–75; Roger Cotterrell, *Law's Community: Legal Theory in Sociological Perspective* (Oxford: Clarendon Press, 1995), pp. 223, 320; Carol M. Rose, 'Property as Wealth, Property as Propriety', in John Chapman (ed.), *Compensatory Justice: Nomos 33* (New York: New York University Press, 1991), p. 233.
54. Peter Linebaugh, *The London Hanged: Crime and Civil Society in the Eighteenth Century* (Harmondsworth: Penguin, 1981), p. 38; Bob Fine and Robert Millar, 'Introduction: The Law of the Market and the Rule of Law', in Bob Fine and Robert Millar (eds), *Policing the Miners' Strike* (London: Lawrence and Wishart, 1985), p. 11. For Smith's use of 'mobbish' see *Wealth of Nations*, pp. 460, 779.
55. E.P. Thompson, *Whigs and Hunters: The Origin of the Black Act* (Harmondsworth: Penguin, 1977), p. 197.
56. I have adopted and slightly adapted this from Juliet Mitchell, 'Introduction', to Daniel Defoe, *Moll Flanders* (1722) (Harmondsworth: Penguin, 1978), p. 10.
57. Linebaugh, *London Hanged*, p. xv. Historically, of course, the vast majority of hangings were for property crimes.
58. Sir William Holdsworth, *A History of English Law*, Vol. II (1903), Third edition (London: Methuen/Sweet and Maxwell, 1923), p. 462.
59. See here Jeffrey Minson, *Questions of Conduct: Sexual Harassment, Citizenship, Government* (London: Macmillan, 1993), p. 61.
60. The account of the triumph of liberalism over police found in the work of the Foucauldians virtually ignores this aspect of 'liberal governmentality'. For them, liberalism is a form of governmentality that 'depends upon a novel specification of the subjects of rule as active in their own government' and encourages individuals to 'govern themselves', to 'master themselves' in fact, to the extent that when the Foucauldians discuss despotism, it is in terms of 'despotism over oneself'. While this highlights the 'individualizing' techniques of liberalism over the 'totalizing' techniques of police science, it conveniently ignores the fact that those who are expected to 'master themselves' are in fact being 'mastered' by capital, having their so-called individuality structured by a particular form of power and logic of order. The phrases given are from Nikolas Rose, 'Government Authority and Expertise in Advanced Liberalism', *Economy and Society*, Vol. 22, No. 3, 1993, pp. 283–99, except for 'despotism over oneself' which is from Marianne Valverde, '"Despotism" and Ethical Liberal Governance', *Economy and Society*, Vol. 25, No. 3, 1996, pp. 357–72, but in general such phrases resonate through the texts of the British Foucauldians.
61. William M. Reddy, *Money and Liberty in Modern Europe: A Critique of Historical Understanding* (Cambridge: Cambridge University Press, 1987), pp. 161, 181, 184; also see Richard Biernacki, *The Fabrication of Labor: Germany and Britain, 1640–1914* (Berkeley: University of California Press, 1995), p. 448. Alan Hunt, *Governance of the Consuming Passions: A History of Sumptuary Law* (New York: St. Martin's Press, 1996), suggests that maybe one reason why sumptuary laws

concerning appropriate forms of dress went into decline is because the 'policing' of dress was increasingly undertaken by the managers of capital, at least within the workplace.

62. Paul A. Samuelson, 'Modern Economic Realities and Individualism', in *The Collected Scientific Papers of Paul A. Samuelson, Volume 2* (Massachusetts: MIT Press, 1966), p. 1408. Even the most liberal of theorists (liberal as in 'libertarian') concede that such a force is necessary. See for example Robert Nozick's concession to a minimal state to provide protection against force, theft and fraud and, of course, to enforce contracts; *Anarchy, State, and Utopia* (Oxford: Blackwell, 1974), Preface.

63. Smith, *Wealth of Nations*, p. 715; also see pp. 710; *Lectures*, pp. 208, 401, 404. As well as the poor, laws and government are also presumably intended to keep down what Smith elsewhere describes as 'factious citizens'. See Letter to George Chalmers, 22 December 1785, in *Correspondence*, p. 290.

64. Michael Dillon, *Politics of Security: Towards a Political Philosophy of Continental Thought* (London: Routledge, 1996), pp. 16, 125.

65. William Shakespeare, *Macbeth*, III, v, 32.

66. In 'Utilitarianism' (1861), for example, John Stuart Mill describes security as 'the most vital of all interests'; in *Utilitarianism, On Liberty and Considerations on Representative Government*, ed. H.B. Acton (London: Dent and Sons, 1972), p. 50. Also note his comment in 'Considerations on Representative Government', published in the same year, that 'security of person and property...are the first needs of society' (p. 355).

67. Smith, *Lectures*, pp. 405, 412, 540, 722–3, 944; Montesquieu, *Spirit of the Laws*, Pt. 2, Book 12, Chap. 2. He makes the same point in Pt. 2, Book 11, Chap. 6. Jeremy Bentham, *Principles of the Civil Code*, in *The Works of Jeremy Bentham, Volume I*, ed. John Bowring (Edinburgh: William Tait, 1843), pp. 302, 307; also see *An Introduction to the Principles of Morals and Legislation* (1789), in *A Fragment on Government and An Introduction to the Principles of Morals and Legislation* (Oxford: Blackwell, 1960), p. 147.

68. Ferguson, *Essay on the History of Civil Society*, p. 143; also p. 221; Paine, *Common Sense*, p. 7; Joseph Priestly, 'An Essay on the First Principles of Government' (1771), in *Political Writings*, ed. Peter Miller (Cambridge: Cambridge University Press, 1993), p. 32; William Paley, *The Principles of Moral and Political Philosophy* (London: R. Faulder, 1785), pp. 444–5; and Wilhelm von Humboldt, *The Limits of State Action* (1792), ed. J.W. Burrow (Indianapolis: Liberty Fund, 1993), p. 84.

69. *Entick v. Carrington* (1765). In this landmark decision in which the Court found that 'every invasion of private property...is a trespass', the Court also argued that the constitution existed to protect liberty and security (*State Trials*, 1765, 1030).

70. Hannah Arendt, 'What is Freedom?', in *Between Past and Future: Six Exercises in Political Thought* (London: Faber and Faber, 1961); Joyce Appleby, *Capitalism and a New Social Order: The Republican Vision of the 1790s* (New York: New York University Press, 1984), p. 17; also see Stephen Holmes, *Passions and Constraint: On the Theory of Liberal Democracy* (Chicago: University of Chicago Press, 1995), p. 245.

71. Smith, *Wealth of Nations*, pp. 710, 944; see also 456, 910. Blackstone, *Commentaries on the Laws of England*, Vol. 1, p. 125, defines the rights of the people of

England as personal security, liberty and private property. Likewise the French
Declaration of the Rights of Man declared that the natural rights of man are
'liberty, property, security, and resistance of oppression'.

72. Karl Marx, 'On the Jewish Question', in Karl Marx, *Early Writings*, trans. Rodney
Livingstone and Gregor Benton (Harmondsworth: Penguin, 1975), p. 230.
73. See Mitchell Dean, *The Constitution of Poverty: Toward a Genealogy of Liberal
Governance* (London: Routledge, 1991), p. 196.
74. Gordon, 'Governmental Rationality', p. 31.
75. Marx, 'On the Jewish Question', p. 230.

Chapter 3

1. Jeanne L. Schroeder, *The Vestal and the Fasces: Hegel, Lacan, Property, and the
Feminine* (Berkeley: University of California Press, 1998), pp. 27–9, 145.
2. G.W.F. Hegel, *Science of Logic*, trans. A.V. Miller (London: George Allen and
Unwin, 1969), p. 107.
3. Translators note to G.W.F. Hegel, *Philosophy of Right*, trans. T.M. Knox
(Oxford: Clarendon Press, 1942), p. 360. The more recent translation, *Elements
of the Philosophy of Right*, ed. Allen Wood and translated by H.B. Nisbet (Cambridge: Cambridge University Press, 1991), is truer to the original in this respect.
4. Translator's note to G.W.F. Hegel, *Lectures on Natural Right and Political Science: The First Philosophy of Right: Heidelberg, 1817–1818*, trans. J. Michael
Stewart and Peter C. Hodgson (Berkeley: University of California Press, 1995),
p. 207.
5. To give but one example, the *Hegel Dictionary* by Michael Inwood contains
no separate entry for this most important of integrating institutions in Hegel's
political philosophy, and only a brief mention in the entry for 'Civil Society'.
Michael Inwood, *A Hegel Dictionary* (Oxford: Blackwell, 1992).
6. Leon Radzinowicz, *A History of English Criminal Law and its Administration from
1750, Volume 3: Cross-currents in the Movement for the Reform of the Police*
(London: Stevens and Sons, 1956), p. 247; T.A. Critchley, *A History of Police in
England and Wales 900–1966* (London: Constable, 1967), pp. 40, 50; Charles
Reith, *The Blind Eye of History* (London: Faber and Faber, 1952), p. 136.
7. Michael Brogden, *The Police: Autonomy and Consent* (London: Academic Press,
1982), p. 137.
8. Mitchell Dean, *The Constitution of Poverty: Toward a Genealogy of Liberal Governance* (London: Routledge, 1991), pp. 194–9.
9. Les Johnston, *The Rebirth of Private Policing* (London: Routledge, 1992), pp.
5–6; Trevor Jones and Tim Newburn, *Private Security and Public Policing*
(Oxford: Clarendon Press, 1998), p. 3.
10. For example, Reith, *Blind Eye*, p. 155; Charles Reith, *A New Study of Police History* (London: Oliver and Boyd, 1956), pp. 24–7; Philip John Stead, 'Patrick
Colquhoun: Preventive Police', in Philip John Stead (ed.), *Pioneers in Policing*
(Montclair, New Jersey: Patterson Smith, 1977), p. 48; Clive Emsley, *The English Police: A Political and Social History*, Second edition (London: Longman,
1996), pp. 21–2; Ben Whitaker, *The Police in Society* (London: Eyre Methuen,
1979), p. 40; Glyn Hardwicke, *Keepers of the Door: The History of the Port of
London Authority Police* (London: Peel Press, n.d.), pp. 30–1; David Ascoli, *The*

Queen's Peace: The Origins and Development of the Metropolitan Police 1829–1979 (London: Hamish Hamilton, 1979), p. 7. Even those works which are not part of 'police studies', but which nonetheless discuss Colquhoun, tend to be drawn to the preventive principle – for example, Dean, *Constitution of Poverty*, p. 66.

11. Hegel, *Elements of the Philosophy of Right*, paras 188, 232, 233, 236, 248, 249; *Lectures on Natural Right*, para. 119.
12. Manfred Riedel, *Between Tradition and Revolution: The Hegelian Transformation of Political Philosophy* (Cambridge: Cambridge University Press, 1984).
13. Hegel, *Elements of the Philosophy of Right*, para. 287. In Part Three of the *Encyclopedia of the Philosophical Sciences* (1830), published as *The Philosophy of Mind*, trans. William Wallace (Oxford: Clarendon Press, 1971), Hegel describes the institution connecting civil society with universality as state-'police' (para. 534).
14. Hegel, *Lectures on Natural Right and Political Science*, para. 101; *Elements of the Philosophy of Right*, para. 189; Norman Waszek, *The Scottish Enlightenment and Hegel's Account of 'Civil Society'* (London: Kluwer Academic Publishers, 1988), pp. 111, 128.
15. For a fuller account see Mark Neocleous, 'Policing the System of Needs: Hegel, Political Economy, and the Police of the Market', *History of European Ideas*, Vol. 24, No. 1, 1998, pp. 43–58.
16. Hegel, *Elements of the Philosophy of Right*, para. 236.
17. Hegel, *Lectures of 1819–1820*, cited in Allen Wood, 'Editorial Notes' to *Elements of the Philosophy of Right*, p. 453; *Elements of the Philosophy of Right*, para. 244.
18. Hegel, *Elements of the Philosophy of Right*, para. 244.
19. Patrick Colquhoun, *A Treatise on the Police of the Metropolis, etc.*, Second edition (London: H. Fry, 1796), pp. 28, 33. Colquhoun's text went through a further five editions, was published in the United States in 1798 and in Europe as *Traite sur la police de Londres* (Paris: L. Collin, 1807).
20. Colquhoun, *Treatise on the Police*, pp. vi, 3–6, 45–7, 188.
21. Colquhoun, *Treatise on the Police*, pp. 7, 282, 299, 334–52.
22. Colquhoun, *Treatise on the Police*, pp. 94–5.
23. Colquhoun, *Treatise on the Police*, pp. 14, 18, 259.
24. Cesare Beccaria, *On Crime and Punishments* (1764), trans. David Young (Indianapolis: Hackett, 1986), p. 74. The text was translated into English in 1767 and by 1809 had been through seven editions. John Fielding, *A Plan for Preventing Robberies within Twenty Miles of London, etc.* (London: A. Millar, 1755); John Fielding, 'To the Acting Magistrates', 19 Oct. 1772, Appendix to Radzinowicz, *History of English Criminal Law, Vol. 3*, pp. 482–3.
25. Philip Rawlings, 'The Idea of Policing: A History', *Policing and Society*, Vol. 5, 1995, pp. 138–9; John Styles, 'Sir John Fielding and the Problem of Criminal Investigation in Eighteenth-Century England', *Transactions of the Royal Historical Society*, Fifth Series. 33, 1983, pp. 127–49; Radzinowicz, *History of English Criminal Law*, pp. 29–62; Critchley, *History of the Police*, p. 34; Charles Reith, *The Police Idea: Its History and Evolution in England in the Eighteenth Century and After* (Oxford: Oxford University Press, 1938), pp. 22–34; Clive Emsley, *The English Police: A Political and Social History* (London: Longman, 1996), pp. 18–19.

26. Henry Fielding fails to integrate an account of police in either his *Inquiry into the late Increase of Robbers, &c.* (1751) or his *Proposal For making an effectual Provision for the Poor, &c* (1753). See Henry Fielding, *An Inquiry into the late Increase of Robbers and Related Writings*, ed. Malvin Zirker (Oxford: Clarendon Press, 1988).

27. Colquhoun, *Treatise on the Police*, pp. 28, 381, 394. The kind of lists and registers Colquhoun has in mind can be seen from those he works with himself. For example, at one point in Chapter VII he lists not only cheats but classes of cheats: cheats impersonating footmen, cheats associating together, cheats impersonating charity collectors, and so on. His work on indigence is also marked by his lists of classes of various types.

28. Colquhoun, *Treatise on the Police*, pp. xviii, 368, 374; Patrick Colquhoun, *A Treatise on the Commerce and Police of the River Thames, etc.* (London: Joseph Mawman, 1800), pp. 245–51.

29. Patrick Colquhoun, *A Treatise on the Police of the Metropolis, etc.*, Seventh edition (London, 1806), Preface.

30. Colquhoun, *Treatise on the Police*, Second edition, pp. 357, 428–35, last two emphases added; *Treatise on the Police*, Seventh edition, pp. 567, 591–601.

31. Patrick Colquhoun, *The State of Indigence and the Situation of the Casual Poor in the Metropolis, explained, etc.* (London: H. Baldwin and Son, 1799), Preface; Patrick Colquhoun, *A Treatise on Indigence, etc.* (London: J. Hatchard, 1806), p. 251.

32. Colquhoun, *State of Indigence*, pp. 16, 25–8.

33. Colquhoun, *State of Indigence*, pp. 18–21.

34. Colquhoun, *Treatise on the Police*, Second edition, p. 99; *State of Indigence*, p. 29.

35. Colquhoun, *Treatise on Indigence*, pp. 219–23, 270.

36. Patrick Colquhoun, *A General View of the National Police System, etc.* (London: H. Baldwin and Son, 1799), p. 25; *An Account of a Meat and Soup Charity, etc.* (London: H. Fry, 1797), p. 13.

37. Colquhoun, *State of Indigence*, p. 18; *Treatise on the Commerce and Police of the River Thames*, p. 155.

38. Colquhoun, *Treatise on Indigence*, pp. 7–8. The increased importance of this distinction to Colquhoun's work is notable from the change in the titles from the *State of Indigence* (1799) to the *Treatise on Indigence* (1806). The full title of the earlier work is *The State of Indigence and the Situation of the Casual Poor in the Metropolis, explained; with reasons assigned why the prevailing system, with respect to This Unfortunate Class of the Community, contributes, in a considerable degree, to the increase and multiplication of crimes: with suggestion, shewing the necessity and utility of an establishment of pauper police, immediately applicable to the casual poor, under the management of responsible commissioners, with their functions explained.* Here the concern is merely with the relationship between the 'unfortunate class' and crime. In the later work, however, the full title makes explicit not only the link between indigence and crime, but also the importance of distinguishing between poverty and indigence. The title is *A Treatise on Indigence; exhibiting A General View of the National Resources for Productive Labour; with Proposition for Ameliorating the Condition of the Poor, and Improving the moral Habits and increasing the Comforts of the Labouring People, particularly the Rising Generation; by regulations of Political Economy, calculated*

to prevent Poverty from descending into Indigence, To Produce Sobriety and Industry, to reduce the Parochial Rates of the Kingdom, and generally to promote the Happiness and Security of the Community at Large, by the Dimunition of moral and penal Offences, and the future Prevention of Crimes.

39. J.R. Poynter, *Society and Pauperism: English Ideas on Poor Relief, 1795–1834* (London: Routledge, 1969), pp. 200–2. Compare Gertrude Himmelfarb, *The Idea of Poverty: England in the Early Industrial Age* (London: Faber and Faber, 1984), p. 85.
40. As Himmelfarb notes, although Bentham had made the distinction between poverty and indigence in his 'Essay on the Poor Laws' in 1796, he himself violated this distinction in the later *Pauper Management Improved*. On the subject of police, in 1789 it was as much as Bentham could do to refer to those public offences which are against 'the preventive branch of police', note the foreign nature of the term and comment on the fact that many of the other functions of the police may be considered under the management of public wealth. See Jeremy Bentham, *An Introduction to the Principles of Morals and Legislation* (1789), in *A Fragment on Government and An Introduction to the Principles of Morals and Legislation* (Oxford: Blackwell, 1960), pp. 321, 323, 325.
41. Himmelfarb, *Idea of Poverty*, p. 77.
42. Frances Gouda, *Poverty and Political Culture: The Rhetoric of Social Welfare in the Netherlands and France, 1815–1854* (Maryland: Rowman and Littlefield, 1995), p. 35, notes that in France a new name for poverty entered public discourse after 1815: pauperism. The word conjured up a fear of chaos, disorder and social plague, and was contrasted to the state of relative deprivation known as poverty. Some writers noted that the term originated in England. We can add that Colquhoun more than anyone helped develop the idea.
43. Colquhoun, *The State of Indigence*, pp. 5, 8; *Treatise on Indigence*, pp. 43–9; *Treatise on the Police*, p. 95; *Minutes of Evidence Taken Before a Select Committee Appointed by the House of Commons, to Inquire Into the State of the Police of the Metropolis* (London: Sherwood, Neely and Jones, 1816), p. 55.
44. Colquhoun, *Treatise on Indigence*, pp. 8–9.
45. Colquhoun, *Treatise on Police*, Seventh edition, pp. 351–80; *Treatise on Indigence*, pp. 79–110. See also his evidence given to the Select Committee on Police of 1816, in which it is apparent that the condition of the poor should be the central focus of police (*Minutes of Evidence*, p. 55).
46. Colquhoun, *Treatise on Indigence*, pp. 69, 82, 87, 90, 94, 109; Colquhoun, *State of Indigence*, pp. 12–15.
47. James Bonar, *Malthus and his Work* (London: Frank Cass, 1966), p. 41.
48. Adam Smith, *Inquiry into the Nature and Causes of the Wealth of Nations,* ed. R.H. Campbell, A.S. Skinner and W.B. Todd (Indianapolis: Liberty Fund, 1979), p. 19. More generally on problems with the idleness of workers see pp. 99, 100, 139, 335–40.
49. Karl Marx, *Capital: A Critique of Political Economy, Vol. 1*, trans. Ben Fowkes (Harmondsworth: Penguin, in association with New Left Review, 1976), pp. 464–5.
50. For the practices and mechanisms in question see Colquhoun, *Treatise on the Police*, Second edition, pp. 34, 37–9, 42–3, 361, 449; *Minutes of Evidence Taken Before a Select Committee*, p. 56; *Treatise on Indigence*, pp. 97–101, 107, 139–56; *A New and Appropriate System of Education for the Labouring People, etc.*

(1806) (Shannon: Irish University Press, 1971), 12, 17–18, 39–40, 64–5, 68; *A Treatise on the Functions and Duties of a Constable, etc.* (London: J. Mawman, 1803), Preface; A Magistrate [Patrick Colquhoun], *Observations and Facts Relative to Public Houses in the City of London and its Environs* (London: Henry Fry, 1794), pp. 16, 23, 38.

51. Other writers then followed Colquhoun along this line. For example, George Mainwaring opens his *Observations on the Present State of the Police of the Metropolis*, Second edition (London, 1822), with the observation that 'the most superficial observer of the external and visible appearances of this town, must soon be convinced, that there is a large mass of unproductive population living upon it, without occupation or ostensible means of subsistence; and, it is notorious, that hundreds and thousands go forth from day to day trusting alone to charity or rapine'. Thus 'in urging the necessity of a change in our present police system...the very operation of a better system will so change the manners and habits of the people, upon whom it is to act, as to *drive them to the pursuits of industry*'.

52. Peter Linebaugh, *The London Hanged: Crime and Civil Society in the Eighteenth Century* (Harmondsworth: Penguin, 1991), p. 427.

53. For example, William Blackstone, *Commentaries on the Laws of England*, Vol. 4 (1769) (London: Dawsons; Blackstone, 1966), pp. 5–9.

54. Jeremy Palmer, 'Evils Merely Prohibited: Conceptions of Property and Conceptions of Criminality in the Criminal Law Reform of the English Industrial Revolution', *British Journal of Law and Society*, Vol. 3, 1976, pp. 1–16; David Lieberman, *The Province of Legislation Determined: Legal Theory in Eighteenth-century Britain* (Cambridge: Cambridge University Press, 1989), p. 46.

55. Colquhoun, *Treatise on the Police of the Metropolis*, Seventh edition, p. 218.

56. Colquhoun, *State of Indigence*, p. 11; also see pp. 17, 28; *Treatise on the Police*, p. 76; *Treatise on Indigence*, p. 90.

57. Colquhoun, *Treatise on the Police of the Metropolis*, Seventh edition, p. 218.

58. Jonas Hanway, *The Defects of Police, etc.* (London: J. Dodsley, 1775). See Donna Andrews, *Philanthropy and Police: London Charity in the Eighteenth Century* (Princeton: Princeton University Press, 1989), pp. 75, 93–5.

59. Colquhoun, *Treatise on the Police*, Seventh edition, p. 562.

60. Colquhoun, *Treatise on the Commerce and Police of the River Thames*, p. 155.

61. Radzinowicz, *History of English Criminal Law, Vol. 3*, p. 282.

62. David Garland, 'The Limits of the Sovereign State: Strategies of Crime Control in Contemporary Society', *The British Journal of Criminology*, Vol. 36, No. 4, 1996, pp. 445–71, p. 466.

63. See Dean, *Constitution of Poverty*, p. 66. Colquhoun has been badly served by the intellectual poverty induced by the excessive specialization within the social sciences. It is indicative of the skewed focus of the discplines of both police studies and social policy that the 'social policy' aspect of Colquhoun's and Hegel's work has been largely ignored. Conversely, one might add that it is indicative of the skewed nature of political theory, political economy and social policy that these disciplines have also failed to note Colquhoun's importance. See for example Raymond Cowherd, *Political Economists and the English Poor Laws: A Historical Study of the Influence of Classical Economics on the Formation of Social Welfare Policy* (Athens: Ohio University Press, 1977), in which Colquhoun is mentioned only in passing.

64. See A.P. Donajgrodzki, '"Social Police" and the Bureaucratic Elite: A Vision of Order in the Age of Reform', in A.P. Donajgrodzki (ed.), *Social Control in Nineteenth Century Britain* (London: Croom Helm, 1977); Geoffrey Kay and James Mott, *Political Order and the Law of Labour* (London: Macmillan, 1982), p. 127.

65. Colin Gordon, 'Governmental Rationality: An Introduction', in Graham Burchell, Colin Gordon and Peter Miller (eds), *The Foucault Effect: Studies in Governmentality* (Hemel Hempstead: Harvester Wheatsheaf, 1991), p. 31.

66. Colquhoun, *Treatise on the Commerce and Police of the River Thames*, p. 38; also see pp. 237–8, 244, 264; *Treatise on the Police*, Second edition, p. 74; *Treatise on the Police*, Seventh edition, p. 218; Hegel, *Elements of the Philosophy of Right*, para. 249; also see paras 203, 230; *Philosophy of Mind*, para. 533.

67. Barry Buzan, *People, States and Fear*, Second edition (London: Harvester Wheatsheaf, 1991), pp. 124, 250.

68. Michael Dillon, *Politics of Security: Towards a Political Philosophy of Continental Thought* (London: Routledge, 1996), p. 16.

69. Dillon, *Politics of Security*, pp. 16, 122.

70. R.N. Berki, *Security and Society: Reflections on Law, Order and Politics* (London: Dent and Sons, 1986), pp. 39, 231; Dillon, *Politics of Security*, pp. 19, 33, 121, 127.

71. James Der Derian, *Antidiplomacy: Spies, Terror, Speed, and War* (Oxford: Blackwell, 1992), p. 75.

72. See David Campbell, *Writing Security:United States Foreign Policy and the Politics of Identity* (Minneapolis: University of Minnesota Press, 1992); Simon Dalby, 'Contesting an Essential Concept: Reading the Dilemmas in Contemporary Security Discourse', in Keith Krause and Michael Williams (eds), *Critical Security Studies: Concepts and Cases* (London: UCL Press, 1997).

73. Security needs calculation, for without calculation security could not be secured. Whatever *is* must thereby be rendered calculable. Security functions as knowledge, relies on knowledge, produces knowledge, and uses its claim to knowledge as licence to render all aspects of life transparent (see Dillon, *Politics of Security*, pp. 17, 21). Police is thus integral to the pursuit of knowledge of civil society by the state. In other words: surveillance.

Chapter 4

1. R.M. Titmuss, *Social Policy: An Introduction* (London: George Allen and Unwin, 1974), p. 88. The first Acts with 'social security' in their titles – the Social Security Act of 1935 in the United States and the Ministry of Social Security Act of 1966 in Britain – both focused on money payments.

2. The Laroque Report – International Labour Office, *Into the Twenty-first Century: The Development of Social Security* (Geneva: International Labour Office, 1984), p. 19; also see Pierre Laroque, 'From Social Insurance to Social Security', *International Labour Review*, Vol. 57, No. 6, 1948.

3. Sir William Jowitt, in *Parliamentary Debates (Hansard)*, Fifth Series, Vol. 404 (H.C. Deb.), 1943–44, p. 984.

4. Note the transformation of the *International Social Insurance Conference* into the *International Social Security Association* in 1947.

5. Vic George, *Social Security: Beveridge and After* (London: Routledge, 1968), p. 7; also see Paul Spicker, *Poverty and Social Security* (London: Routledge, 1993), p. 101.
6. V.A.C. Gatrell, 'The Decline of Theft and Violence in Victorian and Edwardian England', in V.A.C. Gatrell, Bruce Lenman and Geoffrey Parker (eds), *Crime and the Law: The Social History of Crime in Western Europe since 1500* (London: Europa, 1980), p. 268.
7. The Instructions are given in Charles Reith, *A New Study of Police History* (Edinburgh and London: Oliver and Boyd, 1956), p. 135.
8. Wilbur R. Miller, *Cops and Bobbies: Police Authority in New York and London, 1830–1870* (Chicago: University of Chicago Press, 1977), Preface.
9. Kit Carson and Hilary Idzikowska, 'The Social Production of Scottish Policing, 1795–1900', in Douglas Hay and Francis Snyder (eds), *Policing and Prosecution in Britain 1750–1850* (Oxford: Clarendon Press, 1989), p. 271.
10. Richard V. Ericson, *Reproducing Order: A Study of Police Patrolwork* (Toronto: University of Toronto Press, 1982), p. 7.
11. Edwin Chadwick, 'Preventive Police', *The London Review*, 1, Feb 1829; 'On the Consolidation of Police Force, and the Prevention of Crime', *Fraser's Magazine*, 77, Jan 1868, pp. 1–18.
12. Chadwick to Lord Russell, August and September 1836, cited in John Knott, *Popular Opposition to the 1834 Poor Law* (London: Croom Helm, 1986), p. 258; *The Herald*, 4 May 1839, cited in S.E. Finer, *The Life and Times of Sir Edwin Chadwick* (London: Methuen, 1952), p. 178.
13. A.P. Donajgrodzki, '"Social Police" and the Bureaucratic Elite: A Vision of Order in the Age of Reform', in A.P. Donajgrodzki (ed.), *Social Control in Nineteenth Century Britain* (London: Croom Helm, 1977); Carolyn Steedman, *Policing the Victorian Community: The Formation of English Provincial Police Forces, 1856–80* (London: Routledge, 1984), pp. 53, 56–9; Knott, *Popular Opposition to the 1834 Poor Law*; V.A.C. Gatrell, 'Crime, Authority and the Policeman-State', in F.M.L. Thomson (ed.), *The Cambridge Social History of Britain 1750–1950, Vol. 3: Social Agencies and Institutions* (Cambridge: Cambridge University Press, 1990), p. 276. Philip Rawlings, *Crime and Power: A History of Criminal Justice 1688–1998* (London: Longman, 1999), p. 116, notes that at a meeting of the unemployed in Hyde Park in October 1888, a placard referring to the murders of Jack the Ripper read 'The Whitechapel Murders. Where are the Police? Looking after the Unemployed.'
14. Steven C. Hughes, *Crime, Disorder and the Risorgimento: The Politics of Policing in Bologna* (Cambridge: Cambridge University Press, 1994), p. 87. Also see John A. Davis, *Conflict and Control: Law and Order in Nineteenth-Century Italy* (London, Macmillan, 1988), pp. 7, 67–71, 218–22.
15. See Frances Gouda, *Poverty and Political Culture: The Rhetoric of Social Welfare in the Netherlands and France, 1815–1854* (Maryland: Rowman and Littlefield, 1995), pp. 43–8, 72; Elaine Glovka Spencer, *Police and the Social Order in German Cities: The Düsseldorf District, 1848–1914* (DeKalb: Northern Illinois University Press, 1992), pp. 44–6; Carson and Idzikowska, 'Social Production of Scottish Policing', p. 273; Sidney L. Harring, *Policing a Class Society: The Experience of American Cities, 1865–1915* (New Jersey: Rutgers University Press, 1983), pp. 201–23.

16. Cited in Clare Demuth, *'Sus': A Report on the Vagrancy Act 1824* (London: Runnymede Trust, 1978), p. 11. Demuth makes clear the extensive use of such street power up until 1981.
17. Demuth, *'Sus'*; Steedman, *Policing the Victorian Community*, p. 56.
18. Clive Emsley, *The English Police: A Political and Social History*, Second edition (London: Longman, 1996), pp. 51, 82, 154; Steedman, *Policing the Victorian Community*, pp. 53, 58–9. B.J. Davey, *Lawless and Immoral: Policing a Country Town 1838–1857* (Leicester: Leicester University Press, 1983), p. 45, notes that in enforcing the Vagrancy Act 'the Constables saw themselves as the legal agents of the poor law authorities, rather than watchmen controlling street crime'.
19. As noted by Gertrude Himmelfarb, *The Idea of Poverty: England in the Early Industrial Age* (London: Faber, 1984), pp. 383–4.
20. Poor Law Commissioners, *Extracts from the Information received by His Majesty's Commissioners, as to the Administration and Operation of the Poor Laws* (London: B. Fellowes, 1833), pp. 247–8; *First Report of the Commissioners Appointed to Inquire as to the Best Means of Establishing an Efficient Constabulary Force in the Counties of England and Wales* (1839), in *Reports from Commissioners*, Vol. 19, 1839 (hereafter *Report on the Constabulary Force*), p. 67. The link would seem to be Chadwick. The *Report on the Constabulary Force* was authored by Chadwick with Charles Shaw Lefevre and Charles Rowan, and Chadwick's essay 'The New Poor Law', *Edinburgh Review*, 63, 1836, pp. 487–537, reproduces the same passages (at pp. 492–3). A significant part of his argument in the *Report on the Sanitary Condition of the Labouring Population* (1842) was also taken from the Constabulary Force Commission, and is discussed below in the section on medical police.
21. Karl Marx, *Capital: A Critique of Political Economy*, Vol. 1, trans. Ben Fowkes (Harmondsworth: Penguin, in association with New Left Review, 1976), p. 874.
22. Mark Neocleous, *Administering Civil Society: Towards a Theory of State Power* (London: Macmillan, 1996), pp. 117–26.
23. *Report from Her Majesty's Commissioners for Inquiring into the Administration and Practical Application of the Poor Laws*, in *Reports from Commissioners*, I, 1834 (hereafter *Poor Law Report*), p. 156; also Chadwick, 'New Poor Law', p. 500.
24. *Poor Law Report*, p. 127.
25. Chadwick, 'New Poor Law', p. 501.
26. Chadwick, 'New Poor Law', pp. 535, 537.
27. T.S. Ashton, *An Economic History of England: The Eighteenth Century* (London: Methuen, 1955), p. 208.
28. Peter Linebaugh, *The London Hanged: Crime and Civil Society in the Eighteenth Century* (Harmondsworth: Penguin, 1991), p. 379, estimates that chips were a perquisite providing between a third and a half of a worker's weekly earnings in the docks. John Styles, 'Embezzlement, Industry and the Law in England, 1500–1800', in Maxine Berg, Pat Hudson and Michael Sonenscher (eds), *Manufacture in Town and Country before the Factory* (Cambridge: Cambridge University Press, 1983), gives a slightly lower figure of 20 per cent of one worker's earnings. On the other hand, Clive Emsley, *Crime and Society in England, 1750–1900* (London: Longman, 1996), p. 128, reports that in 1801, when the basic daily rate for a skilled shipworker was 2s1d, workers in the Royal Dockyards

were asked how much they would have to be paid to forgo their daily bundle of 'chips'. They estimated the value at 8d. Whichever figure is right, Linebaugh's general point that 'to those having a right to this prescriptive custom, chips were an essential part of their ecology – in housing, in energy, in cooking, in furnishing' rings true. Colquhoun, whose position on this issue is discussed below, cited a rather ridiculous rumour to the effect that regular plunderering allowed 'common labourers...to have their houses furnished in a very superior style and to be possessed of property...to the extent of from £1,500 to £3,000' (Patrick Colquhoun, *A Treatise on the Police of the Metropolis*, Fifth edition [London: H. Fry, 1799], p. 64).

29. Karl Marx, 'Debates on the Law on Thefts of Wood', *Rheinische Zeitung*, Oct. 1842, in Karl Marx and Frederick Engels, *Collected Works*, Vol. 1 (London: Lawrence and Wishart, 1975), pp. 232–3.

30. See Peter Linebaugh's contribution to 'Eighteenth-century Crime, Popular Movements and Social Control', *Bulletin of the Society for the Study of Labour History*, 25, 1972, p. 13.

31. On the Worsted Committee see Barry Godfrey, 'Law, Factory Discipline and "Theft": The Impact of the Factory on Workplace Appropriation in Mid to late Nineteenth-Century Yorkshire', *British Journal of Criminology*, Vol. 39, No. 1, 1999, pp. 56–71; Richard J. Soderland, '"Intended as a Terror to the Idle and Profligate": Embezzlement and the Origins of Policing in the Yorkshire Worsted Industry, c. 1750–1777', *Journal of Social History*, Vol. 31, No. 3, 1998, pp. 647–69; Michael Ignatieff, *A Just Measure of Pain: The Penitentiary in the Industrial Revolution 1750–1850* (Harmondsworth: Penguin, 1989), p. 26. On the West India merchants see Leon Radzinowicz, *A History of English Criminal Law and its Administration from 1750, Volume 2* (London: Stevens and Sons, 1956). On the naval authorities Linebaugh, *London Hanged*, p. 394. On gleaning see David H. Morgan, 'The Place of Harvesters in Nineteenth-century Village Life', in Raphael Samuel (ed.), *Village Life and Labour* (London: Routledge, 1975); and Emsley, *Crime and Society*, pp. 122–5. For a general account, see John Rule, *The Experience of Labour in Eighteenth-Century Industry* (London: Croom Helm, 1981), pp. 124–46.

32. Jason Ditton, 'Perks, Pilferage, and the Fiddle: The Historical Structure of Invisible Wages', *Theory and Society*, Vol. 4, 1978, pp. 39–71.

33. David Philips, *Crime and Authority in Victorian England: The Black Country 1835–1860* (London: Croom Helm, 1977), pp. 188–9. Philips shows (p. 183) that 'industrial thefts' make up over one-quarter of committals for larceny between 1835 and 1860, and over one-fifth of all committals in the same period. On the question of perks in the nineteenth century generally see Emsley, *Crime and Society*, p. 133; Radzinowicz, *History of English Criminal Law, Volume 2*, p. 358; Jennifer Davis, '"The Thief Non-Professional": Workplace Appropriation in Nineteenth-century London', *Bulletin of the Society for the Study of Labour History*, 52, 1987, p. 41, and Jennifer Davis, 'Prosecutions and their Context: The Use of the Criminal Law in Later Nineteenth-Century London', in Douglas Hay and Francis Snyder (eds), *Policing and Prosecution in Britain 1750–1850* (Oxford: Clarendon Press, 1989).

34. Marx, 'Debates on the Law on Thefts of Wood', p. 235.

35. Patrick Colquhoun, *A Treatise on the Commerce and Police of the River Thames, etc.* (London: Joseph Mawman, 1800), pp. 80, 139, 141, 155, 163, 168. He

also estimated (p. 198) that nine-tenths of all crimes in the port were committed by persons whose presence in the area was justified (i.e. workers), that in some groups of workers up to half were delinquents, and that different gangs of different types of thieves work there. Also see Colquhoun, *A Treatise on the Police of the Metropolis, etc.*, Seventh edition (London: Joseph Mawman, 1806), pp. 223–5, 252–6; Colquhoun, *A General View of the Causes and Existence of Frauds, Embezzlements, Peculation and Plunder, on His Majesty's Stores in the Dock Yards, etc.* (London: H. Baldwin, 1799), p. 7; Colquhoun, *A General View of the Depradations Committed on West-India and Other Property in the Port of London, etc.* (London: H. Baldwin, 1799), pp. 10–11.

36. Colquhoun, *Treatise on the Police*, Seventh edition., p. 252; also Colquhoun, *General View of the Causes and Existence of Frauds*, p. 3.
37. Colquhoun, *Treatise on the Commerce and Police of the River Thames*, p. 63.
38. Colquhoun, *Treatise on the Commerce and Police of the River Thames*, pp. 80–9, 159.
39. Colquhoun, *Treatise on the Police*, Seventh edition, pp. 231, 234; *General View of the Causes and Existence of Frauds*, pp. 32–5. Some of the thoughts here have been inspired by Linebaugh, *London Hanged*, pp. 426–35; Ian Macdonald, 'The Creation of the British Police', *Race Today*, Vol. 5, No. 11, 1973, pp. 331–3; Tony Bunyan, *The History and Practice of the Political Police in Britain* (London: Quartet, 1977), p. 61.
40. Brogden, *Police: Autonomy and Consent*, pp. 44–7; also Mike Brogden and Ann Brogden, 'From Henry III to Liverpool 8: The Unity of Police Street Powers', in *International Journal of the Sociology of Law*, Vol. 12, No. 1, 1984, pp. 37–58; Philips, *Crime and Authority*; Godfrey, 'Law, Factory Discipline and "Theft"'.
41. Phil Cohen, 'Policing the Working-class City', in Bob Fine et al. (eds), *Capitalism and the Rule of Law: From Deviancy Theory to Marxism* (London: Hutchinson, 1979), p. 121.
42. Alf Lüdtke, *Police and State in Prussia, 1815–1850*, trans. Pete Burgess (Cambridge: Cambridge University Press, 1989), p. 110; Oskar Negt and Alexander Kluge, *Public Sphere and Experience: Towards an Analysis of the Bourgeois and Proletarian Public Sphere* (1972), trans. Peter Labanyi et al. (Minneapolis: University of Minnesota Press, 1993), pp. 54–95.
43. W.G. Carson, 'Policing the Periphery: the Development of Scottish Policing 1795–1900. Part II – Policing and the Production of Social Order', *Australian and New Zealand Journal of Criminology*, 18, 1985, pp. 3–16, p. 8.
44. Noting the importance of the wage form goes some (though by no means all) of the way to explaining some of the problems which have continued to dog policing in Britain, such as the constant police difficulty with blacks and in particular black youth. The wider historical point to note is that the perception of blacks held by the state from the beginning of mass immigration has been that they are a form of wage labour. With indigenous working-class wage labour increasingly scarce and expensive, British capital turned to the West Indian working class; the influx of black immigrants in the 1950s was as wage labour, and a cheap one at that. The difficulties faced by the British police in subsequent years were thus founded on the widespread prior assumption within the ruling class and the state that West Indians should be engaged in wage labour. Thus following a raid on a black gambling house in February 1957 the Chief Inspector concerned argued that 'when the police find a house

of this description every endeavour must be made to suppress it. The majority of men are not working' (cited in Darcus Howe, 'Fighting Back: West Indian Youth and the Police in Notting Hill', *Race Today*, Vol. 5, No. 11, 1973, pp. 333–7). What has ever since been presented as a problem of 'black crime' is in some sense a problem of 'black wagelessness'; black 'resistance' is understood, first and foremost, as a refusal of the wage. As such the tensions between black youth and the police can be thought of in terms of the historical origins of the police more generally, namely, as tensions arising from the attempt to bring the wageless back into wage labour. On this score it is perhaps worth pointing out that the constant demands by senior police officers, officials of the social police and politicians, that one needs to distinguish between the 'hard-working and law-abiding' black and the 'rebellious' (and usually young) black is a reiteration of the desire in the early nineteenth century to distinguish between poverty and pauperism and thus identify the 'respectable' working class. As well as Howe on this point, see Macdonald, 'Creation of the British Police'; and Stuart Hall, Chas Crichter, Tony Jefferson, John Clarke and Brian Roberts, *Policing the Crisis: Mugging, the State, and Law and Order* (London: Macmillan, 1978), pp. 370, 391, 396. Whether this point can explain the systematic beatings, shootings and 'accidental' deaths of blacks in police custody is another matter of course.

45. *Report from the Departmental Committee on Prisons* (London: HMSO, 1895), p. 410; Peel cited in Emsley, *Crime and Society*, p. 56.
46. Poor Law Commission, *Extracts...as to the Administration and Operation of the Poor Laws*, pp. 247–8; Chadwick, 'New Poor Law', p. 493.
47. Chadwick, 'New Poor Law', pp. 517, 536.
48. *Poor Law Report*, p. 128.
49. *Report on the Constabulary Force*, pp. 25–6, 53, 206.
50. *Report on the Constabulary Force*, pp. 36, 67, 181. Henry Mayhew similarly defined criminals as 'those who will not work', as Volume 4 of his *London Labour and the London Poor* is titled. Frederick Engels, *Anti-Dühring*, trans. Emile Burns (Moscow: Progress Publishers, 1947), p. 117: 'from the moment when private ownership of movable property developed, all societies in which this private ownership existed had to have this moral injunction in common: Thou shalt not steal'.
51. Leon Radzinowicz, *A History of English Criminal Law and its Administration from 1750. Vol. 4: Grappling for Control* (London: Stevens and Sons, 1968), p. 177; Stanley Palmer, *Police and Protest in England and Ireland 1780–1850* (Cambridge: Cambridge University Press, 1988); also see Jennifer Hart, 'Reform of the Borough Police, 1835–1856', *The English Historical Review*, 70, 1955, pp. 411–27; Philips, *Crime and Authority*, pp. 74–87; Peter Laurie, *Scotland Yard* (London: The Bodley Head, 1970), p. 91.
52. E.P. Thompson, 'The Moral Economy of the English Crowd', in *Customs in Common* (Harmondsworth: Penguin, 1993).
53. Karl Polanyi, *The Great Transformation* (New York: Octagon Books, 1980), pp. 186–7.
54. 'The Great Want of New York City – a Government', *New York Qurterly*, 3, April 1854, cited in Miller, *Cops and Bobbies*, p. 8.
55. See Polanyi, *Great Transformation*, p. 187; also see Allan Silver, 'The Demand for Order in Civil Society: A Review of Some Themes in the History of Urban

Crime, Police, and Riot', in David Bordua (ed.), *The Police: Six Sociological Essays* (New York: John Wiley, 1967); Steven Spitzer and Andrew Scull, 'Privatization and Capitalist Development: The Case of the Private Police', *Social Problems*, Vol. 25, No. 1, 1977, pp. 18–29, p. 21.

56. Indeed, since the rationale of police is supposedly the prevention of crime, having social and political struggles dealt with by the police facilitates the 'criminalization of the adversary', the process by which social struggles opposing the ruling class and challenging the bourgeois order are criminalized, depoliticizing an issue and discounting the political dimension of 'disorder'. To give an example: Sir Robert Mark, *In the Office of the Constable* (London: Collins, 1978), p. 138, notes that in 1973 the Metropolitan Police were under strain, 'having to deal with 72,750 burglaries, 2680 robberies and 450 demonstrations during the year'. E.P. Thompson rightly points out the implications of such a claim: 'Football crowds and traffic accidents go unmentioned. The point is the sequence: burglaries-robberies-demonstrations, and to associate in the readers' minds popular democratic manifestations with crime' ('On the New Issue of Postal Stamps', *New Society*, 8 November 1979, pp. 324–6). One might also draw attention to Mark's comment that 'the worst of all crimes is the furtherance of political or industrial aims by violence', and that pickets are in some sense worse than murderers: those picketing in Shrewsbury, he comments, 'had committed the worst of all crimes, worse even than murder, the attempt to achieve an industrial or political objective by criminal violence'. Indeed, not only worse than murder, but worse than mass murder: trying to achieve an industrial or political objective by criminal violence is 'the very conduct...which helped to bring the National Socialist Workers Party to power in 1933' (pp. 152, 325). It is perhaps not insignificant that Mark was writing in such a way at the time when Mrs Thatcher was gearing up for a law and order society by making the same sort of identifications. 'In their muddled but different ways, the vandals on the picket lines and the muggers in our streets have got the same confused message – "we want our demands met or else" and "get out of the way and give us your handbag"' – cited in Michael Brake and Chris Hale, *Public Order and Private Lives: The Politics of Law and Order* (London: Routledge, 1992), p. 15. I have taken the idea of the criminalization of the adversary from Giorgio Agamben, 'The Sovereign Police', trans. Brian Massumi, in Brian Massumi (ed.), *The Politics of Everyday Fear* (Minneapolis: University of Minnesota Press, 1993), p. 63.

57. Disraeli, Speech at Maidstone, 1837, cited in Karl de Schweinitz, *England's Road to Social Security: From the Statute of Labourers in 1349 to the Beveridge Report of 1942* (New York: Perpetua Books, 1961), p. 124; Steedman, *Policing the Victorian Community*, p. 59; also see Linebaugh, *London Hanged*, p. 71.

58. Gatrell, 'Crime, Authority and the Policeman-State', pp. 244–5, 251–2; Martin J. Wiener, *Reconstructing the Criminal: Culture, Law, and Policy in England, 1830–1914* (Cambridge: Cambridge University Press, 1990), p. 11.

59. E.P. Thompson, *Whigs and Hunters: The Origin of the Black Act* (Harmondsworth: Penguin, 1977), p. 194. The account referred to is Pat Rogers, 'The Waltham Blacks and the Black Act', *Historical Journal*, Vol. 17, No. 3, 1974.

60. Paul Rock, 'Law, Order and Power in Late Seventeenth- and Early Eighteenth-century England', in Stanley Cohen and Andrew Scull (eds), *Social Control and the State: Historical and Comparative Essays* (Oxford: Blackwell, 1985),

pp. 212, 215; Steven Spitzer, 'The Rationalization of Crime Control in Capitalist Society', in Cohen and Scull (eds), *Social Control and the State*, p. 319.

61. Thompson, *Whigs and Hunters*, pp. 217–18.

62. Juliet Mitchell, 'Introduction' to Daniel Defoe, *Moll Flanders* (Harmondsworth: Penguin, 1978).

63. Hall et al., *Policing the Crisis*, p. 189. The 17-year-old is cited in Gatrell, 'Decline of Theft and Violence', pp. 264–5. In his study of crime in the Black Country David Philips notes that many thefts 'were committed by people who stole regularly while also having occupations at which they worked for at least part of the time'. Thus many of those tried were 'neither "honest poor", nor "criminal class", but an important third category – people in employment who supplemented their income with theft' – Philips, *Crime and Authority in Victorian England*, p. 198.

64. Chadwick, 'New Poor Law', p. 503.

65. In the twentieth century black people would come to find themselves on the 'wrong' side of this ideological divide. On this score note the comment by Mike Davis, *City of Quartz: Excavating the Future in Los Angeles* (London: Vintage, 1992), p. 270, on the war on gangs as 'an imaginary class relationship'.

66. Michel Foucault, *Discipline and Punish: The Birth of the Prison*, trans. Alan Sheridan (Harmondsworth: Penguin, 1977), p. 283.

67. To give one recent example. On 2 September 1982, 283 people who walked into an unemployment benefit office in Oxford found themselves arrested (under the Prevention of Terrorism Act, no less). The then Department of Health and Social Security (DHSS) had its own mechanism for dealing with benefit fraud, cheaper, less stigmatizing and generally more effective than using the police, yet the whole operation was mounted as a police campaign and the eventual charge (of 175 persons) was for 'offences of obtaining property by deception' under the Theft Act (1968) rather than the Supplementary Benefit Act (1976). See Ros Franey, *Poor Law: The Mass Arrest of Homeless Claimants in Oxford* (London: CHAR/CPAG/Claimants Defence Committee/NAPO/NCCL, 1983).

68. John Alan Lee, 'Some Structural Aspects of Police Deviance in Relations With Minority Groups', in Clifford Shearing (ed.), *Organizational Police Deviance: Its Structure and Control* (Toronto: Butterworths, 1981), pp. 53–4; also see Satnam Choong, *Policing as Social Discipline* (Oxford: Clarendon Press, 1997), p. 50; P.A.J. Waddington, *Policing Citizens* (London: UCL Press, 1999), p. 42. The term is one adopted from the police themselves – see its use by Simon Holdaway, *Inside the British Police: A Force at Work* (Oxford: Basil Blackwell, 1983), pp. 86–9.

69. Himmelfarb, 'Culture of Poverty', pp. 175, 720. See also the discussion of work, idleness and criminality in Jonathan Simon, *Poor Discipline: Parole and the Social Control of the Underclass, 1890–1990* (Chicago: University of Chicago Press, 1993), pp. 39–59. It is also pertinent to note that the idea of the 'dangerous class' was also very imprecise, with its French popularizer Frégier unable to properly distinguish the dangerous class from the working class. See Louis Chevalier, *Labouring Classes and Dangerous Classes in Paris During the First Half of the Nineteenth Century*, trans. Frank Jellinek (London: Routledge, 1973), pp. 141–2, 361, 366–70, 397.

70. See W.G. Carson, 'The Conventionalization of Early Factory Crime', *International Journal for the Sociology of Law*, 7, 1979, pp. 37–60; Emsley, *Crime and Society in England*, p. 135.

71. Foucault, *Discipline and Punish*, p. 87.
72. Ian Taylor, Paul Walton and Jock Young, 'Critical Criminology in Britain: Review and Prospects', in Ian Taylor, Paul Walton and Jock Young (eds), *Critical Criminology* (London: Routledge, 1975), p. 31.
73. Frederick Engels, *The Condition of the Working Class in England* (1845) (London: Granada, 1969), p. 126.
74. For this and countless other cases see Gary Slapper and Steve Tombs, *Corporate Crime* (London: Longman, 1999).
75. Jacques Derrida, *Of Grammatology*, trans. Gayatri Chakravorty Spivak (Baltimore: Johns Hopkins University Press, 1976), p. 26; *Writing and Difference*, trans. Alan Bass (London: Routledge, 1978), pp. 179–83. Some of my thoughts here have been shaped by Patricia Parker, *Literary Fat Ladies: Rhetoric, Gender, Property* (London: Methuen, 1987), pp. 155–77; and Margaret Davies, 'The Proper: Discourses of Purity', *Law and Critique*, Vol. 9, No. 2, 1998, pp. 147–73.
76. Gareth Stedman Jones, *Outcast London: A Study in the Relationship Between Classes in Victorian Society* (Harmondsworth: Penguin, 1976), p. 289; Gatrell, 'Crime, Authority and the Policeman-state', p. 252.
77. For Chadwick on miasma and disease see Edwin Chadwick, *Report on the Sanitary Condition of the Labouring Population of Great Britain* (Edinburgh: Edinburgh University Press, 1965), pp. 371, 375, 409, and 'New Poor Law', p. 498. Also see R.A. Lewis, *Edwin Chadwick and the Public Health Movement 1832–1854* (London: Longmans, 1952), p. 42; Frank Mort, *Dangerous Sexualities: Medico-Moral Politics in England Since 1830* (London: Routledge, 1987), p. 28.
78. The phrase is from Alain Corbin, *The Foul and the Fragrant: Odour and the Social Imagination* (London: Papermac, 1996), p. 55. Incidentally, it is perhaps worth noting that before fingerprints were in use Barruel in France had offered his discoveries on the odour of blood to the police, suggesting the use of 'smell prints' to identify the criminal (Corbin, p. 187).
79. Chadwick, *Report on the Sanitary Condition*, p. 413.
80. Norbert Elias, *The Civilizing Process, Volume 1: The History of Manners* (1939), trans. Edmund Jephcott (Oxford: Basil Blackwell, 1978), pp. 51, 126–9, 134–52; Peter Linebaugh, '(Marxist) Social History and (Conservative) Legal History: A Reply to Professor Langbein', in David Sugarman (ed.), *Law in History: Histories of Law and Society, Volume 1* (Aldershot: Dartmouth, 1996), p. 346. As William Connolly, *Political Theory and Modernity* (Oxford: Blackwell, 1988), p. 13, notes, the quest for order often leads to defining as 'otherness' all conduct and events which do not conform to this order: 'They become dirt, matter out of place, irrationality, abnormality, waste, sickness, perversity, incapacity, disorder, madness, unfreedom.'
81. Himmelfarb, *Idea of Poverty*, pp. 356–8; 'The Culture of Poverty', in H.J. Dyos and Michael Wolff (eds), *The Victorian City: Images and Realities, Volume 2* (London: Routledge, 1973), p. 719.
82. M.W. Flinn, 'Introduction' to Chadwick, *Report on the Sanitary Condition*, p. 60; and see Geoffrey Pearson, *The Deviant Imagination: Psychiatry, Social Work and Social Change* (London: Macmillan, 1975), p. 164.
83. Sigmund Freud, 'Character and Anal Eroticism' (1908), in *The Standard edition of the Complete Psychological Works of Sigmund Freud, Volume IX* (London: The Hogarth Press, 1959), p. 172. Freud cites it in quotation marks, but no source is given.

84. Mary Douglas, *Purity and Danger: An Analysis of the Concepts of Pollution and Taboo* (London: Ark Paperbacks, 1984), pp. 2, 35. Cleanliness may have been next to the virtue of godliness for John Wesley, but for the sanitary reformers of the nineteenth century it was closer to another virtue, that of orderliness: 'a place for every thing, and every thing in its place', as Catharine Beecher put it in her famous *Treatise on Domestic Economy* (1841). The maxim was presented as an alternative to 'cleanliness is next to godliness' on the grounds that most Americans had next to no access to decent plumbing. Beecher also noted that for cleanliness 'there was no one thing, more necessary...than *a habit of system and order*'. See Suellen Hoy, *Chasing Dirt: The American Pursuit of Cleanliness* (Oxford: Oxford University Press, 1995), pp. 21, 32.

85. Richard L. Schoenwald, 'Training Urban Man: A Hypothesis about the Sanitary Movement', in Dyos and Wolff (eds), *Victorian City*, pp. 675–7.

86. Chadwick, *Report on the Sanitary Condition*, pp. 266–8, 308.

87. See Malcolm Young, *An Inside Job: Policing and Police Culture in Britain* (Oxford: Clarendon Press, 1991), pp. 13, 65, 76, 85, 113–14, 130, 134–6, 140, 165, 388. Mike Brogden, *On the Mersey Beat: Policing Liverpool Between the Wars* (Oxford: Oxford University Press, 1991), p. 1; Brogden, *Police: Autonomy and Consent*, p. 60; David Smith and Jeremy Gray, *Police and People in London, Vol. IV: The Police in Action* (London: Policy Studies Institute, 1983); Peter K. Manning, *Police Work: The Social Organization of Policing* (Cambridge, MA: MIT Press, 1977), pp. 112, 236–7.

88. Young, *An Inside Job*, pp. 114, 141.

89. *Police*, September 1970, p. 6, cited in Robert Reiner, *The Politics of the Police*, Second edition (London: Harvester Wheatsheaf, 1992), p. 77.

90. Michel Foucault, *The Birth of the Clinic: An Archaeology of Medical Perception* (1963), trans. Alan Sheridan (London: Routledge, 1973), p. 26.

91. See *A System of Complete Medical Police: Selections from Johann Peter Frank*, ed. Erna Lesky (Baltimore, Maryland: Johns Hopkins University Press, 1976), p. 12. For the influence of the police theorists on Frank see Gertrud Kroeger, *The Concept of Social Medicine as Presented by Physicians and other Writers in Germany, 1779–1932* (Chicago: Julius Rosenwald Fund, 1937), pp. 6–7; George Rosen, 'Cameralism and the Concept of Medical Police', *Bulletin of the History of Medicine*, Vol. 27, 1953, pp. 21–42.

92. John Roberton, *A Treatise on Medical Police, and Diet, Regimen, etc.* (Edinburgh, 1809), p. x.

93. See L.J. Jordanova, 'Policing Public Health in France 1780–1815', in Teizo Ogawa (ed.), *Public Health: Proceedings of the 5th International Symposium on the Comparative History of Medicine* (Tokyo: Saikon, 1981); Leona Baumgartner and Elizabeth Mapelsden Ramsey, 'Johann Peter Frank and his *System einer vollständigen medicinischen Polizey*', *Annals of Medical History*, Vol. V, 1933, pp. 525–32 and Vol. VI, 1934, pp. 69–90; Brenda White, 'Medical Police, Politics and Police: The Fate of John Roberton', *Medical History*, Vol. 27, 1983, pp. 407–22; Finer, *Life and Times*, p. 210.

94. See Thomas Ferguson, *The Dawn of Scottish Social Welfare: A Survey from Medieval Times to 1863* (London: Thomas Nelson and Sons, 1948), pp. 12, 56–7, 97, 143–4. It is perhaps worth noting that Edinburgh University also had a Chair in Medical Jurisprudence and Police.

95. *The British and Foreign Medical Review*, Vol. XIV, October 1842, pp. 446–61.

96. W. Strange, 'Formation of a System of Medical Police and Public Hygiene', *London Medical Gazette*, II, 1846, pp. 452–7, p. 453; James Black, 'Lectures on Public Hygiene and Medical Police', *Provincial Medical and Surgical Journal*, 1844, pp. 275–80, 327–32, 359–64, 391–6, 551–7. For similar trends in America see Hoy, *Chasing Dirt*, pp. 27, 60.
97. Carson and Idzikowska, 'Social Production of Scottish Policing', p. 273.
98. See George Rosen, 'The Fate of the Concept of Medical Police', *Centaurus*, Vol. 5, No. 2, 1957, pp. 97–113, p. 108.
99. Charles Townsend, *Making the Peace: Public Order and Public Security in Modern Britain* (Oxford: Oxford University Press, 1993), p. 140.
100. 'The Police System of London', *The Edinburgh Review*, 96, July 1852, pp. 1–33; Emsley, *English Police*, p. 44, 83; Gatrell, 'Decline of Theft and Violence', p. 260; Thomas Ferguson, *Scottish Social Welfare 1864–1914* (Edinburgh: E. and S. Livingstone, 1958), p. 162.
101. David Dixon, *Law in Policing: Legal Regulation and Police Practices* (Oxford: Clarendon Press, 1997), p. 51.
102. In H. Aubrey Husband, *The Student's Handbook of Forensic Medicine and Medical Police* (Edinburgh: E. and S. Livingstone, 1877), for example, the links between medicine and police are slowly being turned into a question of forensics rather than public health.
103. See George Rosen, *From Medical Police to Social Medicine: Essays on the History of Health Care* (New York: Science History Publications, 1974). Also George Rosen, *A History of Public Health* (New York: MD Publications, 1958), p. 163; 'Fate of the Concept of Medical Police', pp. 101, 108, 111.
104. Brogden, *Police: Autonomy and Consent*, p. 82; Jack Douglas, *American Social Order: Social Rules in a Pluralistic Society* (New York: Free Press, 1971), p. 51.
105. Brogden and Brogden, 'From Henry III to Liverpool 8', p. 47.

Chapter 5

1. Egon Bittner, 'Florence Nightingale in Pursuit of Willie Sutton: A Theory of Police', in Herbert Jacob (ed.), *The Potential of Reform of Criminal Justice* (London: Sage, 1974).
2. V.A.C. Gatrell, 'Crime, Authority and the Policeman-state', in F.M.L. Thompson (ed.), *The Cambridge Social History of Britain 1750–1950, Volume 3: Social Agencies and Institutions* (Cambridge: Cambridge University Press, 1990), p. 245.
3. Paul Gilroy and Stuart Sim, 'Law, Order and the State of the Left', in Phil Scraton (ed.), *Law, Order and the Authoritarian State* (Milton Keynes: Open University Press, 1987), p. 71.
4. See Michael Banton, *The Policeman in the Community* (London: Tavistock, 1964), pp. 2, 7, 127; Egon Bittner, 'The Police on Skid-row: A Study of Peace Keeping', *American Sociological Review*, Vol. 32, No. 5, 1967, pp. 699–715; David Bayley, 'What Do the Police Do?', in William Salusbury, Joy Mott and Tim Newburn (eds), *Themes in Contemporary Policing* (London: Policy Studies Institute, 1996), pp. 31–3; Steven Spitzer and Andrew Scull, 'Privatization and Capitalist Development: The Case of the Private Police', *Social Problems*, Vol. 25, No. 1, 1977, pp. 18–29; A. Keith Bottomley and Clive A. Coleman, 'Criminal Statistics: The Police Role in the Discovery and Detection of Crime', *International Journal of*

Criminology and Penology, Vol. 4, 1976, pp. 33–58; Richard V. Ericson, *Reproducing Order: A Study of Police Patrolwork* (Toronto: University of Toronto Press, 1982), pp. 5–6, 206; Robert Reiner, *The Politics of the Police*, Second edition (London: Harvester Wheatsheaf, 1992), pp. 139–46; Richard V. Ericson and Kevin D. Haggerty, *Policing the Risk Society* (Oxford: Clarendon Press, 1997), p. 19.

5. Reiner, *Politics of the Police*, p. 212.
6. Bittner, 'Florence Nightingale in Pursuit of Willie Sutton', p. 30.
7. The Mental Health Act 1959 allowed an officer to remove a person to a place of safety if they 'appear to him to be suffering from mental disorder'. The Mental Health Act 1983 left the same powers unchanged.
8. In the light of the argument here about police, work and poverty, it is pertinent to point out that 'truant' originally referred to the idle and the vagabond.
9. Michael Brogden, *The Police: Autonomy and Consent* (London: Academic Press, 1982), pp. 23, 206–8; Ericson and Haggerty, *Policing the Risk Society*, p. 127.
10. Maurice Punch, 'The Secret Social Service', in Simon Holdaway (ed.), *The British Police* (London: Edward Arnold, 1979).
11. Reiner, *Politics of the Police*, pp. 139–46.
12. Herbert Packer, *The Limits of the Criminal Sanction* (Stanford, CA: Stanford University Press, 1968).
13. David Dixon, *Law in Policing: Legal Regulation and Police Practices* (Oxford: Clarendon Press, 1997), p. 130; also see Satnam Choong, *Policing as Social Discipline* (Oxford: Clarendon Press, 1997), pp. 9–10. For an account of abuses evident at an early stage see Wilbur R. Miller, *Cops and Bobbies: Police Authority in New York and London, 1830–1870* (Chicago: University of Chicago Press, 1977), pp. 74–7. On the rise of police as prosecutors see Douglas Hay and Francis Snyder, 'Using the Criminal Law, 1750–1850: Policing, Private Prosecution, and the State', in Douglas Hay and Francis Snyder (eds), *Policing and Prosecution in Britain, 1750–1850* (Oxford: Clarendon Press, 1989).
14. Cited in Choong, *Policing as Social Discipline*, p. 10; Dixon, *Law in Policing*, p. 143.
15. Choong, *Policing as Social Discipline*, pp. 11–16, 34 (Mark and McNee cited p. 13); also see John Baxter and Laurence Kofman, 'Introduction', in John Baxter and Laurence Kofman (eds), *Police: The Constitution and the Community* (Abingdon, Oxon: Professional Books, 1985), p. 1; Reiner, *Politics of the Police*, p, 82.
16. Mike McConville, Andrew Sanders and Roger Leng, *The Case for the Prosecution: Police Suspects and the Construction of Criminality* (London: Routledge, 1991), p. 177; Andrew Sanders and Richard Young, *Criminal Justice* (London: Butterworths, 1994), p. 124.
17. Choong, *Policing as Social Discipline*, p. 34. McConville, Sanders and Leng, *Case for the Prosecution*, pp. 175, 188–9; Tom Bowden, *Beyond the Limits of the Law: A Comparative Study of the Police in Crisis Politics* (Harmondsworth: Penguin, 1978); Ivor Jennings, *The Sedition Bill Explained* (London: New Statesman and Nation, 1934), p. 11.
18. Andrew Sanders and Richard Young, 'The Rule of Law, Due Process and Pre-trial Criminal Justice', *Current Legal Problems*, Vol. 47, No. 2, 1994, pp. 125–56, p. 154; Egon Bittner, *The Functions of the Police in Modern Society: A Review of Background Factors, Current Practices, and Possible Role Models* (New York: Jason

Aronson, 1975), p. 34; Gary T. Marx, *Under Cover: Police Surveillance in America* (Berkeley: University of California Press, 1988), p. 190: 'in practice, "due process" has little relevance to contemporary police actions, even for cases that are "shocking to the universal sense of justice"'.

19. Sanders and Young, 'Rule of Law, Due Process and Pre-trial Criminal Justice'.

20. Edwin Chadwick, 'The New Poor Law', *Edinburgh Review*, 63, 1836, pp. 487–537, p. 528; Lord Scarman, *The Scarman Report: The Brixton Disorders 10–12 April 1981* (Harmondsworth: Penguin, 1982), s. 4.58.

21. Sanders and Young, *Criminal Justice*, p. 209.

22. Mike Brogden, *On the Mersey Beat: Policing Liverpool Between the Wars* (Oxford: Oxford University Press, 1991), p. 92. James Wilson, *Varieties of Police Behaviour* (Cambridge, MA: Harvard University Press, 1968), p. 7: 'the police department has the special property...that within it discretion increases as one moves down the hierarchy'. This distinguishes the police from its closest political cousin, the military, the lowest levels of which obey orders with virtually no discretion.

23. Gatrell, 'Crime, Authority and the Policeman-state', p. 278. Also Clive Emsley, *Crime and Society in England 1750–1900* (London: Longman, 1996), p. 23.

24. Duncan Campbell, 'Police Stop Blacks Eight Times More than Whites', *Guardian*, 27 July 1998; Susan Edwards, *Policing 'Domestic' Violence: Women, Law and the State* (London: Sage, 1989), pp. 81–110.

25. Carl B. Klockars, *The Idea of Police* (London: Sage, 1985), p. 92.

26. *The Police and Criminal Evidence Act 1984* (London: Sweet and Maxwell/Police Review, 1985), sections 41, 42, 54, 55, 61, 62; Home Office circular 22/92, and PACE sections 63 and 65 as amended by the Criminal Justice and Public Order Act 1994, cited in Choong, *Policing as Social Discipline*, pp. 98, 219.

27. Following the trial based heavily on the video evidence of the 53 blows rained down on the body of King, the jury decided that no assault had taken place. As P.A.J. Waddington, *Policing Citizens* (London: UCL Press, 1999), p. 179, notes, 'beating someone almost senseless is something that police can do with the utmost propriety *if it is appropriate or necessary for a lawful purpose*'.

28. Doreen McBarnet, *Conviction: Law, the State and the Construction of Justice* (London: Macmillan, 1981), p. 35.

29. Choong, *Policing as Social Discipline*, p. 217.

30. See for example, Ronald Dworkin, *Taking Rights Seriously* (London: Duckworth, 1978), pp. 31–9.

31. Laurence Lustgarten, *The Governance of Police* (London: Sweet and Maxwell, 1986), pp. 10, 15, 30, 68–70; also Christopher L. Ryan and Katherine S. Williams, 'Police Discretion', *Public Law*, 1986, pp. 285–310; Michael Lipsky, *Street-Level Bureaucracy: Dilemmas of the Individual in Public Services* (New York: Russell Sage Foundation, 1980).

32. Lord Devlin, for example, noted in 1960 that 'the Judges' Rules were made for the guidance of the police and not for the circumscription of the judicial power'. It was also held in *R. v. Prager* (1972) that a voluntary confession made in breach of the Rules could not be made inadmissable since that 'would exalt the Judges' Rules into rules of law'; cited in McBarnet, *Conviction*, p. 67. Sanders and Young, *Criminal Justice*, p. 124, note that the obligation on the police to inform suspects of the right to legal advice was, given its place in the Judges' Rules, merely an 'administrative direction'. Also see Sanders and Young,

'Rule of Law, Due Process and Pre-trial Criminal Justice', pp. 128–9; Dixon, *Law in Policing*, p. 135; Choong, *Policing as Social Discipline*, pp. 13–18.

33. Kenneth Culp Davis, *Discretionary Justice: A Preliminary Inquiry* (Urbana: University of Illinois Press, 1971), p. 222.

34. Dixon, *Law in Policing*, p. 142; Sanders and Young, *Criminal Justice*, p. 99.

35. *Council of Civil Service Unions v. Minister for the Civil Service* (1984), cited in D.J. Galligan, *Discretionary Powers: A Legal Study of Official Discretion* (Oxford: Oxford University Press, 1986), p. 263.

36. David Smith and Jeremy Gray, *Police and People in London, Vol. IV: The Police in Action* (London: Policy Studies Institute, 1983), p. 232. Given this wide interpretation and use of 'reasonable suspicion', the number of stops and searches should perhaps not surprise us: in 1998 in Britain police made 1,050,700 stops and searches, only 10 per cent of which led to an arrest; 'Stop and Search at Record Level', *Guardian*, 23 January 1999. Mike Davis, *City of Quartz: Excavating the Future in Los Angeles* (London: Vintage, 1992), p. 272, notes that in Los Angeles wearing red shoelaces has been used as reasonable grounds for arrest.

37. See McBarnet, *Conviction*, p. 167; and 'Legal Form and Legal Mystification: An Analytical Postscript on the Scottish Criminal Justice Act, the Royal Commission on Criminal Procedure, and the Politics of Law and Order', *International Journal of the Sociology of Law*, Vol. 10, 1982, pp. 409–17; Mike Brogden, 'Stopping the People – Crime Control versus Social Control', in Baxter and Kofman (eds), *Police*, p. 94.

38. See Mark Neocleous, *Administering Civil Society: Towards a Theory of State Power* (London: Macmillan, 1996), p. 159.

39. See Alan Booth, 'An Administrative Experiment in Unemployment Policy in the Thirties', *Public Administration*, Vol. 56, 1978, pp. 139–57; Tony Prosser, 'The Politics of Discretion: Aspects of Discretionary Power in the Supplementary Benefits Scheme', in Michael Adler and Stewart Asquith (eds), *Discretion and Welfare* (London: Heinemann, 1981), p. 157.

40. See Neocleous, *Administering Civil Society*, Chapter 5, for a full account.

41. Patrick Devlin, *The Judge* (Oxford: Oxford University Press, 1979), pp. 71, 83. Interestingly, Devlin also distinguishes between types of questioning that the police may make on the grounds that some questioning is judicial and some administrative. 'There is a distinction, clear enough in principle though difficult to apply, between asking for information needed for an investigation and obtaining admissions needed for proof. Questioning in the first category is administrative in character, and in the second judicial' (p. 80).

42. Brogden, *Police: Autonomy and Consent*, pp. 24–5; Waddington, *Policing Citizens*, p. 186.

43. Jeffrey Jowell, 'The Legal Control of Administrative Discretion', *Public Law*, 1973, pp. 178–220, p. 217.

44. The phrase was in the form of a question to the Home Secretary, Lord Melbourne, in 1833 at the inquest into an anti-police demonstration in Clerkenwell which turned into a riot at which one police officer was stabbed to death. Melbourne's answer to the question was a firm 'yes'. The 1834 Report which emerged from the inquiry argued for 'the necessity of finally separating the judicial and executive functions of the Police Magistrates'. See David Ascoli, *The Queen's Peace: The Origins and Development of the Metropolitan Police 1829–1979* (London: Hamish Hamilton, 1979), p. 106.

45. The first Commissioners, Rowan and Mayne, were unclear about their judi-cial-cum-executive position. Ascoli, *Queen's Peace*, p. 103, claims that between April and November of 1832 alone, Mayne wrote eleven letters to the Home Office on this subject.

46. Lustgarten, *Governance of Police*, p. 43.

47. Reiner, *Politics of the Police*, pp. 239–48.

48. Bittner, 'Police on Skid-row', p. 699. For a comment on the 'profound administrative confusion' created by the blurring of the distinction between the police as an executive or judicial body in Australia see Mark Finnane, *Police and Government: Histories of Policing in Australia* (Oxford: Oxford University Press, 1994), pp. 14–17.

49. The first is from David Donnison, *The Politics of Poverty* (Oxford: Martin Robertson, 1982), p. 93, the second from Julian Fulbrook, *Administrative Justice and the Unemployed* (London: Mansell, 1978), p. 201. Also see Christopher Ham and Michael Hill, *The Policy Process in the Modern Capitalist State* (Brighton: Harvester, 1984), p. 156; Michael Adler and Stewart Asquith, 'Discretion and Power', in Adler and Asquith (eds), *Discretion and Welfare*, p. 9. And note Roscoe Pound, *An Introduction to the Philosophy of Law* (New Haven: Yale University Press, 1954), p. 54: 'Almost all of the problems of jurisprudence come down to a fundamental one of rule and discretion.'

50. Galligan, *Discretionary Powers*, p. 91.

51. A.V. Dicey, *An Introduction to the Study of the Law of the Constitution*, Tenth edition (London: Macmillan, 1959), p. 188; F.A. Hayek, *The Constitution of Liberty* (London: Routledge, 1960), p. 213; Bob Jessop, 'The Transformation of the State in Post-war Britain', in Richard Scase (ed.), *The State in Western Europe* (London: Croom Helm, 1980), p. 62. As I comment in *Administering Civil Society*, p. 162, too many writers when discussing law work with simple dichotomies – contract v. status, law v. administration, courts v. tribunals – encouraging us to think of them as historical 'stages', to regard one as more 'modern' than the other and to assume that such things as administration occur somehow *outside* the sphere of law. Worse, such approaches assume that anything which cannot be fitted into the liberal concept of law is some-how a problem.

52. Isaac D. Balbus, 'Commodity Form and Legal Form: An Essay on the "Relative Autonomy" of the Law', in Charles Reasons and Robert Rich (eds), *The Sociology of Law: A Conflict Perspective* (Toronto: Butterworths, 1978), p. 84; and Richard Titmuss, 'Welfare "Rights", Law and Discretion', *Political Quarterly*, Vol. 42, 1971, 113–32, p. 124. Also see Hugh Collins, *Marxism and Law* (Oxford: Oxford University Press, 1982), p. 10.

53. E.P. Thompson, *Whigs and Hunters: The Origin of the Black Act* (Harmondsworth: Penguin, 1977), pp. 265–6.

54. Bob Fine, *Democracy and the Rule of Law* (London: Pluto Press, 1984), p. 175.

55. Fine, *Democracy and the Rule of Law*, p. 175; Bob Fine and Robert Millar, 'Introduction: The Law of the Market and the Rule of Law', in Bob Fine and Robert Millar (eds), *Policing the Miners' Strike* (London: Lawrence and Wishart, 1985), p. 11. It must be said in fairness that Thompson himself has revealed in his own work on this subject the class basis of the rule of law, which makes his comments on its unqualified goodness even odder, but this is not the place to pursue such problems.

154   The Fabrication of Social Order

56. Thompson, *Whigs and Hunters*, p. 260.
57. Thompson, *Whigs and Hunters*, p. 268. Thompson's position is not unconnected to his view that 'in any known society, some of the functions of the police are as necessary and legitimate as those of firemen and of ambulancemen' ('The Secret State' [1976], in *Writing by Candlelight* [London: Merlin, 1980], p. 174).
58. McBarnet, *Conviction*, pp. 4–5.
59. John Baxter, 'Policing and the Rule of Law', in Baxter and Kofman (eds), *Police*, p. 41.
60. Despite the wealth of research to suggest that the equation 'police = law' is fundamentally misleading, it is still common in some academic work. The index entry for 'police' in Barry Buzan, *People, States and Fear*, Second edition (London: Harvester Wheatsheaf, 1991), runs: *see* law. And this despite the fact that where the author mentions police he does so in outside of any discussion of law (pp. 90, 100).
61. Sir Robert Mark, *Policing a Perplexed Society* (London: George Allen and Unwin, 1977), p. 56: 'The fact that the British police are answerable to the law, that we act on behalf of the community and not under the mantle of government, makes us the least powerful, the most accountable, and therefore the most acceptable police in the world.' There is of course just a little anglocentricism at play here: the assumption is often that it is the *British* police that is genuinely consistent with the rule of law, foreigners having to put up with all sorts of undemocratic police organizations (hence their propensity for 'police states'). As Lustgarten, *Governance of Police*, p. 1, notes, some people assume that 'democracy speaks only the Queen's English'.
62. V.A.C. Gatrell, *The Hanging Tree: Execution and the English People 1770–1868* (Oxford: Oxford University Press, 1994), p. 519; Paul W. Kahn, *The Reign of Law: Marbury v. Madison and the Construction of America* (New Haven: Yale University Press, 1997), pp. 67, 96–9, 178, 187.
63. Peter Manning, *Police Work: The Social Organization of Policing* (Cambridge, MA: MIT Press, 1977), pp. 7, 101.
64. Walter Benjamin, 'Critique of Violence' (1920–1), in *One Way Street and Other Writings*, trans. Edmund Jephcott and Kingsley Shorter (London: Verso, 1985), pp. 141–2.
65. See See R.N. Berki, *Security and Society: Reflections on Law, Order and Politics* (London: Dent and Sons, 1986), p. 113; C. Vick, 'An Introduction to Aspects of Public Order and the Police', in J.R. Thackrah (ed.), *Contemporary Policing: An Examination of Society in the 1980s* (London: Sphere Reference, 1985), p. 169; Roger Cotterrell, *Law's Community: Legal Theory in Sociological Perspective* (Oxford: Clarendon Press, 1995), p. 250; Stuart Hall, Chas Crichter, Tony Jefferson, John Clarke and Brian Roberts, *Policing the Crisis: Mugging, the State, and Law and Order* (London: Macmillan, 1978), p. 208.
66. Georg Lukács, 'Legality and Illegality' (1920), in *History and Class Consciousness*, trans. Rodney Livingstone (London: Merlin, 1971), p. 268.
67. V.A.C. Gatrell, 'The Decline of Theft and Violence in Victorian and Edwardian England', in V.A.C. Gatrell, Bruce Lenman and Geoffrey Parker (eds), *Crime and the Law: The Social History of Crime in Western Europe since 1500* (London: Europa, 1980), pp. 254–5.
68. Lustgarten, *Governance of Police*, p. 15; Jerome H. Skolnick, *Justice Without*

Trial: Law Enforcement in Democratic Society, Second edition (New York: John Wiley, 1975), pp. 6–7.

69. Scarman, *The Scarman Report*, s. 4.58. In the previous paragraph Scarman rationalizes such prioritization by describing order as 'the normal state of society'.
70. Zygmunt Bauman, *In Search of Politics* (Cambridge: Polity Press, 1999), p. 14.
71. The comment is from a New South Wales police officer, cited in Dixon, *Law in Policing*, p. 49; also see McConville, Sanders and Leng, *Case for the Prosecution*, pp. 175, 188–9.
72. Ericson, *Reproducing Order*, pp. 16, 197. As he notes (p. 200), the campaign for law and order should in fact read 'order, and law'; also McConville, Sanders and Leng, *Case for the Prosecution*, p. 43.
73. Slavoj Žižek, *Tarrying with the Negative: Kant, Hegel, and the Critique of Ideology* (Durham: Duke University Press, 1993), p. 234.
74. Malcolm Young, *In the Sticks: Cultural Identity in a Rural Police Force* (Oxford: Clarendon Press, 1993), p. 177; Simon Holdaway, *Inside the British Police: A Force at Work* (Oxford: Basil Blackwell, 1983), p. 82; also Ericson, *Reproducing Order*, p. 9. Malcolm Young, *An Inside Job: Policing and Police Culture in Britain* (Oxford: Clarendon Press, 1991), p. 175, notes one case in which officers interviewed a man regarding a case of indecent exposure, in which a woman had complained about a man appearing from the bushes in a park brandishing what she described as 'his weapon'. The weapon in question turned out to be made from a piece of nylon stuffed with cotton wool. This posed the problem of what charge, if any, could be made, since 'flashers' are required in law to have 'wilfully, openly and obscenely exposed the person'. The problem for the officers was that the act appeared *disorderly* but was *ambiguous* in terms of the law. Young reports one officer raising the problem with his senior: 'we may have one insulted female, boss, but we haven't got a real prick, so what's the offence?' The officers then searched diligently through the reference books to *fix* the behaviour ('try looking up the Waggling of Wool Willies Act', commented one officer). The officers were concerned with making the offence in question 'fit known patterns of disorder' and thus erase the ambiguity by imposing a classificatory system for the ordering of offences on something previously unknown. The officers could not function without ordering the disorderly.
75. G.W.F. Hegel, *Lectures on Natural Right and Political Science* (1817–1819), trans. J. Michael Stewart and Peter C. Hodgson (California: University of California Press, 1995), p. 213: 'For the police official, I am a subjectively strange individual.'
76. Douglas A. Smith and Christy A. Visher, 'Street-level Justice: Situational Determinants of Police Arrest Decisions', *Social Problems*, Vol. 29, No. 2, 1981, pp. 167–77, p. 172; McConville, Sanders and Leng, *Case for the Prosecution*, pp. 25, 197.
77. Walter Benjamin, 'Theses on the Philosophy of History' (1940), in *Illuminations*, trans. Harry Zohn (London: Fontana, 1973), p. 259; Giorgio Agamben, 'The Sovereign Police', trans. Brian Massumi, in Brian Massumi (ed.), *The Politics of Everyday Fear* (Minneapolis: University of Minnesota Press, 1993), p. 62.
78. McConville, Sanders and Leng, *Case for the Prosecution*, pp. 203–4.
79. Allan Silver, 'The Demand for Order in Civil Society: A Review of Some Themes in the History of Urban Crime, Police, and Riot', in David Bordua (ed.), *The Police: Six Sociological Essays* (New York: John Wiley, 1967).

80. See Karl Marx, 'Critique of Hegel's Doctrine of the State', in *Early Writings*, trans. Rodney Livingstone and Gregor Benton (Harmondsworth: Penguin, 1975), p. 107.
81. Geoffrey Pearson, *Hooligan: A History of Respectable Fears* (London: Macmillan, 1983), p. 230; also see Gatrell, 'Crime, Authority and the Policeman-state', p. 244; Gatrell, 'Decline of Theft and Violence', p. 249; McConville, Sanders and Leng, *Case for the Prosecution*, p. 208.
82. Roland Barthes, 'Writing Degree Zero', in *A Barthes Reader*, ed. Susan Sontag (London: Jonathan Cape, 1982), p. 43.
83. See Sanders and Young, *Criminal Justice*, p. 82; Dixon, *Law in Policing*, pp. 52–3. The provision in PACE, section 24 (6) and (7), breaks this legitimizing myth.
84. Charles Reith, *A New Study of Police History* (Edinburgh: Oliver and Boyd, 1956), p. 287. The anglocentricism already noted is frequently present in such assumptions. Reith, *The Blind Eye of History* (London: Faber and Faber, 1952), p. 20, differentiates between two kinds of police: 'the kin police or Anglo-Saxon police system, and the ruler-appointed *gendarmerie*, or despotic totalitarian police system. The first represents, basically, force exercised indirectly, by the people, from below, upwards. The other represents force exercised, by authority, from above, downwards.' Quite how police power is directed 'upwards' by the people is never explained.
85. Brian Chapman, *Police State* (London: Macmillan, 1971), pp. 118–19.
86. See Mark Neocleous, *Fascism* (Milton Keynes: Open University Press, 1997), pp. 38–53.
87. Reiner, *Politics of the Police*, pp. 2, 92–3, 121–4.
88. As one major court judgment – *Fisher v. Oldham* (1930) – held, the police officer 'is a servant of the State, a ministerial officer of the central power, though subject in some respects, to local supervision and local regulation'. The judgment has been confirmed in subsequent rulings.
89. Hannah Arendt, *The Origins of Totalitarianism* (1950), (San Diego: Harcourt Brace and Co., 1973), p. 435.
90. McConville, Sanders and Leng, *Case for the Prosecution*, p. 180.
91. Richard Quinney, 'Crime Control in Capitalist Society: A Critical Philosophy of Legal Order', in Ian Taylor, Paul Walton and Jock Young (eds), *Critical Criminology* (London: Routledge, 1975), p. 196.
92. Manning, *Police Work*, p. 361.
93. Benjamin, 'Critique of Violence', pp. 141–2.

Index

absolutism, 3
Administering Civil Society, xiii, xiv, 65, 69
administration
  against critique, xv
  and law, 102–7
  and welfare, 32, 90
  police as, xiii, xiv, 4, 65–6, 91, 94–5, 99–108, 118
  poverty and, 16
  see also political administration
Agger, B., xiv
Anderson, P., 19, 34
Appleby, J., 43
Aquinas, T., 6
Arendt, H., 43, 117
Aristotle, 9–11
arrest, 95–9
Ashton, T.S., 71
Associated Provincial Picture Houses v. *Wednesbury Corporation* 1948, 102–3
Association of Chief Police Officers, 106

Bacon, F., 10
Balbus, I., 107
Barthes, R., xiv
Bauman, Z., 112
Baxter, J., 109
Beccaria, C., 32, 49
Benjamin, W., 111, 118
Bentham, J., 10, 43, 53
Bittner, E., x, 93, 117
Black Act 1723, 79
Brogden, M., 74, 91, 99
Brown, V., 23, 25
Butler, J., xiv

cameralism, 12–21, 30, 32, 48, 57
capital, xi, xii, 1–2, 5, 7, 11–21, 27–9, 34, 37, 39–41, 60, 72
Carson, K., 75
Caygill, H., 24

Chadwick, E., 66, 67, 70, 76, 81, 85–7, 88, 99
Chapman, B., 9, 116
Choong, S., 97, 98
civil society, *see* state
claimants, 81–2
class
  and crime, 53–6, 70–84, 100
  and law and order, 40–1, 114–15, 118
  and liberalism, 38–9,
  and security, 44, 59, 61–2
  as dirt, 85–8
  fabrication of, xii, 16–20, 65, 70–84
  Hegel on, 47–8,
  Colquhoun on, 53–6
  subsumption of struggle, 103
cleanliness, *see* hygiene
Colbert, J.B., 18, 28
Colquhoun, P., 44, 45, 46–7, 49–59, 67, 70, 72–4
communism, 61
consent, xi
County and Borough Police Act 1856, 67
Cowan, R., 88, 89
crime, xiv, 4, 64, 68, 91
  as myth, 92–5
  class and, 53–6, 70–84, 100
  Colquhoun on, 49–56
  custom and, 69–76
  poverty and, 66–78
  Smith on 23–4
Criminal Law Act 1967, 98, 101
criminology, ix, xi–xii, xiii, 92–4
Critchley, T.A., 46
Culp Davis, K., 102

Dean, M., 6
Delamare, N., 4, 5, 15
Der Derian, J., 61
Derrida, J., 84
Devlin, P., 96, 101

157

Dicey, A.V., 107
Dillon, M., 60
Diplock, Lord, 102
dirt, 84–8
discipline, ix, 17, 41
discretion, 99–106, 112
discrimination, 99–100
disease, 84–9
Disraeli, B., 79
Dithmar, J.C., 12
Ditton, J., 72
Dixon, D., 96
Dobb, M., 14
Donoughmore Committee 1932, 104
Dorwart, R.A., 9, 11
due process, 95

Elias, N., 86
Elton, G.R., 10
Engels, F., 83
executive power, 101–2, 104–6

Factory Act 1833, 83
fascism, 116
Federalists, 31
Ferguson, A., 27, 43
fetishism, 107, 109–10
feudalism, x, 1–3
Fielding, H., 49–50, 57
Fielding, J., 49–50, 57
Flinn, M.W., 86
Forbes, D., 26
Ford Motors, 84
Foucauldians, ix–x
Foucault, M., ix, xiii, 8, 18, 19, 20, 83, 88
Frank, J.P., 88
Frederick the Great, 24
Freud, S., 86

Galligan, D.J., 107
Garfinkel v. *Metropolitan Police*
   Commissioner 1972, 98
Gatrell, V.A.C., 64, 66, 92, 100, 111
Ghani v. *Jones* 1970, 98
Gordon, C., 44
governmentality, ix
Gunn, J.A.W., 34

Habitual Criminals Act 1869, 100

Hall, S., 81
Hayek, F.A., 107
Hecksher, E., 14
Hegel, G.W.F., xiii, 44, 45–9, 54, 57–9
Herbert, C-J., 26, 27, 35
hierarchy, 38, 40, 114
Highways Act 1835
Himmelfarb, G., 82, 86
Hirschman, A., 35
Hirst, P., xiii
Hobbes, T., xi, 3, 7, 43, 61
Holdaway, S., 113
Holdsworth, W., 40
Holgate-Mohammed v. *Duke* 1984, 98,
   101, 102
Hooker, R., 7, 38
Houghton and Franciosy, 97
Hughes, S., 67
Hull, I., 14
Humboldt, W. v., 30–1, 43
hygiene, 23, 84–9

idleness, *see* vagrancy
independence, 34–41
indigence, *see* vagrancy; poverty
interest, 34–41

James I, 7
Jefferson, T., 31
Jessop, B., 107
Jowell, J., 105
Jowitt, W., 63
Judges' Rules, 95, 96, 97, 98
Justi, J.H.G.v., 12–13, 14, 30

Kant, I., 29–30, 35–6, 57
Kaplan, S., 26, 28
Knemeyer, F-L., 5

Laroque Report (1984), 63
Lasker, E., 29, 110
law, xii, xiii, 29–34, 37, 39, 40–1, 83–4,
   91, 94, 95–118
LeDonne, J., 10
legitimacy, xi, 109–14
Leibniz, G.W., 30
Lemaire, J-C., 4, 16
liberalism, xi, xiii–xiv, 21, 22–44, 45,
   59, 61, 101, 107, 108, 110, 116–17

Linebaugh, P., 40, 55
Locke, J., 38, 39
Louis XIV, 19
Louis XV, 4, 26
Lüdtke, A., 75
Lukács, G., 111
Lustgarten, l., 102, 106

McBarnett, D., 109
Malthus, T., 53, 54
Manning, P., 110
marine police, 73–4
Mark, R., 97
market, see capital
Marx, K., xiii, 16–17, 39, 43–4, 69, 71, 114
marxism, xii, xiii
Master and Servant Act 1823, 83
medical police, 88–9
mercantilism, 13–14, 22, 28, 34
Metropolitan Police, x, 64, 65, 97, 105
Metropolitan Police Act 1829, 105
miasma, 85–7
Miller, P., 28
Minson, J., 6
Mitchell, J., 80
McNee, D., 97
Mohl, R.v., 32
mob, 40
Montesquieu, C. de S., 37, 43
myth,
    of crime, 92–5
    of law and order, 109–15
    of liberalism, xiii–xiv, 32, 106, 110, 113, 115–17

new police, 46–7, 64, 66, 68, 74–5, 96
new poor law, 64, 66–70, 76–7
Nightingale, F., 85
Novak, W., 32

Oestreich, G., 11, 19

.

Paine, T., 22, 31, 43
Paley, W., 43
Palmer, S., 78
Pashukanis, E., xii
Pasquino, P., 16
Peace of Westphalia, 8, 13

Peel, R., 76
Pergen, J.A., 33
perquisites, 70–4
Peter the Great, 5
Philips, D., 74
pigs, 87–8
Pocock, J.G.A., 28
Polanyi, K., 78
Police and Criminal Evidence Act 1984, 95, 98, 102
political administration, xiii, xiv–xv, 65, 99–108
polizeistaat, police state, 1, 8–9, 10, 29, 30, 32, 33, 116–17
pollution, 85–7
poverty, xii, 16–21, 45, 48–9, 51–9, 65, 70–7, 81–4, 90–1
prevention, 46–7, 64, 65, 66
Prevention of Crimes Act 1871, 100
Priestly, J., 43
proper, the, 84
property, 34–41, 47–8, 56–8, 65, 74–6, 82
propriety, 39, 84

Quesnay, F., 27

R. v. Gavin 1885, 96
Raeff, M., 6, 20
raison d'état, 8, 33
Radzinowicz, L., 46, 58, 78
Raleigh, W., 10
Rau, W.T., 88
reasonable suspicion, 102
Reiner, R., 93, 94, 117
Reith, C., 46
riots, 77–8
Rock, P., ix
Rosen, G., 90
rule of law, see law

Samuelson, P., 42
Sanders, A., 99
Scarman, Lord, 99
security, xii, 23, 30, 34, 41–4, 45–62, 64
sexuality, x, 14–15
Shaaban Bin Hussein v. Chong Fook Kam 1970, 101

Shakespeare, W., 7, 42
Shapiro, M., 33
Silver, A., 114
Smith, A., 22–9, 34, 35, 38, 39, 41, 43, 48, 54, 55, 57, 85
social contract, xi
social insurance, 63
social police, xi, 57–8, 61, 64–77, 81, 87–9, 91, 93–4, 118
social policy, xi, 58, 63, 93–4
social security, xi, 59–62, 63–91, 103–4, 116–17
Sonnenfels, J.v., 4, 13, 18
sovereignty, xi, 25, 30, 33, 39, 43
Soviet revolution, 111
stalinism, 116
state,
    absence of in other work, x–xii
    and civil society, xiii, 11–21, 33, 37–8, 47–8, 61–2, 87, 114, 117–18
    and order, 1, 115–18
    and property, 59–62, 82
    and security, 59–62, 111–12
    and violence, x, 118
    as police, xi–xii, 5, 58, 59–62, 111–12, 115–18
    cameralism on, 12–16
    Hegel on, 47–9
    liberalism on, 29–34, 37–8, 110–11, 115–17
    stages of, 5
Stedman Jones, G., 85

Steedman, C., 79
Steuart, J., 28, 48
sublation, 45
Sunday Observance Act 1677, 75
'sus' law, 67

Thompson, E.P., 40, 79–80, 108–9
Tilly, C., 15
Titmuss, R., 107
Tomlins, C., 31
Turgot, A.R., 27

vagrancy, 2, 16–21, 50, 67–8, 75, 89, 100, 105
Vagrancy Act 1824, 67, 75, 100, 105
violence, x, xi, 100–1, 118

Walker, M., 32
'Ways and Means Act', 112
Weber, M., xi, 14
Wednesbury Rules, 102–3
welfare, 8, 9, 30, 32, 54, 63, 77, 89–91, 103, 107, 116–17
Wild, J., 80
Winch, D., 28
Wright v. Court 1825, 96

Young, M., 87, 113
Young, R., 99

Žižek, S., 113

CPSIA information can be obtained
at www.ICGtesting.com
Printed in the USA
FFOW03n2134130917
39914FF